NO MISSION IS IMPOSSIBLE

ALSO BY MICHAEL BAR-ZOHAR

FICTION

The Third Truth

The Man Who Died Twice

The Secret List

Enigma

The Deadly Document

The Phantom Conspiracy

Double Cross

The Unknown Soldier

The Devil's Spy

A Spy in Winter

Brothers

NONFICTION

Suez, Top Secret (French and Hebrew)

Ben-Gurion: The Armed Prophet

The Hunt for German Scientists

Embassies in Crisis

The Avengers

The Paratroopers' Book (with Eitan Haber, Hebrew)

Spies in the Promised Land: Isser Harel and the Israeli Secret Service

Arrows of the Almighty

Ben-Gurion: A Biography (3 Volumes, Hebrew)

Ben-Gurion: A Biography

The Quest for the Red Prince
(with Eitan Haber, reprinted in 2005 as Massacre in Munich)

Facing a Cruel Mirror: Israel's Moment of Truth

Lionhearts: Heroes of Israel (editor)

Bitter Scent: The case of L'Oreal, Nazis, and the Arab Boycott

The Book of Valor (editor, Hebrew)

Beyond Hitler's Grasp: The Heroic Rescue of Bulgaria's Jews

To Be a Free People: The Saga of Israel (editor)

Yaacov Herzog: A Biography

Shimon Peres: The Biography

Mossad: The Greatest Missions of the Israeli Secret Service
(with Nissim Mishal)

NO MISSION IS IMPOSSIBLE

THE DEATH-DEFYING MISSIONS OF THE ISRAELI SPECIAL FORCES

MICHAEL BAR-ZOHAR AND NISSIM MISHAL

Translated from the Hebrew by Michael Bar-Zohar and
Nathan K. Burstein

ecco

An Imprint of HarperCollins Publishers

HarperCollins books may be purchased for educational, business, or sales promotional use. For information please e-mail the Special Markets Department at SPsales@harpercollins.com.

A hardcover edition of this book was published in 2015 by Ecco, an imprint of HarperCollins.

FIRST ECCO PAPERBACK EDITION PUBLISHED IN 2016.

Designed by Shannon Nicole Plunkett

Library of Congress Cataloging-in-Publication Data has been applied for.

ISBN 978-0-06-237900-9

HB 06.21.2021

For my comrades who fought at my side
The living and the dead
Conquerors of Sinai in the "Six Days"
Bravehearts across the Suez in "Yom Kippur"
Defenders of the North in "Peace for Galilee,"
Carrying the dream of peace in their hearts.

—Michael Bar-Zohar

For my grandchildren
Idan, Yoav, Or, Guri, Noam and Noa
I am praying that you'll see, one day,
The dove of peace with an olive branch.

—Nissim Mishal

CONTENTS

PREFACE
TWO COMBATS

Since Israel's Independence War, its army has been involved in two never-ending combats. A combat on the front lines with Israel's enemies, who never give in, and an inner combat—the effort to conceive and apply strict moral and humane principles, unequaled by any other army.

The combat with Israel's enemies has been and will remain uneven. In 1948, the year the Jewish State was created, its population numbered 650,000 people, who had to face an invasion by five Arab nations numbering more than 30 million. In 2015, when the Israeli population had risen to 8 million, made up of 80 percent Jews and 20 percent Israeli Arabs who don't serve in the army, the population of the states surrounding it had reached 140 million, and the gap continues to grow. Egypt and Jordan, who have signed peace treaties with Israel, should be taken out of this equation, but a new, redoubtable power has joined the enemy camp: the 75 million–strong Iran, whose fanatic Islamist leaders have sworn to wipe Israel off the map, with conventional or unconventional weapons.

The IDF (Israel Defense Forces), therefore, has had to develop military techniques to compensate for the alarming gap between it and the Arab armies. This has been accomplished by equipping the army with the most modern and sophisticated weapons, many of them conceived and produced in Israel; by basing its war strategy on containment of the enemy on two fronts while concentrating the main effort on a third; by building a formidable air force and excellent intelligence services; and, especially, by forming several units of special forces, composed of deeply motivated volunteers, centered on physical and mental excellence, rigorous training, and, most of all, inspired by creative, inventive planning to surprise the enemy and to hit them at the most unexpected and vulnerable points, allowing a small number of soldiers—sometimes just a few—to carry out a mission normally requiring companies and battalions. This is how Unit 101, the paratroopers; the special commandos such as Sayeret Matkal, Shayetet 13, Kingfisher, Duvdevan, Shimshon, Maglan; the commando units in every IDF brigade; and others were created. The experience and the tactics of these select units would later be shared with the main bodies of the army. "We could not resist you," a captured Egyptian general admitted after the Six Day War. "You are an army of commandos!"

The battle for moral conduct in times of peace or war is based on an ethical code originating in the Haganah underground, which operated before Israel was even created. The concept of "purity of arms" was forged by the Haganah, meaning that combatants' weapons shouldn't be soiled by hurting civilians, women, children or unarmed enemy soldiers. Several trials of IDF soldiers, in the past and present, have been based on that commandment. A famous court ruling speaks of a "black flag" flowing over any military order that counters the law; the soldiers should oppose it rather than execute it. This concept is enforced by the IDF, and any infractions, including some during the last confrontation with the Palestinians in Gaza, are brought before the courts.

As it tries to protect enemy noncombatants, the IDF strives to protect its own. A principle conceived under fire in the Independence War was never to abandon a wounded or stranded soldier in enemy territory but to rescue him at all costs. Rescuing endangered Jews and Israelis abroad has also become a major commandment, be they terrorist hostages, as in Entebbe (1976), or a community at risk, as the Ethiopian Jews in 1981 to 1991.

Another distinctive term is "Follow me!" The officers in the combat units should not only instruct and train their men and women; they should always be the first to engage the enemy, charging ahead of their soldiers, giving them a personal example of courage and devotion. "Follow me!" has become the battle cry of the Israeli Army and explains the large proportion of officers among IDF war casualties.

The moral values, the strong motivation, the special training, and the unorthodox strategy of the Israel Defense Forces have come together to produce a soldier for whom no mission is impossible.

NO MISSION IS IMPOSSIBLE

On October 6, 1973, on Yom Kippur
(the Jewish Day of Atonement), Syria and Egypt
launched a surprise attack on Israel, simultaneously
invading the Golan Heights in the north and the Sinai
Peninsula in the south. After several painful losses, Israel
defeated her enemies, but at a heavy cost. Three years after the
Yom Kippur War, Israel is still licking her wounds, having lost
2,700 soldiers and much of her deterrent protective power.
Golda Meir has resigned as prime minister and been replaced
by Yitzhak Rabin; Moshe Dayan has been replaced by Shimon
Peres as defense minister. Rabin and Peres distrust and dislike
each other, but they have to work together to deal with the
unending attacks of terrorist groups on Israel.

CHAPTER 1
ENTEBBE, 1976

A German couple boarded an Air France plane in Athens on June 27, 1976, quietly took their seats in first class and placed their bulky carry-on bags beneath the seats in front of them. The man was of slight build, his brown hair and beard framing an oval face, a mustache drooping over a pointed chin and blue beady eyes. Apparently tired, he leaned back in his seat and closed his eyes. His companion, wearing a summer pantsuit, was a tall, blond woman with a pretty face, slightly marred by a prominent jaw.

The Airbus A300 Flight 139 from Tel Aviv to Paris, with a short stopover in Athens, carried 246 passengers—105 of them Jewish and Israeli—and twelve crew members. During the Athens stopover, more people boarded. The passengers from Tel Aviv cast indifferent eyes on two Middle Eastern–looking men in dark suits who were shown to their economy-class seats by a smiling blond hostess.

At 12:35 P.M., fifteen minutes after the aircraft took off from Athens, the two Germans opened their handbags. The man took out a large gaily painted candy box and removed its tin cover. The woman produced a champagne bottle and started spinning it in her hands. Suddenly the man drew a miniature submachine gun out of the candy box and leapt to his feet. He darted to the cockpit and pointed his weapon at the pilots. At the same time, the woman unscrewed the bottom of the champagne bottle and pulled out a handgun and two grenades.

"Hands up!" she yelled at the first-class passengers. "Don't move from your seats!"

Similar shouts could be heard in Economy, where the two Middle Eastern men had jumped from their seats, brandished small submachine guns, and easily subdued the other passengers. The excited voice of the male German hijacker boomed from the loudspeakers. He announced in accented English that he was the new captain of the aircraft and identified himself as Basil Kubaissi, commander of "the Che Guevara Commando of the Gaza Strip,", belonging to the Popular Front for the Liberation of Palestine.

Panic swept the passenger compartments—shouts of fear and anger, and weeping, erupted from almost every seat. The horrified passengers realized that they had been hijacked and were the prisoners of terrorists. The "new captain" and his companions ordered the passengers to throw all weapons in their possession down in the aisles. Some set down pocket knives. Immediately afterward the hijackers submitted the male passengers to thorough body searches. And meanwhile the plane turned and headed south.

In the midst of a cabinet meeting in Jerusalem, a note was quietly handed to Shimon Peres. The fifty-three-year-old defense minister had been David Ben-Gurion's devoted assistant; Peres was credited with establishing Israel's alliance with France in 1956 and with carrying out a "mission impossible"—the building of a secret nuclear reactor close to the southern town of Dimona.

Peres passed the note to Prime Minister Yitzhak Rabin, who put on his glasses and read it. A year older than Peres, with graying blond hair and a pinkish complexion, Rabin had been a fighter in the Palmach, Israel's elite troops during the War of Independence. He had assumed office in 1974, after serving as the IDF (Israel Defense Forces) chief of staff and as Israel's ambassador to the U.S. He had run in the Labor Party primary for prime minister against Peres, but in spite of the support of the party apparatus he had won by only a few votes. The two men loathed each other and Rabin had been forced to accept Peres as defense minister against his own judgment.

These two, in spite of their sour relations, had to cooperate in dealing with Israel's security. Both Rabin and Peres knew the Popular Front well—a terrorist organization led by Dr. Wadie Haddad, a Safed-born physician who had abandoned his profession and devoted himself to the struggle against the Jewish State. He had carried out several bloody hijackings and also used the services of foreign recruits, including the notorious Carlos, an Venezuelan-born terrorist with a chilling record of bombings, kidnappings, and assassinations, that had made him the most wanted man in Europe. Haddad had been the first to organize the hijacking of an Israeli plane, in 1968, and was known to be a devious, cruel fanatic.

The 1967 Six Day War had radically changed the character of the relations between Israel and its enemies. In June 1967, threatened with annihilation by Egypt's president Gamal Abdel Nasser and his allies, Israel had launched a preventive war that had crushed the armies of Egypt, Syria and Jordan; Israel had emerged from the war controlling huge chunks of territory—the Sinai Peninsula, the Golan Heights and the West Bank of Palestine, After Israel's astounding victory, the Arab armies had been largely replaced by newly born terrorist organizations, which claimed that they were continuing the struggle of the Arab world against Israel. They replaced confrontation in the battlefield with hijackings, bombings and assassinations, directed mostly against Israeli civilians. Wadie Haddad's Popular Front was among the most ruthless groups Israel had to face.

After receiving the news about the hijacking, Rabin and Peres called an urgent council of ministers and senior officials. As the group convened, more information about the hijacking arrived. Among the fifty-six passengers who boarded in Athens, four were transit passengers who had arrived in Greece with a Singapore Airlines flight from Kuwait. They were believed to be carrying forged passports. The Mossad,

Israel's national intelligence agency, quickly identified the Germans as Wilfried Böse, a founder of the German Revolutionary Cells terrorist group, formerly associated with Carlos and now of the Popular Front; and Bose's female companion, Brigitte Kuhlmann, as a known member of the Baader-Meinhof terrorist gang. The two others were recognized as Palestinians, Abu Haled el Halaili and Ali el Miari.

The intelligence reports also pointed out that the security personnel at Athens airport had carried out only a perfunctory search of the passengers' bags, and they had missed the four Scorpion miniature submachine guns and the hand grenades that had been concealed in tin candy boxes and a champagne bottle. Additionally, several packages of explosives had been hidden in the hijackers' hand luggage.

At midnight, while the plane still appeared to be heading toward the Middle East, Peres met with Yekutiel "Kuti" Adam, the forty-nine-year-old IDF chief of operations, a brilliant general whose huge, bushy mustache betrayed his family's origins in the Caucasus. They set about to make sure that the IDF would be prepared to storm the aircraft if it landed at Ben Gurion Airport. They took an army jeep and set off for the base of Sayeret Matkal, the IDF's elite commando unit, which had already begun rehearsing an attack on a large Airbus, in case the hijacked plane landed in Israel.

The newly appointed commander of the Sayeret was thirty-year-old Yoni Netanyahu, one of the three Netanyahu brothers, who, according to Peres, "had already become a legend—three brothers, fighting like lions, excelling both in their deeds and in their learning." The brothers, Yonatan "Yoni," Binyamin "Bibi" and Ido, sons of renowned scholar Ben-Zion Netanyahu, were all current or former members of Sayeret Matkal. New York–born Yoni, a handsome, tousle-haired lieutenant colonel, combined his military skills with a deep love for literature, mostly poetry. After the Six Day War, Yoni had spent a year at Harvard and six months at Hebrew University before returning to military service. Tonight Peres and Adam hoped to find him at the Sayeret base; he was away, though, off leading an operation in the Sinai, so the rehearsal was supervised by his deputy Muki Betzer, one of the Sayeret's best fighters.

They did not stay long as Peres, shortly after arriving, was informed that the hijacked plane had made a refueling stop in Benghazi, in Libya, and then was continuing to its destination in the heart of Africa: Entebbe airport, outside Kampala, the capital of Uganda. The first news to come from Entebbe revealed that Uganda's dictator, General Idi Amin, had warmly received the terrorists and had declared them "welcomed guests." It now appeared that the landing in Entebbe had previously been coordinated with Amin.

Amin was a cruel and fearsome ruler who governed his country with an iron fist. A huge man, his uniform covered with scores of medals, he had been called the "wild man of Africa" by *Time* magazine. Once a lowly private, he had climbed the army hierarchy until he became chief of staff, then seized power in a bloody coup and pronounced himself "His Excellency President for Life, Field Marshall Alhaji Dr. Idi Amin Dada, Master of all the animals on land and all the fish of the seas, Conqueror of the British Empire in all of Africa, and especially in Uganda." Until recently, Amin had been Israel's ally and had gone through paratrooper training in the IDF parachuting academy, as the guest of former defense minister Moshe Dayan. Peres had met him at a dinner in Dayan's house and remembered that he was both attractive and scary, "like a jungle landscape, like an indecipherable secret of Nature."

Amin later broke off diplomatic relations with Israel when Prime Minister Golda Meir refused to sell him Phantom jets. He also expelled all Israelis from his country and befriended Israel's worst enemies—hostile Arab nations and terrorist organizations. During the 1973 Yom Kippur War, he even claimed to have sent a Ugandan Army unit to fight against the IDF. And this unscrupulous despot now held in his hands the lives of 250 hostages in Entebbe airport, 2,500 miles from Israel.

When news of this broke in Israel, a storm erupted. Israelis were swept up by feelings of fury and helplessness. Heated debates over the appropriate reaction raged in the media. Many of the hostages' families teamed up to exert pressure on the government. They all made the same demand: free our loved ones.

In the days that followed the situation became clearer. At Entebbe, more terrorists had been waiting for the plane. Amin had sent his private plane to Somalia, to bring over Wadie Haddad and a few of his henchmen. The hostages were being held in the old terminal at the airport, guarded by terrorists and Ugandan soldiers. The terrorists then separated the Jewish passengers from the others, reviving atrocious memories of the Holocaust "selection" by the Nazis in World War II. One of the German terrorists, Brigitte Kuhlmann, was especially cruel. She verbally abused the Jewish passengers with foul anti-Semitic remarks.

Upon arrival, Wadie Haddad gave Amin a list of jailed terrorists in Israel and in other countries whom he demanded be exchanged for the hostages. And the list came with an ultimatum: if Israel did not agree to Haddad's demands before the deadline he set, his men would start executing the hostages. Amin sent the list to Israel.

Prime Minister Rabin appointed a ministerial committee to deal with the crisis. At the committee's meeting on June 29, Rabin asked his chief of staff, General Mordechai ("Motta") Gur, if he thought there could be "a military option."

Gur was something of a legend. After fighting in the War of Independence, he had joined the paratrooper corps and participated in many combat situations beside Ariel Sharon. He had been wounded in a battle against Egyptian troops in 1955. In 1967 he had led the 55th Paratroopers Brigade in conquering East Jerusalem and had been the first Israeli soldier to reach the Temple Mount. "The Temple Mount is in our hands!" he had shouted in his radio as his armored half-track had emerged at the Jewish people's holiest place. After the Yom Kippur War, Gur had been appointed Israel's tenth chief of staff; Rabin held him in high esteem but thought Gur had no solution for the Entebbe affair.

"Yes, there is a military option," Gur responded to everyone's surprise. He proposed parachuting a unit of the IDF somewhere close to Entebbe airport, perhaps over nearby Victoria Lake. His soldiers would attack the terrorists and protect the hostages until it became possible to bring them all home. But the committee rejected the plan. First, it became clear that, after landing, the paratroopers would have great difficulty reaching the airport. Second, the plan did not include any solution as to how the hostages would be brought back to Israel. Rabin would later call this plan a "Bay of Pigs," like the botched U.S. invasion of Cuba in 1961.

Rabin and Peres fought bitterly with each other from the outset. Rabin believed that he had no choice but to negotiate with the hijackers and to agree to release the Palestinian terrorists. But Peres was determined not to free the terrorists because of the negative impact such a deal would have both on Israel's international image and on its ongoing anti-terrorist struggle. The rift between the two men was amplified by their strained personal relations, which had been creating a foul atmosphere at the cabinet meetings.

After the meeting Peres left his office on the second floor of the Ministry of Defense, and through a nearby door entered the western part of the building, which housed the offices of the IDF general staff. Peres urgently summoned the chief of staff and some of his generals.

"I want to hear what plans you have," he said to the group of generals in their olive-colored summer uniforms.

"We have no plans," Kuti Adam answered.

"Then I want to hear what you don't have," Peres said.

It was quickly revealed that while no formal plans had been drafted, some of the men had ideas. Kuti Adam suggested a joint operation with the French army—after all, he argued, Air France was a French company, and the French government should be involved. Benny Peled, the forty-eight-year-old IAF (Israeli Air Force) commander, had an "insane" but original idea. A founder of the IAF, this heavy-set, courageous and cool-headed fighter pilot was gifted with a fertile imagination. He proposed they fly a large number of elite troops to Uganda, conquer Uganda, free the hostages and bring them back home. He suggested employing the squadron of fourteen large Hercules ("Rhino") aircraft for this. They could fly from Israel to Entebbe and then back.

Peres had bought the Rhinos during a visit to Georgia in the United States, a few years before; he had at the time presented Governor Jimmy Carter with his book David's Sling. Carter had said to Peres, "All that David needed was a sling but today's David needs more than a sling, he needs a Hercules!"; he had talked Peres into buying several Georgia-made Rhinos.

Peres was intrigued by Peled. At first look, his plan seemed to him and to others like lunacy, but after weighing all other options, he deemed it "quite realistic." His colleagues, though, did not share Peres's assessment. Motta Gur, in particular, was negative; the plan, he declared, "was unrealistic, nothing but a fantasy," and ought to be scrapped.

Peres, however, set aside these doubts and pursued discussions with a small group of senior officers. Among them were the chief of staff; generals Kuti Adam, Benny Peled and his deputy, Rafi Harlev; Dan Shomron (chief infantry and paratroopers officer); Shlomo Gazit (head of military intelligence); Yanosh Ben-Gal (IDF assistant head of operations); and a few colonels, including Ehud Barak, a brilliant officer and former head of Sayeret Matkal(and a future prime minister of Israel). Their discussions were held in utmost secrecy.

The very morning of these discussions, Peres received the list of jailed terrorists whose release the hijackers had demanded. It was most complicated. Forty of the prisoners were held in Israel, among them the notorious Kozo Okamoto, a Japanese terrorist whose group had massacred twenty-four people and wounded seventy-eight in Lod airport in May 1972. Also included were six terrorists jailed in Kenya, where the local authorities denied having them. Another five were in Germany, including the leaders of the ferocious Baader-Meinhof Gang. One was in France and another in Switzerland. A quick glance and Peres realized it was an impossible demand. How could he possibly organize the release of terrorists held in so many countries, subject to different laws and for different crimes? And what if some or all those countries refused?

Rabin, however, continued to insist that Israel negotiate immediately, fearing that when the terrorists' ultimatum expired, they would start killing innocent people. But Peres stood his ground—he contended that Israel could push back the ultimatum, which had been set for Thursday, July 1, at 11:00 A.M. At the same time, he agreed with the decision to negotiate, but stressed he would be doing so only as a "tactical maneuver" to gain time.

On Wednesday, June 30, Peres decided to explore another angle. He summoned three IDF officers who had served in Uganda and had worked with Idi Amin. He asked them to describe Amin's character, behavior and attitude toward foreigners. These men thought Amin would not dare massacre the hostages, but they also felt certain Amin would not confront the terrorists. Peres asked Colonel "Borka" Bar-Lev, who had been friendly with Idi Amin, to telephone the Ugandan ruler. Bar-Lev was unable to reach him despite repeated efforts.

In the meantime, Peres again summoned his top officers. Beni Peled's plan was discussed once more but now with a narrowed focus. Its goal now became not to conquer Uganda but simply to win control over Entebbe airport, release the hostages and fly them back. Peled laid out a revised plan calling for a thousand paratroopers to be dropped from ten Rhino aircraft. Shomron and Ben-Gal estimated that such an operation could be successfully carried out with two hundred men and three Rhinos.

Kibbutz-born Dan Shomron, a paratrooper and a hero of the Six Day War, was opposed to any parachuting. He told Peled that "by the time your first paratrooper hits the ground, you won't have anybody left to rescue anymore." Soft-spoken, but sharp and cool, this future chief of staff was certain that as soon as the terrorists saw paratroopers descending, they would massacre the hostages. So Shomron, who now became the key coordinator, started drafting a plan to land planes carrying his soldiers directly onto the Entebbe runways. Kuti Adam pointed out the need for a stopover base close to Uganda, in case of an emergency. They all agreed it would have to be in Kenya, whose government maintained friendly relations with Israel while loathing Idi Amin. Peres asked the Mossad head, General Yitzhak ("Haka") Hofi, to check discreetly with his Kenyan contacts to ascertain if their country would authorize such a stopover at Nairobi airport. Peres, however, felt dubious about this approach, as Haka seemed to him reserved and skeptical.

Additionally, the emerging mission continued to have an important and stubborn antagonist: Chief of Staff Motta Gur, who strongly believed it could not succeed and insisted that Israel had no military option. He stressed the complete lack of intelligence about what was happening in Entebbe. He called the group working with Peres "the Fantasy Council."

Meanwhile, one far-fetched aspect of the plan did progress—Borka Bar-Lev at long last established a telephone connection with Idi Amin. The talk was discouraging, though. Uganda's ruler bluntly advised him that Israel should accept the hijackers' demands without delay.

This was also the opinion of Rabin, who now had the cabinet's backing to start negotiations right away. He further informed his ministers that the opposition leader, Menachem Begin, agreed with his decision to negotiate. Rabin criticized Peres for using "demagogical lightnings . . . and ornate phrases that sounded totally ridiculous." Indeed, Rabin regarded Peres's responses throughout the crisis as pure demagogy. He did not believe that Peres even meant what he was saying. Most of the ministers agreed that Israel had no military option. Rabin also kept nervously demanding that France immediately be informed of Israel's acceptance of the terrorists' conditions, so that the French foreign ministry could immediately establish contact with Entebbe.

Amid all the angry politicking, some good news came on July 1: the terrorists had by themselves postponed their deadline for capitulation to Sunday, July 4. This stemmed from Idi Amin's departure to an African nations' conference in Mauritius. He was supposed to return in a couple of days. The terrorists wanted Amin to be present when the negotiations took place. So Peres and his "Fantasy Council" now suddenly had a little more time.

Kuti Adam and Dan Shomron thus were able to present the plan they had drafted: The mission would sortie at night, under cover of darkness. The Rhinos would land at Entebbe, and the IDF would acquire control of the airport, kill the terrorists and rescue the hostages.

The whole operation, Dan Shomron emphasized, would not last more than an hour, making all possible use of surprise and speed. First to land would be a Rhino, not asking permission from the control tower. It would arrive at 11:00 P.M., right after a British airliner that was scheduled to come in at the same time. With the Rhino landing in the shadow of the British aircraft, the airport radar would not detect it. Two armored cars laden with commandos would emerge from the Rhino and race toward the Old Terminal, where the hostages were being kept. Five or ten minutes later another Rhino would land and disgorge two more cars, with soldiers who would gain control over the New Terminal, the main runway and the fuel reservoirs. After these men in the first two planes had fulfilled their assignments, two more Rhinos would land, load up the hostages and return home.

Peres now asked the head of the Mossad for his input, but Hofi kept stressing the risks—what if the Ugandan soldiers fired an RPG (rocket-propelled grenade) or a machine-gun burst into the Rhino fuel tank and set off an explosion? In that event, one or more planes might have to be abandoned, ruining the delicate interdependencies of the plan. And then there were the potential human costs—what if soldiers and hostages were killed or wounded? What if the terrorists simply blew up the Old Terminal with all the hostages? Hofi was—to say the least—unenthusiastic.

Peres's council then tore apart every detail of the mission—what snags might occur; whether, if the first Rhino was hit or damaged, the other planes would be able to return; what to do if the airport had antiaircraft guns; whether there were Ugandan MiG jet fighters stationed there, and would there be enough fuel left for the takeoff from Entebbe? . . .

Peres then asked the military for their opinions. Dan Shomron said, "If we start in Entebbe at midnight, we can take off for the flight back at one A.M." He estimated the chances of success were close to 100 percent. Benny Peled thought 80 percent and Kuti Adam, between 50 and 80 percent.

Peres finally approved the plan and set the deadline for carrying it out at Saturday night, July 3, the night before the terrorists' deadline. The generals all agreed, except for Motta Gur, who still stubbornly objected.

"Such an operation without adequate intelligence," he said, "is charlatanism!"

"Motta," Peres asked, "will you reconsider?"

"Without intelligence there is no chance that I'd recommend such an operation. Some of the things I have heard here aren't worthy of an army's general staff. If you want Goldfinger, that's a different story. If you want James Bond—not with me!"

Peres then pulled Gur into an in-depth discussion that lasted all through the night, but Gur still would not budge. And without the chief of staff's support, Peres could not bring the go-ahead to the cabinet for its approval.

Gur, despite his opposition, did agree to assemble the task force—Sayeret Matkal, paratroopers and other units—in a training facility to prepare for the assault, but it would move forward only if the situation were to change. The facility was sealed, and to prevent any leaks, no one was allowed to leave. Shomron was appointed mission commander. An advance command post was to be established in a big air force Boeing that would accompany the Rhinos to Ugandan airspace and control the operation from the sky. Models of the old and new Entebbe terminals were built in the facility, and the soldiers repeatedly rehearsed for an attack and for the rescue.

Peres now set out to freeze the efforts to reach a compromise with the hijackers. Israel's former ambassador to France, Arthur Ben-Natan, had just arrived in Paris to talk with the French about a joint initiative to deal with the terrorists. He was Peres's longtime friend and a former director general of the defense Ministry. Peres telephoned him and conveyed a veiled hint, using "typical" Parisian banter, to delay his talks with the French. "If you meet the French girl tonight," Peres advised, "please don't get too excited. At most, content yourself with a vague flirtation. As a friend, and not only as a friend, I am telling you: don't take your clothes off." Ben-Natan laughed but clearly understood the message and let nothing come out of his "flirtation" with the French.

Two encouraging reports then arrived the following morning, Friday, July 2. The first, from Hofi, the head of the Mossad, informed Peres that Kenya, Uganda's neighbor, had agreed to authorize a stopover for the Israeli planes. The second came from an unexpected source—Paris. The Sayeret operation planner, Major Amiram Levin, had been sent to France to debrief the non-Israeli hostages who had just been released. But most, still terrified, confused and unfocused, could supply no useful information. Suddenly an older Frenchman approached Levin, introducing himself as a former French Army colonel. "I know what you need," he said. He sat down beside Levin and gave him a succinct description of the Old Terminal, where the hostages were being kept, the layout of the various halls and the positioning of the terrorists. He also drew for Levin detailed sketches of the building.

Various sources reported that the total number of terrorists was thirteen, including two Germans and a South American who was apparently the hijackers' commander. The other terrorists were Palestinians. Four had participated in the hijacking while the others had been waiting for the plane in Entebbe. Their rapport with the Ugandans was cordial. The captors were armed with small submachine guns, revolvers and hand grenades. The hostages were being held in the main hall of the Old Terminal, and the French crew of the Air France plane (which had refused the opportunity to be released out of loyalty to their passengers) were confined to the women's restrooms.

Additionally, the Ugandan military unit said to be watching over the prisoners was sixty men strong—but less than a battalion, as earlier reports had stated. In the Old Terminal a wall of crates had been erected, which the terrorists claimed were full of explosives. But intelligence sources indicated that these crates were not connected to any wires and no preparation for blowing them up appeared to have been made.

The Mossad, in preparation for the mission, should it be given a green light, had sent to Entebbe a foreign aircraft that allegedly had mechanical problems. The plane circled over the airport while radioing calls for help and secretly photographing the buildings, runways and equipment, as well as the military aircraft stationed there—two helicopters and eight MiG-21 jet fighters.

Armed with all this new information, Peres hurried to Motta Gur's office and presented him with these new reports. He noticed that on hearing the news, "Gur's eyes shone." The chief of staff reacted with enthusiasm and completely reversed his position. Gur, reassured that he now had enough information, became a staunch supporter of the Entebbe rescue.

Peres hurried to the prime minister's office. Rabin's headquarters was located in a picturesque small house a stone's throw from the Ministry of Defense, in the modest, book-filled room where David Ben-Gurion had planned major moves in the War of Independence. Peres described the plan to Rabin. The prime minister's reaction was lukewarm. He lit a cigarette and asked, "What would happen if the Ugandans identified the plane as it landed and fired at it?"

Peres told him that the IAF commander was certain that the plane could be landed without any response from the ground. Hofi, who had joined the meeting, for the first time expressed cautious support for the operation.

At the next Fantasy Council meeting, one of the officers suggested preparing a "double" of Idi Amin. When the Rhinos started landing in Entebbe, Amin would still be at the African nations' conference. So it might work to have a black Mercedes, similar to Idi Amin's, drive at the head of the Israeli troops. Inside would be an Israeli soldier with his face painted black. At midnight the Ugandans wouldn't clearly notice the figures inside the "presidential" car, and they'd clear a path out of respect for their leader. On the spot, Gur ordered his people to find a large black Mercedes that could be used.

The black Mercedes on its way to Entebbe. *(IDF Spokesman)*

Gur ensured that the elite units chosen for the mission were kept exercising without respite. Their commanders were measuring every yard and counting out every minute in the operational plan, every soldier's assignment and every vehicle's course. The critical moment, of course, would be the first Rhino's landing. Gur detailed the timetable: "From the turning on of the plane's landing lights and until it stops—two minutes. Two more minutes to get the men out of the plane. Five minutes to reach the target. Five more to complete the operation . . . "

Peres, Gur and Hofi hurried to Rabin's office. Gur presented the plan in detail and received guarded approval from Rabin, who ruled that the final decision would be made by an extraordinary cabinet meeting on Saturday, shortly before the planes were set to leave for Entebbe. The code name was to be "Thunderball."

During the meeting, Peres wrote a note and slipped it to Rabin:

Yitzhak—here is the last refinement in the planning: instead of a military ground service vehicle—a large Mercedes with flags will descend. Idi Amin will appear to be coming home from Mauritius. I don't know if it is possible, but it is interesting. —

The IDF planners couldn't find a black Mercedes similar to Idi Amin's, but they did find a white one of the same size in Gaza. It was immediately brought into the departure area and painted black. Amin's double was at hand, and the Sayeret mixed black dye to paint his face.

Then, just as all the pieces seemed to be coming tenuously together, an unexpected problem arose. Peres was scheduled to host a distinguished foreign visitor for dinner at his home: Polish-American professor Zbigniew Brzezinski, the future U.S. national security adviser during the Carter administration. Gur was also invited, but he had to cancel when his father-in-law suddenly died.

Brzezinski was cordially received, and Sonia, Peres's wife, cooked her specialty for him: honey chicken. Mid-dinner, Brzezinki surprised his hosts by throwing a direct question at Peres:

"Why don't you send the IDF to rescue the hostages at Entebbe?"

For a moment, the defense minister was speechless. But then, determined to preserve the secrecy, he explained why the mission was impossible: Entebbe was too far, Israel didn't have enough intelligence and MiG fighters and Ugandan battalions were stationed at the airport.

Brzezinski was not convinced.

A t the Fantasy Council's last meeting, the participants felt confident that the mission would succeed. The officers asked Peres a few-last minute questions:

"If the control tower asks our aircraft to identify themselves, should we answer?"

Peres and Gur decided that the pilots shouldn't answer.

"And what about the Air France crew?"

"Bring them home," Peres said. "We should treat them as Israelis in every way."

With the final cabinet meeting approaching to decide if the mission would occur, Peres asked Gur, "When should the planes take off?"

After considering this, the chief of staff answered, "From Ben-Gurion Airport to Sharm el Sheikh in Sinai—at one P.M.; then from Sharm el Sheikh—between four and five P.M."

This meant the planes should leave before the decisive cabinet meeting even took place. Peres then authorized the planes to take off before getting approval from the top. He reasoned that if the cabinet decided against the mission, the planes could still be turned around and brought back.

On Saturday, at 2:30 P.M., the cabinet met; having a meeting on the Sabbath was unusual and it had happened only a few times in Israel's history. Rabin expressed his full support of the operation, so now all three main players—the prime minister, the minister of defense and the chief of staff—were united. After a brief discussion, the cabinet voted and unanimously approved Thunderball.

A t 3:30 P.M. the good news was radioed to Sharm el Sheikh, and fourteen minutes later four Rhinos took off. They carried 180 elite soldiers and their arms and vehicles, and the black Mercedes. The soldiers spread swiftly over the large bellies of the Rhinos, curled on the metal floor and tried to get some sleep. A bit later, the flying command post, an Oryx (IAF Boeing), took off, and yet another Oryx, one carrying medical teams and equipment, flew toward Nairobi. The four-thousand-kilometer journey had begun.

A t 11:00 P.M., the pinpoint lights of Entebbe began to emerge from the darkness. The Rhinos had flown at an extremely high altitude, so as to elude all radar stations along their way. A minute later, the first Hercules landed on the illuminated runway, hiding from Ugandan radar behind the British airliner that had landed just before it. It rolled forward on the tarmac, miraculously unnoticed by the control tower.

Soldiers of the Doron and Tali units leapt from the plane and placed lit torches by the runway lights. Their assumption was that in a few minutes the built-in runway lights would be turned off by the Ugandans as a defensive measure, and so only their torches would illuminate the runway for the planes yet to come. The soldiers ran ahead of the Rhino and placed their torches intermittently along 540 yards. The aircraft then stopped, and out of it drove the black Mercedes and two Land Rover jeeps; they sped toward the Old Terminal. In the Mercedes, beside the black-painted "Idi Amin," crouched Yoni Netanyahu, Muki Betzer, Giora Zussman and their men.

They were barely one hundred meters from the old control tower when two Ugandan soldiers appeared in front of them. One ran away but the second pointed his weapon at the Mercedes and tried to stop it. Yoni and Giora drew their silenced handguns. "Don't shoot," Muki grunted, certain that the Ugandan was only going through the motions and probably wouldn't open fire; but when the Ugandan did not lower his weapon the two men shot him, first with their handguns and then with a Kalashnikov. Their shots echoed loudly in the night and cost the Israelis their element of surprise. Instead of reaching the Old Terminal gates the cars were forced to stop fifty yards from the old control tower, where the commandos jumped out of their vehicles and sprinted toward the building, killing another Ugandan soldier who tried to block their path.

Muki and his men broke into the Old Terminal through a side door.

The former departure hall was illuminated, and the hostages were lying on the floor inside, most of them asleep. With bursts from their guns Muki and his men killed the four terrorists who were guarding the hall's corners. Only one of the terrorists managed to fire back; the others were all killed before drawing their weapons. Using portable megaphones, the soldiers warned the hostages, in Hebrew, to stay down where they were. Some unfortunately got up and were shot at once. Six were wounded and three killed. Despite this tragic loss, the first stage of the mission was a success, with only fifteen or so seconds having passed between the shooting of the first Ugandan and the takeover of the departure hall. Phase one was now completed, and four terrorists lay dead.

While Muki Betzer was scanning the departure hall, he received a call over his radio; it was Captain Tamir Pardo, the twenty-three-year-old Sayeret communications officer (and a future head of the Mossad), who informed him that Yoni had been shot in the garden adjacent to the hall entrance. "Muki, assume command!" Pardo urgently said. He had just killed the Ugandan soldier who had shot Yoni. Some later claimed Yoni had been shot by Ugandans firing from the old control tower; others believed he had been shot by a terrorist.

An IDF doctor soon arrived and got Yoni to the Rhino. Muki picked up his radio transceiver and announced that he was assuming command.

Other commandos systematically mopped up the remaining passages and halls in the building. In the "small hall" behind the departure hall they found no one, but when Giora's detail moved into the VIP lounge they clashed with two Ugandan soldiers and killed them. Suddenly, two European-looking men appeared before the Israelis, ignoring their calls to identify themselves. At first the commandos thought they were hostages, but when they didn't answer the Israelis' calls, the commandos realized they were terrorists and opened fire. One of the terrorists was carrying a grenade, which exploded, and both were killed.

During the mopping up of the VIP lounge, the customs hall and the second floor, more Ugandan soldiers were killed, but nearly all of the sixty Ugandans stationed at the airport escaped and fled. In total, twelve Ugandans were killed in various firefights.

Suddenly, the lights in the entire airport were cut off, and Entebbe was plunged in darkness. Luckily, the runway where the first aircraft had landed was illuminated by the commandos' torches, and the remaining Rhinos landed easily and discharged more soldiers and armored vehicles.

Back in Israel, Rabin, Peres and Gur anxiously listened to the direct reports radioed from Entebbe. At 11:10 P.M. Dan Shomron's slightly hoarse voice came on, saying, "Everything is fine. I'll report later." Eight minutes passed, and Shomron again radioed: "Low tide." That was the code phrase that all the planes had landed safely. He followed this up with the code word "Palestine," announcing the assault on the Old Terminal. Shomron himself drove his jeep to that building and continued commanding from there.

As gunfire was still blasting in and around the Old Terminal, the just-arrived units had set off on their assignments. The half-tracks of Major Shaul Mofaz silenced the old control tower with a lethal burst. Another Mofaz paratrooper squad killed eight Ugandan soldiers in two clashes. They then joined the forces still mopping up the Old Terminal.

Colonel Matan Vilnai led his forces to the New Terminal. After their breaking in, the brightly illuminated building suddenly went completely dark, and the operation had to be continued with no lights. In accordance with the plan, Vilnai's men did not open fire on the Ugandan soldiers they encountered, allowing them to escape, and in two cases arrested Ugandans and locked them up in the terminal offices. It was then that Vilnai heard two shots from the north of the terminal. On the stairs he found one of his soldiers, Sergeant Surin Hershko, lying wounded, probably shot by a Ugandan security officer. Hershko was quickly evacuated, and his comrades kept advancing, but because of the darkness they couldn't find the entrance to the new control tower.

Yet, even as Vilnai and his men struggled in this confusion, the battle had already reached its finale. The IDF had conquered the airport. Its commanders had located the fuel dumps but decided not to refuel the Rhinos in Entebbe, as that would have delayed their departure by two hours. Matan Vilnai and the captain of the first Rhino, Colonel Shani, advised Shomron now not to delay their departure unless absolutely necessary, so Shomron agreed that they would refuel in Nairobi. There an IDF unit was already waiting, commanded by Ehud Barak, along with an airborne field hospital with twelve doctors and two operating rooms, which had arrived from Israel.

In the Entebbe Old Terminal the liberated hostages were stunned. The arrival of the Israelis and the lightning speed of the encounter, which had left their captors dead, seemed to them a miracle. When they came to their senses they clustered around the soldiers, hugging and embracing them in an explosion of joy and gratitude. Some wept, others joined in prayer. But the troops swiftly put an end to the euphoria. They told the hostages and the Air France crew to gather their belongings and in orderly fashion led them out of the building. They escorted them in the dark and kept counting them, to ensure that all the hostages were accounted for.

At 11:32 P.M. the code word "Jefferson" echoed in radio receivers in Tel Aviv. It meant the evacuation of the hostages had begun. And a minute later: "Move everything to Galila," meaning the hostages were boarding the Rhinos.

The soldiers carried the wounded and the bodies of the hostages killed in the crossfire into an aircraft. One woman was missing: an elderly Israeli, Dora Bloch, who had taken ill earlier and been transferred to a Kampala hospital. Soon she would be murdered by the Ugandans.

Everything else proceeded according to plan, but at 11:50 P.M. the powerful antennae at the Ministry of Defense in Tel Aviv intercepted a worrying message radioed from "Almond Grove," the Sayeret of Yoni Netanyahu, to the unit's medical officer in Entebbe. It was a laconic call for medics, mentioning "Two Ekaterina"—code for "two wounded." But nothing was said about the identity of the wounded.

The military vehicles and units drove back into the Rhinos. The soldiers of Lieutenant Omer Bar-Lev, son of a former chief of staff, blew up the eight MiG jets stationed at the airport to prevent them from chasing and attacking the much slower Rhinos on their way home.

At 11:51 P.M. the radio message everyone in Tel Aviv was praying for finally came—"Mount Carmel." It meant the end of the evacuation. The operation was completed and all the planes had taken off.

"The heart jumps with joy," Shimon Peres wrote jubilantly in his diary.

After the planes took off from Entebbe, Peres instructed Borka Bar-Lev, Idi Amin's former friend, to call Amin from Tel Aviv. Perhaps the Ugandan dictator had now returned from Mauritius, Peres thought. To Borka's surprise, Amin himself picked up the phone. He had returned a bit earlier to Kampala.

Borka spoke to him using a well-rehearsed scenario, one intended to create the impression that Amin had been secretly involved in the rescue; that might ignite a conflict between him and the terrorists he had so eagerly assisted. The phone conversation was recorded by the IDF.

"I called to thank you, Mr. President, for what you did!"

"Yes," Amin said, "I advise you to accept my friends' demands."

Borka was taken aback. "I want to thank you for what you did for the hostages."

"Yes, yes," was Amin's response. "You should negotiate with my friends and make the exchange with them. The hostages will be released, and so would the prisoners."

This dialogue continued for a few minutes, until Borka understood: Amin did not know that the hostages had been liberated! He was sitting in his palace, discussing the ultimatum and upcoming negotiations, completely ignorant of the fact that the Israelis had been to Entebbe, freed the hostages and taken off. None of his officers had dared to inform him that a few miles from his palace a firefight had taken place, the terrorists were dead and the Israeli hostages were on their way back home!

"Thank you, sir," Borka mumbled and hung up, dismayed.

All the aircraft landed safely in Nairobi. The IDF medical team treated the wounded as the Rhinos refueled. Shortly afterward, the planes took off and headed for Israel.

Very few of the liberated hostages slept during the long journey. They were too excited by this extraordinary experience. When the IDF spokesman published a short communiqué about the mission, "IDF forces tonight rescued the hostages from Entebbe airport, including the Air France crew," an unprecedented wave of enthusiasm and rejoicing swept the country.

An elated outburst shook the IDF general staff when Motta Gur informed his officers of the mission's success. He also made a speech, saying, "I cannot sum up the operation even in this early stage without stressing the drive and the influence on its execution that were centered in one man . . . who pressed on and pushed in every direction, both up and down, for the operation. And this is the defense minister, who deserves all the credit."

In the prime minister's office, Rabin and Peres exchanged excited greetings with Knesset members Begin and Elimelech Rimalt and Yitzhak Navon, chairman of the Defense and Foreign Affairs Committee. Rabin briefed the president and Golda Meir, while Peres woke up his wife, Sonia. The fantastic news spread throughout the world, and messages of amazement and admiration poured in from all over.

But then, in the wee hours all this joy was painfully interrupted. Gur came to the defense minister's office. Shimon Peres was lying on his narrow couch, trying to get some sleep.

"Shimon, Yoni is dead," Gur said. "He was hit by a bullet in the back. Apparently he was shot from the old control tower. The bullet pierced his heart."

Peres, devastated, burst into tears.

The following day, the Fourth of July, 1976 (the two-hundredth anniversary of the United States), the rescue planes landed in Israel and were received by a festive, flag-waving crowd. The operation became legendary in Israel and in the outside world. Flowery articles, books, TV shows and movies hailed the glory of the IDF soldiers. Foreign nations regarded the operation as a symbol of courage, dedication and impressive military capability.

All the terrorists who had participated in the hijacking and the imprisonment in Entebbe had been killed, with the exception of Wadie Haddad, head of the Popular Front, who had left Entebbe before the IDF raid. Knowing he was now in the crosshairs of the Israelis, he found refuge in Baghdad, hoping he would be protected there. It took nearly two years for the Mossad to reach him. Israeli agents discovered Haddad's weakness: he adored fine Belgian chocolate. The Mossad laced a box of mouth-watering Godivas with an untraceable poison and recruited one of Haddad's trusted lieutenants, who brought him the deadly box. Haddad gobbled down the chocolates, all by himself. A few weeks later, the ailing arch-terrorist was urgently flown, in critical condition, to an East German clinic, where he died in March 1978.

That same year, Idi Amin's regime collapsed following a war he instigated against neighboring Tanzania. Amin escaped to Libya and later to Saudi Arabia, where he lived until his death in 2003.

The IDF mission in Entebbe had been an astounding success. And yet, Yoni Netanyahu's death left a dark shadow over the popular rejoicing. The IDF changed the name of Operation Thunderball to Operation Yonatan. Peres eulogized Yoni at his funeral:

"What burdens didn't we load on Yoni and his comrades' shoulders? The most dangerous of the IDF's tasks and the most daring of its operations; the missions that were the farthest from home and the closest to the enemy; the darkness of night and the solitude of the fighter; the taking of risks, over and over again, in times of peace and in times of war. There are times when the nation's fate depends on a handful of volunteers. . . . Yonatan was a commander of valor. He overcame his enemies by his courage. He conquered his friends' hearts by the wisdom of his heart. He didn't fear danger and victories didn't make him vain. By falling he caused an entire nation to raise her head high."

Shimon Peres quoted King David's biblical verses mourning his friend Jonathan: "I am distressed for thee, my brother Jonathan; very pleasant hast thou been unto me; thy love to me was wonderful" (2 Samuel 1:26).

SHIMON PERES, LATER ISRAEL'S NINTH PRESIDENT

"From the first moment I was determined not to yield to the terrorists. We had to find a way to liberate the hostages. I had the support of a fine group of generals—Shomron, Adam, Peled, Gazit and their close colleagues. At the beginning our plans were vague. We perfected and honed the project hour by hour. But I felt I was completely alone in that matter.

"The prime minister was ready to exchange the jailed terrorists for the hostages. Most of the cabinet thought like him. Even Menachem Begin, the bold activist, agreed with him. Motta Gur, the IDF chief of staff, ridiculed my little group, compared our plans to James Bond stories and called us the 'Fantasy Council.' I knew that even if I had a good plan, I couldn't get it approved by the cabinet over the objection of the chief of staff and the reluctance of the prime minister. I decided to try obtaining the support of some cabinet ministers. I went to Hayim Tzadok, the minister of justice, a strong supporter of Prime Minister Rabin, but also a very wise and objective man. In utmost secrecy I revealed the plan to him. 'An excellent plan,' he said, 'I'll support it at the cabinet.'

"I got another encouragement from my friend Moshe Dayan, the former defense minister. I found Moshe in the Tel Aviv Capricio restaurant, in the company of Australian guests. I admired Dayan and valued his opinion. We ordered two glasses of wine and moved to a nearby table. I told Dayan about the plan. I remember how his eye sparkled. 'That's a great plan,' he said, 'and I support it a hundred percent.'

"But Motta Gur kept refusing to endorse the project. Only at the very last moment, on Friday morning, I brought him a new and detailed intelligence report about Entebbe, the hostages and the terrorists guarding them. This report made Motta change his mind. He became a staunch supporter of the mission.

"Now, at last, we could go to Rabin and ask for his support."

TAMIR PARDO, SAYERET MATKAL'S COMMUNICATIONS OFFICER, LATER HEAD OF THE MOSSAD

"There were many heroes in this mission. Everybody who took part in this operation—in every category—deserves a place in the Entebbe pantheon. The mission was well prepared but the guy who planned the air force part deserves special appreciation. To fly four Hercules aircraft to the heart of Africa; to land those without being detected; to discharge the forces without being fired at, even one shot; and to get them back after the rescue of the hostages—this is an act deserving our praise. Ido Ambar, who was a colonel in the IAF and head of the planning team, deserves special honors. True, military orders are always signed by generals and senior commanders, while the men who worked day and night, and brought to the task so much talent and creativity, remain sometimes in the shadows.

"We, the takeover force, had trained well, and each and every one of us knew exactly what his place was and what his role in the operation was. During the long flight all I did was try to sleep and to not throw up because of the violent shaking and jumping of the planes that flew at different altitudes and chose different paths.

"I was a twenty-three-year-old captain. In the assault of the Old Terminal I was in the first Land Rover, the jeep that moved ahead of the Mercedes. When our attack started I was beside Yoni. He was about a yard away from me when he was killed. In front of us stood a Ugandan soldier and he kept firing at us. I killed him. I think he was the one who shot Yoni, but there is another version—that Yoni was killed by a soldier firing from the old control tower or by a terrorist.

"I had a lot of esteem for Yoni as a commander. I saw him in action, and he had a very important part in the success of the Entebbe mission. When he fell, I bent over him and saw that he was seriously wounded. I alerted the doctor at once and radioed Muki Betzer, his deputy, to assume command. Later I joined Giora Zussman's detail, and together we entered the Old Terminal. The operation itself took barely a few minutes.

"The following day we came back to Israel with the hostages. I was sent to Jerusalem, to the home of the Netanyahu family, to tell them about Yoni's last moments. That was a painful task."

PART ONE

How It All
Started

On May 14, 1948, the British Army and administration
leave Palestine after thirty years of British rule. That
same afternoon Israel's independence is proclaimed
by David Ben-Gurion in the Tel Aviv Museum of Art.
The United Nations, by a vote taken six months before,
on November 29, 1947, has decided to partition Palestine
into a Jewish and an Arab state, but the Arabs reject partition.
The local Palestinian Arabs and the armies of Egypt, Syria,
Lebanon, Jordan and Iraq, as well as units of Arab volunteers
from all over the Middle East, set out to invade and destroy the
Jewish State. David Ben-Gurion is elected prime minister and
minister of defense. The acting chief of staff is Yigael Yadin,
a future world-renowned archaeologist.

CHAPTER 2

TO SAVE JERUSALEM, 1948

On May 24, 1948, while Israel's Independence War was raging, David Ben-Gurion summoned Yigael Yadin. He approached the map of Palestine, hanging on the wall in his office, and pointed at a crossroads marked "Latrun."

"Attack! Attack at all costs!" he forcefully said.

Yadin refused.

Ben-Gurion, "the Old Man," was sixty-two years old, a stocky Polish-born man with a defiant face, a jutting chin, piercing brown eyes—all this crowned with two tufts of snow-white hair hovering like wings over his temples. Yigael Yadin was half his age—a thin young man, balding and with a luxuriant mustache. Before the war he had studied at Hebrew University, following in the footsteps of his father, a noted archaeologist.

Ben-Gurion was haunted by the situation in Jerusalem. The Jewish part of the city was under siege, surrounded by the Arab Legion—Jordan's first-rate army. Starved, thirsty, its defenders and weapons insufficient, Jerusalem was in immediate danger of collapsing.

Ben-Gurion believed that if Jerusalem fell, the newborn Jewish State wouldn't survive. The fortress of Latrun, near a Trappist monastery, controlled the road from the coastal plain to Jerusalem; it had been occupied by elite units of the Arab Legion. To break the siege, Latrun had to be conquered.

But Yadin had other priorities. The Arab armies had penetrated deep into Israeli territory. The Syrians had reached the Jordan Valley; the Iraqis were close to the Mediterranean coast, threatening to cut the country in two; and the Egyptian expeditionary force had set up camp on the shore of the Lakhish River, thirty-five kilometers from Tel Aviv. Yadin believed he had to stop the Egyptians first.

Latrun, Ben-Gurion repeated, had to be taken. Nothing else mattered as much. A heated exchange erupted between the two, and Yadin angrily slammed his hands on the glass plate covering Ben-Gurion's desk, breaking it. But the Old Man wouldn't budge. While respecting Yadin and even admiring his fiery character, he stuck to his guns. Yadin finally gave in, and in a telegram to the commander of the Seventh Brigade repeated Ben-Gurion's order: "Attack at all costs!"

Wave after wave of Israeli soldiers stormed the Latrun fortress over the next weeks; time after time their attacks ended in failure. Hundreds of Israelis were killed and wounded, but the Arab Legion repelled all the attacks. In the meantime UN envoys were feverishly trying to broker a temporary cease-fire between Jews and Arabs. Ben-Gurion knew that the cease-fire agreement would "freeze" the situation on the different fronts. This meant that if the cease-fire was achieved while Jerusalem was still under siege, that fact would be finalized in the UN reports, and Israel wouldn't be allowed to supply Jerusalem with reinforcements and weapons. The Holy City would fall, and Israel with it.

While Latrun fortress still blocked the road, Aryeh Tepper, a platoon commander in the Harel Brigade, which was fighting near Jerusalem, reported to the brigade commander, a young officer named Yitzhak Rabin. He asked permission to try to reach—by foot—the coastal plain. His brother had fallen in battle, Tepper said, and he wanted to visit his bereaved mother. Rabin not only approved the request but ordered three more soldiers to join Tepper. At nightfall, the four men made their way down steep slopes and tortuous arroyos, quietly slipped by an enemy patrol and finally reached kibbutz Hulda in the plain.

The kibbutz members were stunned. It turned out that following some recent battles the Israeli forces had gained control over a strip of land between Hulda and the approaches to Jerusalem, west of Latrun and concealed from the enemy's eyes by a mountain ridge. This discovery was almost unbelievable: there might be a chance to develop an alternative road to Jerusalem that would bypass the deadly Latrun fortress.

A few days later, 150 soldiers reached Jerusalem by the new route; they were the first reinforcements to Rabin's Harel Brigade. Yet the IDF did not need a footpath but a real road for the transport of weapons to the besieged city. The front commander, General David Marcus, decided to try reaching Jerusalem from the plain by jeep. Marcus, tall, jovial and smart, was an American colonel, a Brooklyn boy who had graduated from West Point and law school. He had volunteered for the U.S. Army during World War Two and parachuted over occupied Normandy on D Day with the 101st Airborne Division. He became a Zionist after witnessing the horrors of the German death camps. The Jewish people, he thought, while preparing legal briefs for the Nuremberg trials, must have a homeland. As a volunteer again, he had come to fight in Israel's Independence War under the pseudonym Mickey Stone and had been appointed by Ben-Gurion as the first Israeli general. Now a senior officer in the IDF, he shared Ben-Gurion's thoughts about the importance of saving Jerusalem.

One night he set out from the plain on a jeep with two Harel officers, Gavrush Rapoport from kibbutz Beit Alfa and Amos Horev, a future general. The jeep slowly advanced through the gullies and up the hills, and the three officers discovered a route connecting with the Deer Path, a steep, sinuous trail that led to the Jerusalem road, far beyond the reach of Latrun fortress. Horev and Gavrush repeated their trip the following night, and after an exhausting three-hour drive suddenly bumped into another jeep that came from Jerusalem, carrying two other Harel officers. They joyfully hugged their comrades; they had proved that it was possible to reach Jerusalem from the plain by jeep!

After several failures and mishaps, jeeps started moving along the new trail and even brought heavy mortars to Jerusalem. To shorten the process, the jeeps would bring their load to a rendezvous point with trucks coming from Jerusalem and transfer the food and the equipment. On their way back the jeeps brought wounded soldiers and civilians from Jerusalem to the plain. But it soon became clear that the jeeps could not transport enough food to the Jerusalem civilian population, which suffered from acute hunger. The city military governor, Dov (Bernard) Joseph, dispatched desperate requests for food, water and fuel.

The engineering department of the Seventh Brigade, using all the heavy equipment it could find, started to build a real road, where trucks could pass, but the Achilles' heel of that enterprise was the sheer Beth Sussin slope, where a four-hundred-foot abrupt drop separated two road portions.

At Ben-Gurion's order hundreds of porters were mobilized—some of them from Tel Aviv and some—about two hundred—volunteers from Jerusalem, who each carried a load of twenty kilograms of flour, sugar and other vital products; night after night they climbed the steep slopes and brought the food to Jerusalem. The army also tried to use some mules and three camels, but those were not very helpful.

Time was running out, and Ben-Gurion ordered an all-out engineering offensive against the treacherous Beth Sussin slope. Every piece of equipment that could be found in Israel—bulldozers, tractors, compressors—was brought to the site. Israel's major construction company, Solel Boneh, sent over its best engineers and workers. Expert stonecutters from Jerusalem were also mobilized, and the roadwork continued day and night. The feverish road paving was not only a technical endeavor but also a heroic operation: hundreds of soldiers and volunteers carried heavy loads on their backs, climbed the slopes, pushed or towed trucks and equipment. Jerusalem's chief rabbi, Yitzhak HaLevi

Herzog, authorized work on the road on the Sabbath and even called it "a great mitzvah [a good deed]."

Nevertheless, the only way to vanquish the steep hill rising over the heads of the workers was to quarry into the rock a succession of serpentines—snakelike paths that would enable the trucks to reach the top.

Suddenly, one night, explosions rocked the Jerusalem Hills, and a murderous shelling swept the new road site. The Arab Legion had detected the feverish activity close to its positions; it ignored what the Israelis were doing there, but started an intense bombardment of the area. The legion batteries relentlessly shelled the site and fired on the IDF soldiers and volunteers, who suffered heavy losses. Egyptian Spitfire planes also strafed and bombed the area several times.

Yet the work continued in a race against the clock. In a few days the UN would announce a temporary truce that would freeze all activities on the ground. Building or paving roads was forbidden as long as the truce was in effect. If the road to Jerusalem was not open, the city would remain besieged for the duration of the truce and probably would collapse even before the fighting resumed. If Israel wanted to continue supplying Jerusalem during the truce, it had first to prove to the United Nations that there was a road to Jerusalem entirely controlled by the IDF.

Forty-eight hours before the cease-fire, the road workers were stunned to see a group of foreign correspondents visiting their construction site. They had been led to the new road by Israeli press officers. Unwittingly, the journalists became of tremendous help to Israel. Their reports in the world press that Israel had secretly built an alternative road to Jerusalem were proof that the city was not under siege anymore.

The *New York Herald Tribune* star reporter Kenneth Bilby called the new road Burma Road, after the highway built in the years 1937 to 1938 between Burma and China that provided supplies to the Chinese Army in spite of the Japanese blockade.

The Israeli Burma Road was completed on the night before the truce began, on June 11, 1948. The work, however, quietly continued till July

14, when the UN observers visited the site and saw the Israeli trucks climbing all the way to Jerusalem. Later, when the Burma Road was paved and officially inaugurated, it was renamed the Road of Valor.

The Burma Road being built behind the back of the Jordanian Legion.
Hans Pinn, GPO (Israel's Government Press Office)

David Marcus, who had contributed so much to the Road of Valor, did not live to see it completed. Unable to sleep on the night before the truce began, he wrapped himself in a sheet and took a walk beyond the perimeter of his advanced command post. A sentry mistook the white-robed figure for an enemy. He shouted at the man in white, asking for that night's password. Marcus failed to identify himself with the password, and the sentry fired at him, one single shot. Marcus collapsed, fatally wounded. His coffin was flown to the U.S. and buried with full military honors. A little-known IDF officer, his left eye covered with a black patch, escorted Marcus's coffin to New York. He was named Major Moshe Dayan.

Years later, Marcus's story would be made into a film, *Cast a Giant Shadow*.

A few hours before the truce began, the trucks rolled on Burma Road, and Jerusalem was saved.

YITZHAK NAVON, LATER ISRAEL'S FIFTH PRESIDENT

"During the siege of Jerusalem, I was the head of Intelligence's Arabic division. With the outbreak of war, we could no longer use Arab agents and had to rely mainly on monitoring our enemies' phone conversations. Thus, for example, when our fighters—among them future generals Dado Elazar and Raful Eitan—were about to retreat from the San Simon Monastery, in the Katamon neighborhood, we overheard a transmission from the Arab commander announcing that his soldiers were exhausted and he had decided to withdraw. As a result, we took control of Katamon. A similar thing happened to us at Allenby Camp. By contrast, when we picked up a discussion about a plan to set a trap for the Bloc Etzion relief convoy (the Bloc is a cluster of Jewish settlements south of Jerusalem), we passed it on to the military staff; but they didn't take us into account, and the convoy departed. On its way back, it was attacked by the Arabs at Nebi Daniel, with lethal consequences. I then resigned my position—what's the use of intelligence if it isn't exploited?—but they convinced me to stay.

"There was great hardship during the siege. The governor of Jerusalem, Dov Joseph, informed the government that the city's entire stock was five days' margarine, four days' noodles and ten days' dried meat. He introduced rationing—two hundred grams of bread per day for adults (plus an egg for children), fifty grams of margarine per week, one tin of sardines every other week, one hundred grams of legumes, fifty grams of sugar and fifty grams of rice. We also ate mallow (malva), which I would pick in a field, and we made soup from grass. Water was distributed in measuring cups.

"And then they broke through on the Burma Road!

"One day, I went down to Tel Aviv on the Burma Road for an interrogation of prisoners. And, to my surprise, I was able to buy candles and matches and sardines—as much as I wanted. Sardines: what a feast!"

The Independence War is crowned with an
Israeli victory. At the end of 1953, Prime Minister
Ben-Gurion, sixty-seven, has resigned and settled in
kibbutz Sde Boker in the Negev, but in February 1955
he is convinced to return as defense minister under
Prime Minister Moshe Sharett. Ben-Gurion accuses
moderate Sharett of weakness and irresolution.
This is also the opinion of the chief of staff,
forty-year-old Moshe Dayan, who is a close ally
of the director general of the defense ministry,
thirty-two-year-old Shimon Peres. The incursions
of terrorists into Israel and the growing
threats of a new war publicly made by Egypt's
president Gamal Abdel Nasser lead Ben-Gurion to
adopt a tough policy toward Israel's neighbors.
After each terrorist act Israel will now hold responsible
the state from whose soil the terrorists have come—
and launch retaliatory raids against its military bases.

CHAPTER 3
BLACK ARROW, 1955

On February 28, 1955, after nightfall, six IDF paratroopers under the command of Captain Saadia ("Suppapo") Elkayam crossed the border into the Egyptian-occupied Gaza Strip. The border was not fenced—just a deep ditch dug by tractors. Suppapo's small advance team quietly moved between two Egyptian army positions, but a couple of Egyptian soldiers in a concealed ambush farther up the road opened fire on the Israelis. Suppapo and his men killed the Egyptians with hand grenades and submachine-gun fire and continued to advance. Very soon they were joined by a column of paratroopers of the 890th Paratroop Battalion. At their head was an already famous officer: Ariel ("Arik") Sharon.

Sharon was escorted by two staff observers and his deputy, the calm, bearded Aharon Davidi. Born in Tel Aviv, a volunteer in the Palmach (storm units of the IDF during the Independence War) since the age of fourteen, Davidi had been nicknamed "the coolest soldier in the army." His tranquillity under fire was legendary. Even in the heat of battle this former Palmach officer would perform his duties unruffled, as if the bullets and the grenades and the bombs were not of his concern. Nobody knew that Davidi worked out in secret before every battle, doing physical exercises that helped him hide his fear from his soldiers. His pockets were full of bread and he would munch crusts during the battle, drawing calm and composure from the food. His soldiers admired his serenity and tried to emulate him.

While Sharon and Davidi led their column into Gaza, another paratrooper unit, led by the battle-scarred Danny Matt, crossed the border close to kibbutz Be'eri, farther to the south. They bypassed some villages and set an ambush on the Gaza–Rafah highway to prevent any reinforcements from reaching Gaza.

After two hours of strenuous marching, the paratroopers stopped in an orchard that offered a view of the railroad station and a large Egyptian military base.

On Sharon's order, the paratroopers charged.

Operation Black Arrow, also called the Gaza raid, was under way.

The Israeli government made the decision to launch Black Arrow after several incidents on the Gaza border. The most recent had been an incursion into Israel of an Egyptian intelligence-gathering detail that had collected information, carried out several sabotage operations and murdered a civilian close to Rehovot. When the identity of the perpetrators was exposed, the IDF decided to deal a severe blow to the Egyptian Army.

In the last few years scores of incidents had erupted on Israel's borders, and many infiltrators had entered the country, stealing and murdering civilians. The IDF had tried to retaliate with raids in enemy territory—and failed. The names of these Arab villages and military positions had aggregated into a long list of shame that the IDF tried to repress. Out of all those failed operations, the fiasco that stunned IDF Head of Operations General Moshe Dayan was the miserable failure of the Givati Brigade at the Jordanian village Falame. On January 28, 1953, 120 soldiers attacked the village, which was defended only by locals, shelled it with mortars and after four and a half hours retreated without accomplishing their mission. Dayan, furious, published a new order: "In the future, if any unit commander failed to carry out his mission claiming that he could not overcome the enemy force, his explanation would not be accepted unless he had suffered 50 percent casualties."

This was a very tough order. But things did not change until Arik Sharon entered the scene.

Arik, the son of Russian-born farmers in moshav ("cooperative village") Kfar Malal, was different. A born rebel, bold and tempestuous, the handsome officer was twenty years old when he was badly wounded in the battle of Latrun. He lay bleeding in a wheat field, watching the Arabs who descended from the hills rushing to murder the wounded Israelis with guns and knives. Another soldier, also wounded, grabbed Arik's arms and dragged him toward the Israeli lines. The other soldier had been wounded in the jaw and couldn't speak. The two men silently crawled across the battlefield, while the desperate cries of their wounded comrades, left behind, resounded in their ears. That experience had a long-lasting effect on Sharon—in the future he would not leave a wounded soldier in the battlefield.

After he recovered, he went back to fighting, then spent four years in the army before becoming a student at Hebrew University in Jerusalem. But his heart was not in it. One evening he lay in wait by the prime minister's office in Jerusalem, and when Moshe Dayan came out of the building he handed him a short note: *I am a student now, but I exist. If you have operations in mind—I am ready.*

Dayan remembered him from the days when he was commander of the Northern District and Sharon his intelligence officer. One day the Jordanian Legion had captured two IDF soldiers and refused to release them. Dayan, back from a general staff meeting, casually asked Sharon, "Tell me, is it possible to capture two legionnaires around here as hostages?"

"I'll check that out, sir," Arik had replied.

He got into a pickup truck with another officer and drove to the Sheikh Hussein Bridge, on Jordan's border, drew his handgun and came back with two legionnaires. Dayan was very impressed: "I only asked if it were possible," he said, "and he went out and came back with two legionnaires as if he had just gone to pick fruits in the garden."

One evening in Jerusalem, while Arik was reading about Duke Godfrey de Bouillon, who had led the Crusaders into Palestine in the eleventh century, he was summoned to the office of Colonel Mishael Shaham, commander of the Jerusalem District. Shaham asked him to assemble a small team of irregulars, cross the border and blow up the home of the Palestinian gang leader Mustafa Samueli in the village of Nebi Samuel. Arik recruited a small group of comrades from the war—Shlomo Baum from Kfar Yehezkel, Yitzhak ("Gulliver") Ben-Menahem and Yehuda Dayan from the university, Uzi and Yehuda Piamenta from Jerusalem, Yoram Lavi from Kfar Malal, and Saadia, the Palmach sapper. The group crossed the border and reached Nebi Samuel undetected. The mission was not exactly a success—they blew up the wrong house and Samueli survived. The Jordanians opened a murderous fire on Arik's men, but they retreated in an orderly way and returned home unscathed. In spite of the failure the conclusion was clear: the men had done their best to execute their mission. If they had been better trained, they certainly would have succeeded.

Arik suggested to Colonel Shaham that they establish a secret unit for special missions across the border. Moshe Dayan embraced the idea in spite of the angry objection of his colleagues. And so, in August 1953, Unit 101 was born.

Unit 101 was to become a legend, even though it was a tiny unit that existed barely five months. There was no mission its irregulars refused: deep reconnaissance incursions into enemy territory, raids on terrorists in their lairs, risky operations amid hostile crowds. One-oh-one produced a group of warriors that inspired the entire army with a new spirit. "Three men revolutionized the IDF," a 101 veteran told us. "The commander who pushed the change from above and believed in it—Moshe Dayan; the officer who initiated operations, conceived and proposed, and relentlessly sought combat with the enemy—Arik Sharon; and the fighter who invented new methods and was a teacher to all of us in his tactical planning—Meir Har-Zion."

Meir ("Har") Har-Zion was a young, fearless kibbutz member with extraordinary scouting instincts, a creative mind and an apparently limitless knowledge of the geography of Israel and Palestine. At the age of seventeen he had been captured by the Syrian Army while hiking with his sister Shoshana north of the Lake of Tiberias; after his release, he had crossed the Jordanian border with a female friend and visited the magnificent ancient city of Petra, in spite of the Jordanian patrols that shot fourteen other Israeli adventurers in the 1950s.

Meir joined the army and was recruited by Sharon. With his friend Shimon ("Katcha") Kahaner and a few other comrades he carried out several daring incursions into neighboring countries. One of their night missions was to reach Hebron by foot, twenty-one kilometers from the Israeli border, kill three terrorists, blow up their house and retreat—another twenty-one kilometers. The mission was a success, but on their way back the 101 fighters clashed with a large unit of the Jordanian National Guard. Meir attacked the Jordanians, killed their commander and led his friends back to Israel, carrying the slain Jordanian officer's handgun.

Sharon and Har-Zion were considered heroes but they also had their questionable sides. Ben-Gurion considered Sharon one of the greatest warriors of Israel but repeatedly noted in his diary that Sharon "is not telling the truth," an accusation that was shared by many senior officers.

Meir Har-Zion, too, had attracted scathing accusations by civilian and military leaders for an act of personal vengeance carried out in enemy territory. His beloved sister Shoshana was captured and murdered with her boyfriend by Bedouins while trekking across the Jordanian border. Meir and three of his comrades crossed the border, caught the five murderers and killed four of them, sending the fifth to tell his tribe about the vendetta. Ben-Gurion had Meir Har-Zion arrested on his return, and he was expelled from the army for six months.

At the end of 1953, Moshe Dayan was appointed chief of staff of the IDF. Soon after, 101 merged with the paratroopers, and Sharon became their commander.

And that February night in 1955, he led his paratroopers into Gaza.

Sharon distributed the missions to his officers. Force B would secure the route of entry and exit of the soldiers to and from the Gaza Strip. Force C, the 101 veterans commanded by Danny Matt, would ambush any reinforcements coming from Rafah. Force D, led by a young officer named Motta Gur, would attack the railway station. Another unit of twenty paratroopers would serve as Arik's reserve.

Force A, charged with the major task—attack and destroy the Egyptian base—was under Suppapo's command. Suppapo was a brave officer, a younger version of Sharon. He was a warhorse, always volunteering for the most dangerous missions. Battle scars were scattered all over his body, but he kept joking, "The bullet that would kill me has not been made yet." His A company was always charged with the most dangerous missions. A few weeks before, when Arik had decided to send Motta Gur's D Company on a raid to Beth Zurif, in the Hebron hills, instead of A Company, Suppapo burst into tears and didn't speak to Motta for several days.

But that night Suppapo was delighted. Arik had instructed him to capture the Egyptian base and blow up its main structures. That very morning Danny Matt had met Suppapo and his young bride in Tel Aviv. They were on their way to receive the keys to their new apartment, Suppapo revealed proudly.

He now led the charge of his men but made a fatal mistake. He mistook a water-pumping facility, surrounded by army tents and positions, for the enemy base. The Egyptians at the facility opened automatic fire on the attackers. After a short firefight, the paratroopers captured the camp.

Suddenly, shots were heard and bullets rained on the paratroopers from the dark compound across the road. The soldiers heard Davidi's voice: "Suppapo, that's a mistake! The camp is on your right!"

Suppapo realized his mistake and darted toward the gate of the compound, followed by two of his men. The enemy's fire increased.

A bullet hit Suppapo's eye and exited through his forehead. A platoon commander, Lieutenant Uzi Eilam, dragged Suppapo's body to a ditch beside the road, where some of the wounded lay. Uzi himself had been wounded; a bullet had shattered his hand, but he kept fighting.

The heavy machine guns kept firing. Company A was dispersed and confused. A feeling of defeat started spreading among the men.

Suddenly Davidi appeared beside them, calmly walking on the road as if the Egyptian bullets were not flying around him. He stood by a eucalyptus tree, exposed to the enemy's fire. Uzi jumped up and stood by him.

"What's going on, Uzi?" Davidi asked evenly.

"Suppapo was killed and we have quite a few wounded."

"Where are they firing from?" Davidi asked.

Uzi pointed: "From here and from there."

Davidi and Uzi threw hand grenades on the Egyptian positions, and one of the soldiers blew up the closest machine-gun nest. Davidi assembled the company and Uzi shouted loudly, "Those of my men who are unhurt—follow me!" He and four of his men found a hole in the camp fence and entered. A paratrooper was killed, but Uzi surprised the Egyptians from the back, blasting their positions one after the other. Several Egyptians were killed while others escaped. In a matter of minutes the paratroopers conquered the entire compound. The battalion sapper led the "porters," laden with explosives, into the camp, and soon all the buildings were blown up. Davidi had Suppapo's men prepare stretchers for the wounded and the dead. Breaching his legendary calm Davidi called out to the men, "Company A lions! Carry on as you did so far. Go on like tigers!"

South of the compound, four Egyptian military trucks came from Rafah, carrying reinforcements. Danny Matt's men were ready. When the first truck approached, Katcha jumped on it and squeezed his trigger into the driver's cabin. The vehicle stopped and the paratroopers attacked the Egyptians with submachine guns and hand grenades. Another man jumped on the canvas top of the truck and fired long bursts on the Egyptians below. The other trucks stopped, and the Egyptian soldiers ran into the fields, firing at the Israelis from afar but not daring to approach.

One after the other the paratroopers' companies returned toward the border, carrying their eight dead and twenty wounded comrades. Sharon radioed, "We are on our way back, we are very heavy." The staff officers who waited for him didn't understand, but his wife, Margalit

("Gali"), who had come to take care of the wounded, understood that they were heavy with casualties. Many of the wounded were carried on improvised stretchers made of rifles and shirts. At the last moment, after he had crossed a large gully and was approaching the border, Uzi heard that one of the wounded had been left behind. He ran back, found the abandoned Major Michael Karten, a staff observer, and carried him on his shoulders to Israel. He did not know that Karten was already dead.

The Egyptians had thirty-six dead and twenty-eight wounded. Twenty-two of them had been killed by Danny Matt's men.

Following the battle Moshe Dayan awarded the Medal of Valor to three of the fighters: Uzi Eilam, Aharon Davidi and the late Suppapo.

A week after the battle Ben-Gurion visited the paratroopers' base, watched their parade and spoke to them. He called them "trailblazers"—the volunteers who march ahead of the nation.

Legendary paratroopers and commanders. Standing, from right to left: Assaf Simhoni, Moshe Efron, Danny Matt, Moshe Dayan, Ariel Sharon, Meir Har-Zion. Crouching: Rafael Eitan, Yaakov Yaakov, Aharon Davidi.

Abraham Vered, Bamachane, IDF (Israeli Defense Forces) archives

Black Arrow inaugurated the era of night retaliation raids. From then on, the IDF would respond to acts of murder and sabotage carried out by the paramilitary Arab infiltrators—called "fedayeen"—with attacks on the enemy's army bases and military targets. This mission started a vicious cycle of terrorist acts and reprisal raids that continued up to the Sinai campaign of 1956.

Ben-Gurion explained forcefully to a reporter, "These raids also have a moral and educational purpose. These Jews [whose settlements are close to the border] come from Iraq, Kurdistan, North Africa. . . . There their blood was free. . . . Here we have to reassure them that the Jewish people has a state and an army, and their life and property have a price. We have to make them stand tall, instill in them a feeling of independence and pride, for they are citizens of a sovereign nation that is responsible for their lives and safety."

UZI EILAM, LATER DIRECTOR GENERAL OF THE ISRAELI ATOMIC ENERGY COMMISSION

"When Suppapo was killed, I was thirty feet away. Suddenly, Davidi appeared next to me, strolling calmly under heavy fire. I stood next to him—it wasn't pleasant sitting when the deputy battalion commander was standing. I learned from him to stay calm and controlled during every battle. This gives tremendous confidence to people, who believe that you know exactly what you want and where you're going.

"I decided to attack with four soldiers, the only ones from my unit who weren't wounded. We cut through the fence and cleaned out the base from behind. Eventually, with just one other soldier, I reached the command building. There were two platoons of Egyptian soldiers there, and a portion of them fled. Then I informed Davidi that it was possible to blow it up; the battalion's sappers arrived and we blew up the two buildings, and also the water-pumping facility.

"After the operation, I was in the hospital for a series of surgeries on my hand, and I was sent to a rehabilitation center.

I escaped, and during the Husan action [a retaliatory raid] I
was in a Piper Cub flying over the troops. I also flew in a Piper
during the Qalqilya raid. On the eve of the Sinai campaign I was
appointed company commander with Motta, and the doctor
finally cut off my cast.

"Two months after the Sinai campaign I was discharged.
Three years later, when I got married, I left the kibbutz. They
were very angry with me, and 'forgave' me only after I took part
in the liberation of Jerusalem during the Six Day War."

PART TWO

PART TWO

The Sinai
Campaign

In the fall of 1955, Egypt signs a formidable arms deal with Czechoslovakia, acting as a proxy for the Soviet Union. Egypt will receive hundreds of jet fighters and bombers, tanks, cannons, and other weapons with which it can wipe Israel off the map. In response, Ben-Gurion wants to launch a preemptive war against Egypt. In July 1956, Egyptian president Nasser nationalizes the Suez Canal, and Israel suddenly finds two major allies for an attack on Egypt—France and Great Britain—who want to take over the canal and dethrone Nasser. A secret deal among the three nations is reached in October 1956—they will launch an attack on Egypt.

CHAPTER 4

"BRING DOWN THIS PLANE!" 1956

On a pitch-black night in October 1956, the Israeli Air Force pilot Yoash ("Chatto") Tzidon took off on the commands of his Meteor 13 night fighter, a sleek British-made jet, its black nose cone carrying a rounded radar device.

Chatto knew that his dangerous mission was crucial for the outcome of Israel's next war. Accompanying him in his Meteor was the navigator Elyashiv ("Shibi") Brosh. The pair knew that their assignment, if it succeeded, would stay top-secret for decades to come. Chatto also already knew that, the next day, October 29, Israel would launch its attack on Egypt. Ironically, his squadron, nicknamed "the Bat," hadn't been assigned a significant role; yet somehow, now, at the last minute, it had been tasked with Operation Rooster.

Chatto Tzidon's Meteor nightfighter.
Air Force Journal (AF Archive)

Chatto was accustomed to dangerous assignments. A fighter in the Palmach from the age of seventeen, he had served in a naval unit, departing for Europe in mid-1945 as a founder of the Gideons, an underground group of wireless operators that ran the communications network among the Aliya Bet (illegal immigration to pre-state Israel) command in Europe, illegal-immigrant camps, ships at sea and the Aliya Bet headquarters. He had escorted illegal immigrant ships, established a secret wireless station at a detention camp in Cyprus and participated in a sabotage mission against the British vessel *Ocean Vigour,* which was involved in expelling illegal Jewish immigrants. In Cyprus he met a nurse from Israel, Raisa Sharira, whom he made his wife. During the War of Independence, Chatto would command a military convoy to Jerusalem and, at the fighting's conclusion, would enroll in the first pilot-training program in Israel.

As a combat pilot, he had made the transition to jet aircraft, and in 1955 was assigned to train a squadron of "night-fighter all-weather" jets. He called the squadron Zero Visibility.

In the last week of October 1956, Chatto was urgently recalled from

England, where he was completing his training for nighttime dog fights. In Israel, his superiors informed him, in total secrecy, of the upcoming Sinai campaign, or Operation Kadesh. "In a couple of days," they said, "we'll be at war."

On October 28, Chatto was transferred to the Tel Nof airbase, closer to the future theater of war. It was there, at 2:00 P.M., that he was urgently summoned to the IAF headquarters in Ramleh. The air force command dispatched a Piper plane to Tel Nof to bring him immediately, even though the trip from Tel Nof to Ramleh lasted barely twenty minutes by car. The head of the Air Department, Colonel Shlomo Lahat, locked the door of his office and explained the assignment to Chatto.

Lahat spoke succinctly, after swearing Chatto to secrecy. "You know," he said, "that a joint command treaty was recently signed by Egypt, Jordan and Syria. We have learned that the Egyptian and Syrian military chiefs of staff are now conducting talks in Damascus. All the senior staff of the Egyptian Army, Navy and Air Force is participating in the discussions, which are run by Marshal Abdel Hakim Amer, chief of staff of the Egyptian Army.

"Trusted intelligence sources," Lahat added, "report that the Egyptian delegation will return to Cairo tonight on a Soviet-made plane, Ilyushin ll-14.

"Your mission," Lahat told Chatto, "is to bring down the plane."

Chatto understood the tremendous significance of the assignment. If he shot down the plane, the Egyptian armed forces would be left without a military staff and a supreme commander on the eve of a war. The outcome of the entire conflict might hinge on his success.

Lahat expected that the Egyptian plane would choose a flight path far from Israel, outside the range of its fighter planes. He proposed that Chatto take off in his own aircraft and circle above Damascus while he waited for the Egyptian Ilyushin to take flight.

Chatto disagreed. "If they discover my presence, I could get in trouble with their interceptors. Or my fuel tanks could run out before they've even taken off."

Lahat asked what he proposed instead.

Chatto knew that the up-to-the-minute information would be reported by the IDF special units listening to the Egyptian-Syrian communication channel. "Call me half an hour after takeoff," Tzidon said, "when the plane is over the Mediterranean, in range of our radar."

Lahat looked at him in surprise. "Do whatever you think is best," he eventually said.

The Piper jet brought Chatto promptly to Ramat David airbase, where he had parked his Meteor. Shibi Brosh, the navigator, was already there. The pair prepped the plane, even conducting a nighttime test flight. Chatto knew that his principal problem was that the Ilyushin Il-14 was a relatively slow piston aircraft, and that his own Meteor was fast. To hit the Ilyushin, he would need to slow his plane down as much as possible—to landing speed or even less; but at such a speed, his aircraft might stall with its nose upward, and then dive and crash. An idea came to him about how to overcome the problem—by partially lowering the landing flaps, which he practiced midair.

Night fell. The call came several hours after dinner. Chatto, with nerves of steel, had even managed to sleep for about thirty minutes, when, at ten-thirty, he was awakened. The Egyptian plane had taken off from Damascus, he was told, and it had turned toward the sea in a wide arc. It was somewhere at the edge of the Meteor's range of action, advancing toward Egypt at a height of ten thousand feet, or thirty-two hundred meters.

At 10:45, Chatto and Shibi took off into the night. All of Israel was dark; there wasn't a trace of moon in the sky. Chatto had never seen such darkness.

The Meteor advanced through the total blackness, with the cockpit faintly illuminated by infrared light so that the pilot's and navigator's night vision wouldn't be diminished. On the two-way radio, Chatto listened to the flight controllers on the ground, identifying among them the serene, restrained voice of Dan Tolkovsky, the IAF commander.

Then the first glitch occurred: Chatto discovered that the fuel in the detachable tanks wasn't transferring into the main tanks. The plane had taken off with two reserve wing tanks, each containing 350 liters of fuel, and Chatto realized, just like that, that he had lost seven hundred liters. With no other choice, he detached the reserve tanks from the wings and dumped them into the sea. A short time later, he heard Shibi's excited voice on the internal two-way radio: "Contact! Contact! Contact!"

"Contact!" Chatto radioed to the ground controller.

Shibi sent him precise instructions: "Boogie [unidentified plane] at two o'clock! Same altitude, three miles away, straight forward, moving to three o'clock, now moving to four o'clock, taking a hard right. Lower your speed! Pay attention, you're closing in fast!"

Chatto couldn't see a thing, but he followed Shibi's instructions to the letter, not cluing him in to the problem that would arise when he needed to bring his own speed into line with that of the slow transport plane.

"Eleven o'clock," Shibi continued. "Descend five hundred. Lower your speed. Distance: seven hundred feet."

Chatto strained to see. At first, it appeared that he could make out the Egyptian plane's silhouette; then he discerned a "faint, hesitant" flame emitting from the pipes of the piston engines.

"Eye contact," he reported to ground control.

Tolkovsky's voice echoed in his earphones. "I want a confirmed ID of the vessel whose outline you've observed. Confirmed beyond a shadow of a doubt. Understood?" The air force commander wanted to avoid any mistake that might unnecessarily cost human lives.

Chatto was now behind the Egyptian plane. Out of the corner of his eye, he spotted its exhaust pipe and maneuvered left, until he could discern the stronger light of the passenger windows. He approached the Egyptian plane, coming to it "nothing less than wing to wing."

Gradually, the silhouette of the entire plane became perceptible. The shape of the windows in the passenger section resembled those of windows on a Dakota aircraft, but the cockpit windows were bigger, a feature unique to the Ilyushin Il-14. Chatto could also identify the shape of the Ilyushin's tail.

As he approached the windows, he could make out people in military uniforms walking in the aisle between the seats. Those in the seats also appeared to be wearing uniforms. Flying in close to the Ilyushin had cost him at least ten minutes of fuel, but it had been necessary to confirm the initial identification.

"I confirm ID," he radioed to ground control.

"You are authorized to open fire only if you have no doubt whatsoever," Tolkovsky instructed.

The moment had arrived to test the maneuver Chatto had attempted earlier. He lowered the landing flaps by a third, thereby preventing a stall.

"Firing," he announced into the two-way radio, and pressed the trigger.

Two malfunctions immediately occurred. Someone had loaded the cannons with munitions that included tracing bullets, which, for a moment, blinded him. The second glitch was a blockage in the cannon on the right, which brought about the same effect as an engine breakdown. The Meteor went into a spin, but Chatto regained control and steadied it. Although the Ilyushin had been darkened, he hadn't lost it, and he could see a flame that flickered from the left-side engine. He reported the hit.

"Finish it off, at any cost," Tolkovsky's voice commanded. "I repeat: at any cost!" Chatto knew that if the plane wasn't brought down right now, Israel would lose the surprise factor during its attack on Egypt the following day.

The Ilyushin was now flying with one engine, much slower than the Meteor's landing speed. Firing again—with unequal kickback from the cannons, now that one was blocked—would surely throw the Meteor into a spin. Chatto again lowered the landing flaps, increased the power of the engines, and lurched at the Ilyushin. Suddenly another danger materialized: a collision with the Egyptian plane.

Chatto put this fear out of his mind and sped toward the Ilyushin. When he came within fifty meters of it, he heard Shibi shout, "Change course! Change course! We're going to hit it. I see it on both sides of the cockpit."

Shibi's command probably saved them both. At the last second, Chatto squeezed the trigger and suddenly found himself "in the midst of hellfire."

His shells exploded into the Ilyushin, barely a few feet from the muzzle of the Meteor's cannon. Fire engulfed the Egyptian plane, shooting across it at the same instant that an explosion transformed it into a fireball. Flaming parts flew past the Meteor. The burning Egyptian plane spun and dived—and, because of uneven kickback from its own blocked cannon, so did the Meteor. Both planes plunged. "A fireball and a darkened plane spun one beside the other, and one above the other," Chatto later wrote, "both out of control, as if performing a sickening, surreal dance."

At the last moment, Chatto was able to exit the spin, at an altitude estimated at between 150 and three hundred meters. Simultaneously, he saw the Ilyushin smash and explode into the waves of the Mediterranean.

Chatto climbed to fifteen thousand feet and reported, "Accomplished!"

Tolkovsky wanted to be sure. "You saw it crash?"

"Affirmative. It crashed." Chatto then looked at the fuel gauge and was horrified. "I'm low on fuel—very low. Give me directions to the closest base."

He had no idea where he was. The sole radar that located the Meteor was an aircraft battery device on the Hatzor airbase. The battery's commander took it upon himself to direct "the Bat" to the landing strip.

"I'll fly in this direction as long as I have fuel," Chatto radioed.

"You think you can make it?" The controller's voice sounded dubious.

Chatto attempted to keep things light. "I poured the fluid from Shibi's cigarette lighter into the fuel tank."

Tolkovsky cut him off: "No names!"

The fuel gauge dropped to zero. One minute, two minutes, three . . . Suddenly, Chatto could make out the lights of the Hatzor runway, which had been illuminated for him despite the blackout. The plane glided toward the landing strip, and Chatto touched down.

As the plane barreled down the runway, the engines shut off, one after the other. The final drops of fuel had run out, but the Meteor was on the ground.

The base's whiz technician reached the plane first. "You did it?" he asked.

"Yes."

"So the war has started."

Ezer Weizman, the base commander and a nephew of Israel's first president, arrived immediately.

"Congrats!" Never one to miss a chance to show off, he went on, "Notice, it was only Hatzor that could bring you in." He added, "They're waiting for you at headquarters. There's a problem."

At headquarters, Lahat, Tolkovsky, and Chief of Staff Moshe Dayan were waiting for Chatto and Shibi. They shook hands.

"What's the problem?" Chatto inquired.

"At the last minute, Amer decided not to fly on the Ilyushin. He's going to take off later, on a Dakota."

The spirit of battle overcame Chatto. "If there's time, we'll refuel and go out on a second run," he offered, and Shibi nodded in agreement.

"It would be too obvious and would expose intelligence sources," Dayan said. "Let's leave him be. The moment you wiped out the general staff, you won half the war. Let's drink to the other half."

Dayan pulled out a bottle of wine, and everyone toasted.

The 1956 War had thus begun, yet only a handful Israelis knew.

Operation Rooster would remain top-secret for thirty-three years, with details reaching the public only in 1989. The Egyptians never reported the downing of the aircraft, probably because they weren't aware that it had been targeted; in Cairo, rumors spread that the plane had crashed close to a desert island, and that the army senior staff was still there, awaiting rescue.

Marshal Amer, the Egyptian chief of staff at the time, would commit suicide after the Six Day War.

YOASH ("CHATTO") TZIDON, COMBAT PILOT

In March 1993, four years after details of Operation Rooster were released, a young Egyptian unexpectedly reached out to Chatto Tzidon. He was Ahmed Jaffar Nassim, the son of an adviser to President Nasser, who had died during Chatto's operation. The dramatic meeting between the son and the man who had killed his father took place at the Tel Aviv Hilton.

The meeting, Chatto later said, was "emotional but without bitterness." Jaffar, a disabled man in a wheelchair, wanted to know if it was true that his father had fallen into Israeli captivity and been tortured to death after his plane made a forced landing. Chatto clarified that there had been no forced landing, that the operation had been one of "door-to-door service."

Two years later, Chatto helped Jaffar Nassim gain admission for surgery at Rambam Hospital, in Haifa. "The desire to aid him came out of a feeling of sharing in his sorrow over his father's death . . . as well as the thought that my own son could have found himself in a similar situation."

This was just one way in which Chatto showed an unusual streak of sensitivity toward others. His spouse, Raisa, recalls how on the eve of the 1956 War, at a dinner at the home of friends in London, Chatto met the sister of the hostess, an Auschwitz survivor. She was on her way to Israel and remarked "how much she would have liked to see Paris."

"Why don't you stop on your way?" Chatto asked. The woman replied, "I have a one-year-old baby. I can't."

Chatto had a solution: "I'll take the baby to Israel."

And, just like that, he took responsibility for the little girl, caring for and feeding her on the plane. When they stopped in Rome for a layover, he selected an excellent hotel, entrusting the baby to the hotel matron. The next day, he flew on with the infant to Israel. His wife was waiting for him at the airfield. and when she saw a man in a tweed suit with a baby in his arms, didn't recognize him.

"How did you end up responsible for a baby?" Raisa asked.

He looked at her in surprise. "Her mother had never seen Paris," he said.

In October 1956, while the Soviet Union is involved
in revolts in Warsaw and Budapest against its dictatorship,
and the U.S. is in the final stage of its presidential campaign—
Dwight Eisenhower is running for a second term—Israel attacks
Egypt and achieves a dramatic victory that makes Moshe Dayan
a legendary hero. The British and the French, however,
fail in their campaign to occupy the Suez Canal.

CHAPTER 5
KADESH, 1956

On Monday, October 29, 1956, at 4:59 P.M., Major Rafael ("Raful") Eitan jumped from a Dakota plane in Western Sinai and kicked off the Kadesh mission.

Three hundred ninety-four paratroopers jumped after him from sixteen aircraft. They had been preceded, two hours earlier, by two Mustang aircraft that had torn surface phone lines over Sinai with their propellers and wings, in order to disrupt the Egyptian communications systems.

In Tel Aviv, Chief of Staff Moshe Dayan dispatched an official communique to Kol Israel radio:

"The IDF spokesman announces that IDF forces entered and attacked Fedayeen units at Ras el Nakeb and Kuntila and took positions in proximity to the Suez Canal."

The paratroopers' drop, close to the Suez Canal, deep in Egyptian territory, was the opening shot of the Sinai campaign and the conclusion of a top-secret political operation with Ben-Gurion, Dayan and Peres as the main players.

In September 1955, Israel had suffered a painful blow when the Soviet Union, using Czechoslovakia as a proxy, concluded a huge arms deal with Egypt. The USSR was going to supply Egypt with about 200 MiG-15 jet fighters and Ilyushin Il-28 bombers, and training and cargo planes; 230 tanks; 200 armored troop carriers; 600 cannons; and various naval vessels—torpedo boats, destroyers and 6 submarines. The weapons Egypt was about to receive were of unprecedented quality and quantity. With them, the balance of power in the Middle East could collapse, and Israel risked losing its deterrent power, the guarantee for its existence. Another reason for worry was the establishment of a joint Egyptian-Syrian military command.

A wave of anxiety swept Israel. She had only thirty jet fighters. The numbers of her tanks, troop carriers and cannons were ridiculous when compared to what Egypt was about to receive. Distraught Israelis spontaneously donated money, jewelry and property deeds to a "defense fund" created for the purchase of weapons. Fiery Ben-Gurion wanted to launch an attack on Egypt immediately. Foreign Minister Moshe Sharett, however, dovish and moderate, defeated his motion in a cabinet vote. A few months later, Ben-Gurion hit back by removing Sharett from the cabinet and appointing a new foreign minister—hawkish Golda Meir.

In the meantime, Shimon Peres invested tremendous effort in establishing an alliance between France and Israel. And in spite of the criticism, even the mockery, in government circles at home, his efforts in France bore fruit: he succeeded in obtaining large quantities of weapons and in establishing relations of trust and friendship with French cabinet ministers, army officers and members of parliament. In June 1956, Israel signed the *Ge'ut* ("High Tide") deal with France for a massive supply of weapons to Israel.

A month later, in a surprise move, Egyptian president Nasser nationalized the Suez Canal. France and Great Britain, the main holders of Suez Canal stock, immediately started planning a military operation against Egypt, to bring the canal back under their power. French and British generals debated successive invasion plans in a World War

II bunker under the Thames. Soon the French leaders realized that the British wouldn't attack Egypt without a solid pretext. Therefore, they turned to Israel.

The paratroopers were dropped close to the Suez Canal.
(Abraham Vered, GPO)

Shortly before sunset on October 22, 1956, several cars stopped by a secluded villa in Sevres, a Parisian suburb. The passengers furtively slipped into the house gates. These were French Prime Minister Guy Mollet, Foreign Minister Christian Pineau, Defense Minister Maurice Bourgès-Maunoury, the army chief of staff, and several high-ranking generals. Their secret guests, who had arrived by special plane, were Israeli Prime Minister Ben-Gurion, hiding his distinctive shock of white hair under a wide-brimmed hat; General Moshe Dayan, concealing his black eye patch under large sunglasses; and Shimon Peres. The two delegations met in a cordial atmosphere. Later in the evening, though, they were joined by British Foreign Secretary Selwyn Lloyd.

With Lloyd's arrival, a cold wind seemed to penetrate the villa. The British foreign secretary apparently couldn't forget that only eight years before, Britain was still the ruler of Palestine and Ben-Gurion was its most formidable opponent. "Britain's Foreign Secretary may well have been a friendly man, pleasant, charming, amiable," Dayan wrote. "If so, he showed near-genius in concealing these virtues. His whole demeanor expressed distaste—for the place, the company and the topic."

But Lloyd was there—and the most secret summit after World War II was under way.

After a first round of talks that continued into the night, Lloyd left to report to British Prime Minister Anthony Eden. "It seems that Lloyd didn't fall in love with Ben-Gurion," Peres noted that night, "but there is no doubt at all that this feeling was mutual from the moment they met."

The conference continued the following day. Several ideas about an action that could justify an Anglo-French intervention were discussed. The various ploys were rejected, one after the other. The French and the British suggested that Israel attack Egypt, conquer the Sinai Peninsula and create a threat to the Suez Canal; France and Great Britain would then intervene to "protect" the canal from the fighting forces.

But Ben-Gurion refused to launch an all-out war against Egypt, just to provide France and Britain with a pretext; he also feared that Israel would have to carry the brunt of such a war on her frail shoulders for several days, perhaps a week, until the Franco-British invasion started.

The following day, while the French and the Israelis were having lunch, General Maurice Challe, the French deputy chief of staff, asked to speak. He suggested that the Israeli Air Force stage an attack on Be'er Sheva and bomb the city. Egypt would be accused, and the Anglo-French forces would intervene immediately. Ben-Gurion, his face flushed with fury, jumped from his seat. "Israel is strong because she fights for a just cause," he said. "I shall not lie, either to the world public opinion or to anybody else." In the sepulchral silence that settled over the room Challe sat down, his face red with embarrassment. The others buried their noses in their plates. The conference seemed about to collapse.

And then Moshe Dayan conceived the magical formula.

Dayan, born in kibbutz Degania, raised in the cooperative village of Nahalal, was a charismatic Israeli hero. A member of the Haganah—the

Jewish defense organization under the British mandate—he had grown up among Nahalal's Arab neighbors, knew them well and respected them. In War World II he had participated in a British patrol operating against the French Vichy forces in Lebanon. An enemy sniper's bullet shattered his binoculars, driving the eye piece into his left eye socket. The eye was lost but the pirate patch that replaced it made the face of Dayan famous all over Israel and later the world. A gifted orator, a lover of poetry, an amateur archaeologist and a womanizer, he also was a fearless warrior. As chief of staff he transformed the IDF into a lean, tough force and commanded the reprisal raids against Israel's restive enemies. Yet, he soon realized that reprisals could not solve the growing tension between Israel and her neighbors, especially Egypt. He supported the idea of attacking Egypt before it mastered the massive influx of arms from the Soviet bloc and was a willing participant in the Sevres conference.

Ben-Gurion, however, kept refusing to launch an all-out war against Egypt. So how to start a war without starting a war? At that crucial moment, when the entire conference depended on a solution to the pretext dilemma, Dayan came up with a plan.

Let's start the war from the end, Dayan said. He suggested parachuting a small Israeli force into the Sinai, about thirty miles east of the Suez Canal, creating an apparent threat on the waterway. France and Great Britain would declare the canal in danger and dispatch ultimata to Egypt and Israel to retreat to new lines, ten miles on each side of the canal. That meant that Egypt would be asked to evacuate the entire Sinai Peninsula, allowing Israel to conquer it and reach the vicinity of the canal. Israel would accept the ultimatum, while Egypt would certainly reject it. That would be the pretext for the French and the British to launch their military operation against Egypt thirty-six hours after the Israelis.

Ben-Gurion hesitated, but after a sleepless night accepted Dayan's plan. When meeting with Dayan and Peres in the villa garden the following morning, he asked Dayan to draw the projected campaign for him. Nobody had any paper, so Peres tore his cigarette pack, and Dayan

sketched on it the Sinai Peninsula; a dotted line represented the flight of
the planes that would drop the paratroopers, and three arrows showed
the main axes of the subsequent Israeli offensive. Ben-Gurion, Dayan
and Peres signed, laughing, the small piece of cardboard, and it became
the first map of the Sinai campaign.

Back in the villa, Dayan's plan was unanimously adopted and on
October 24 a secret agreement was signed among France, Great Britain
and Israel. On his return to Tel Aviv Ben-Gurion called a cabinet meeting. He didn't tell the ministers about his trip to France or the agreement
they had made, a copy of which he carried in his breast pocket. Yet, he
obtained the cabinet consent for an operation against Egypt. As always
when in a state of utter tension, Ben-Gurion fell sick with high fever.
But that night Menachem Begin, Ben-Gurion's staunch rival, was invited
to Ben-Gurion's home for the first time in his life. While Begin sat on a
stool beside Ben-Gurion's cot, the Old Man described the decision to go
to war, and Begin congratulated him warmly.

On October 29, Raful Eitan and his paratroopers jumped deep behind enemy lines, reached their destination and dug in for the
night. In the wee hours, Israeli aircraft parachuted jeeps, recoilless guns
and heavy mortars.

While Raful's men were still in the air, Arik Sharon crossed the Egyptian border with the paratrooper brigade, riding armored troop carriers and reinforced by AMX tanks. The column advanced through Sinai,
conquering several Egyptian fortresses in fierce battles and after thirty
hours approached Raful's compound.

While waiting for Arik, Raful jokingly prepared a cardboard sign:
STOP! FRONTIER AHEAD! Shortly after 10:00 P.M., on October 30, the armored column reached the sign. Davidi and Sharon, covered with fine
desert dust, jumped from their jeeps and hugged Raful. The mission was
accomplished.

Or so it seemed. Sharon had other thoughts. In the last two years
he had turned the paratrooper corps into an elite commando unit that
had carried out most of the reprisal raids against Israel's neighbors. The

price had been heavy—many of the best fighters had been killed and Meir Har-Zion himself had almost died during the al Rahwa raid in September 1956. A bullet had blasted his throat and he was choking to death when the unit doctor, Maurice Ankelevitz, drew a pocketknife, stuck it in his windpipe, performing an improvised tracheotomy under fire, and saved his life.

Yet, in spite of the wounded and the dead, the paratrooper corps was submerged by a wave of volunteers, most of them members of kibbutz and moshav agricultural settlements. The battalion became a brigade. Sharon, now a lieutenant colonel, had become the best fighter in the IDF. Dayan liked him and Ben-Gurion admired his fighting skills, even though he criticized his integrity. On October 30, 1956, Sharon was, as always, hungry for battle.

He had barely finished hugging Raful when he decided to conquer the famous Mitla Pass—a winding canyon road in the nearby mountain ridge—and be the first to reach the canal with his paratroopers.

The pass seemed to be empty of enemy forces. The day before, an armored convoy coming from Egypt had crossed the canal and penetrated the pass, but Israeli jets had attacked and destroyed it completely. The black carcasses of the burned vehicles still smoked all along the Mitla road.

Sharon sent a radio message, asking permission to take the Mitla Pass. But the General Staff radioed him a clear order: "Don't advance, stay where you are." Sharon, Raful and the other commanders didn't know that the goal of the paratroopers' drop at the Mitla approaches was not fighting or conquering, but to serve as a pretext for the Anglo-French intervention.

In the early morning another message arrived from the staff: "Do not advance!" But Arik did not give up. At 11:00 A.M. Colonel Rehavam ("Gandhi") Ze'evi, the Southern Command chief of staff, arrived at the compound in a light Piper Cub plane. Arik again requested permission to enter Mitla, but Gandhi allowed him only to send a patrol to the pass, on the condition that he wouldn't get entangled in fighting.

Arik immediately assembled a "patrol team" under the command of Motta Gur. At the head of the column Arik placed six half-tracks;

behind them the half-track of the tanks force commander Zvi Dahab and Danny Matt; then three tanks; then the brigade deputy commander, Haka Hofi's, half-track; six more half-tracks full of paratroopers; a battery of heavy 120-millimeter mortars; and several equipment-carrying trucks. The paratrooper commando joined the column not as fighters but as tourists who came to enjoy the trip to the canal. Davidi made a funny hat out of a newspaper, to protect himself from the sun.

And Arik called all this battalion-sized convoy a "patrol."

At 12:30 P.M. the convoy entered the pass. They quickly advanced in the narrow canyon, between two towering mounts.

And there the Egyptians were waiting.

Hundreds of Egyptian soldiers were entrenched in dugouts, natural caves in the rock and behind low stone fences. On the roadside, camouflaged by bushes and bales of thorns, stood armored cars carrying Bren machine guns. Companies of soldiers were positioned above them, armed with bazookas, recoilless guns, anti-tank guns and mid-sized machine guns. And on a third line above, in positions and cubbyholes in the rock, lay soldiers armed with rifles and automatic weapons.

At twelve-fifty, the half-tracks advancing in the pass were hit by a lethal volley of bullets and shells. A hail of bullets drummed on the half-tracks' armored plates. The first half-track swayed to and fro and stopped, its commander and driver dead; the other soldiers, some of them wounded, jumped off the vehicle and tried to find cover.

Motta Gur's half-track was about 150 yards behind. He ordered his men to advance toward the damaged vehicle. Three half-tracks reached the immobile vehicle and were hit too. Motta got around them and tried to escape the ambush, but he was hit as well. He and his men sought refuge in a shallow ditch beside the road.

Haka, who was in the middle of the column, realized that his men had blundered into a deadly ambush. He ordered Davidi to get back and stop the vehicles that had not entered the pass yet. Davidi unloaded the mortars and opened fire on the hills. Haka himself broke through the enemy lines with a company and two tanks. The armored vehicles bypassed the stuck half-tracks and emerged on the other side of the pass, two kilometers down the road.

Mitla, full of burned, smoldering vehicles from the Egyptian convoy from the day before, now became a killing field for the paratroopers. Four Egyptian Meteor jets dived toward the column, blew up eight trucks carrying fuel and ammunition, and hit several heavy mortars.

Motta sent an urgent message to Haka, asking him to come back into the pass and rescue the trapped soldiers. He also requested from Davidi that Micha Kapusta's commando should attack the Egyptian positions from behind.

Micha's commando—the finest paratrooper unit—climbed to the tops of the hills. His platoon commanders started moving down the northern slope, annihilating the Egyptian positions. But at this point a terrible misunderstanding occurred.

The commando fighters that destroyed the enemy positions on the northern slope clearly saw the road. They didn't notice that the slope turned to a sheer drop almost at their feet, and most of the Egyptians were entrenched there. They also failed to notice other Egyptian positions that were located on the southern slope, across the road.

Suddenly, Micha's men were hit by a hail of bullets and missiles from the southern slope. Micha thought that the trapped paratroopers by the road were firing at him. Furious, he yelled at Davidi on his radio to make Motta's people stop firing, while Motta, who couldn't see the enemy positions on the southern slope that were firing at the commando, did not understand why Micha didn't continue his advance.

These were tragic moments. "Go! Attack!" Davidi yelled at Micha, while Micha saw his men falling. The paratroopers dashed forward under heavy fire. Some reached the edge of the rocky drop without noticing it and rolled down, in full sight of the Egyptians, who shot them.

Facing heavy fire, Micha decided to retreat to a nearby hill. But another Israeli company appeared on top of that hill and mistakenly started firing on Micha's men. Micha's fury and pain echoed in the walkie-talkies. His soldiers were fired at from all sides, by Egyptians and by Israelis.

At last Davidi understood the mix-up that had caused Motta's and Micha's contradictory reports. He made a fateful decision: send a jeep that would attract the enemy fire into the pass. Davidi's observers would then locate the sources of the Egyptian fire.

For that mission he needed a volunteer who would be ready to sacrifice his life.

"Who volunteers to get to Motta?" he asked.

Several men jumped right away. Davidi chose Ken-Dror, his own driver.

Ken-Dror knew he was going to his death. He started the jeep and sped to the pass, immediately becoming the target of heavy fire. The jeep was crushed and Ken-Dror collapsed beside it. His sacrifice was in vain. Motta and Micha didn't succeed in pinpointing the sources of enemy fire.

Davidi sent a half-track with four soldiers and a lieutenant to the pass. The carrier reached Motta, loaded some wounded soldiers and returned, unharmed.

And the sources of the shooting still were not discovered.

Davidi again ordered Micha to storm the Egyptian positions. His soldiers ran again down the slope. Another platoon was hit by crossfire from the southern hill. And Micha suddenly saw the abrupt drop at his feet and understood where the Egyptian positions were.

At that moment he was shot. A bullet pierced his chest, he lost his breath and he felt he was going to die.

"Dovik!" he shouted at his deputy. "Take over!"

A bullet hit Dovik in the head. The two wounded men started crawling up the hill. In front of them they saw other paratroopers. They feared their comrades would shoot them by mistake. "Davidi! Davidi" they shouted hoarsely.

At 5:00 P.M. a rumble of tanks suddenly echoed in the narrow canyon. Haka's two tanks returned from the western exit of the pass and turned the tide. They first set their guns toward the southern hill and blasted many of the enemy positions. Egyptian soldiers started fleeing in a disorderly way but were mown down by the paratroopers' machine guns. Simultaneously, two paratrooper companies reached the crests of the two ridges rising on both sides of the road. They came from the western entrance to the pass and systematically mopped up the Egyptian positions. They agreed that their finishing line would be a burning Egyptian half-track in the center of the canyon. Other fighters would come from the east and destroy the remaining enemy positions on the northern and southern hills.

At nightfall fifty paratroopers scaled the hills—half of them, commanded by a twice-decorated veteran, Oved Ladijanski, turned to the southern ridge; the other half, under the leadership of a slim and soft-spoken kibbutz member, Levi Hofesh, attacked the northern one. Their goal was to reach the burning half-track with no Egyptian soldier left behind.

Oved's unit moved up the hill in silence, holding their fire. They reached a fortified machine gun position, hewn in the rocky slope. They attacked it from below with hand grenades, but some of those bounced off the rock and exploded. Oved threw a grenade toward the machine gun, but the grenade rolled down. "It's coming back," Oved whispered to the soldier beside him, pushed him aside and covered him with his body. The grenade exploded against Oved's chest and killed him. One of his comrades succeeded in dropping a grenade into the position, burst in and killed the Egyptians cowering inside.

The survivors of Oved's unit kept advancing and destroying the enemy positions. Levi Hofesh did the same on the northern hill. He realized that the Egyptians had placed their forces in three tiers, one above the other. He divided his soldiers in three detachments, and each mopped up one of the enemy lines. The fighting was desperate; the trapped Egyptians had nothing to lose. It took the paratroopers two hours to advance three hundred yards. Shortly before 8:00 P.M., Levi completed his operation, leaving behind ninety Egyptian dead.

The paratroopers now were the masters of the Mitla Pass. During the night, cargo planes landed nearby and evacuated the wounded—Dovik and Micha, Danny Matt and another 120 paratroopers. Among the seriously wounded was also Yehuda Ken Dror, hanging to life by a thread. In a few months he would succumb to his wounds.

Thirty-eight paratroopers and two hundred Egyptian soldiers died in the Mitla battle. Four more Israelis would die later of their wounds. Dayan seethed with fury, accusing Sharon of losing so many lives in a totally unnecessary battle. Ben-Gurion, alerted, refused to interfere in a row between two senior officers whom he especially liked. But the Mitla battle actually sent Sharon to an informal exile and delayed his advancement in the IDF by several years.

The Mitla battle was gratuitous, indeed. Yet it was a bravely fought battle, in which Sharon's paratroopers demonstrated his principles that one doesn't abandon comrades on the battlefield, even if it costs human lives, and an IDF team doesn't bend, doesn't give up and doesn't retreat until the mission is achieved.

The Sinai campaign lasted seven days and ended with an Israeli victory. Israel had beaten the Egyptian Army and conquered all of the Sinai Peninsula. The Franco-British invasion, on the other hand, failed miserably. The Israeli triumph marked the beginning of eleven years of de facto peace on the southern border that would abruptly end with the Six Day War.

RAFAEL "RAFUL" EITAN, COMMANDER OF THE 890TH PARATROOP BATTALION AND LATER THE CHIEF OF STAFF

[From an excerpt from his book, *A Soldier's Story: The Life and Times of an Israeli War Hero*, written with Dov Goldstein, Maariv, 1985]

"I was standing closest to the aircraft door. A bit of excitement always hits you over the parachuting site, even if you've done it many times before. All the more so at the start of a large-scale military campaign, at such a distance from Israel. You're plunging into the unknown, into enemy territory. The cockpit of the next plane in the formation was directly across from me, mere feet away. I waved to the copilot. He held his head in both hands, as if to say, 'What you're about to do . . .'

"Red light. Green light. I'm in the air, floating down, over the Mitla crossroads. It's five in the afternoon, dusk. The sun is setting. You can hear a few shots. My feet hit the ground. I release myself from my parachute, get organized quickly. We take our weapons out of their cases. We hold positions in the staging territory. The companies spread out. It's already dark. We put barriers into place. We lay mines. We dig in, hole up. There are trenches there from the days of the Turks. This makes our work easier. Our two forces take positions at the Parker Memorial, to the west, and en route to Bir Hasna, to the north. We mark the ground intended for receiving the supplies being parachuted in.

"At night I went to sleep. . . . One must muster his forces before experiencing the pressure of combat. One must remove the stress and the emotions to a secluded corner. I dug myself a foxhole, padded it with the cardboard from the parachuted supplies, spread down one or two parachutes, and tucked myself in. Good night by the Mitla."

PART THREE

The Six
Day War

The Suez campaign brings Israel almost eleven years
of peace. In 1963, Ben-Gurion resigns and is replaced by
Levi Eshkol. The chief of staff is Yitzhak Rabin. Ben-Gurion,
Dayan and Peres are the leaders of a small party, Rafi, created
after a violent clash between Ben-Gurion and Eshkol.
On May 15, 1967, Egypt's President Nasser suddenly triggers
a sequence of military moves that threaten Israel with
annihilation: he announces that the end of Israel is near.
Israel's efforts to obtain the support of the Great Powers
end in failure. France switches camps; President De Gaulle,
Israel's great ally, unexpectedly imposes an embargo on
weapons for Israel. Under popular pressure Eshkol
reluctantly appoints Moshe Dayan as defense minister in
a Government of National Unity in which opposition leader
Menachem Begin is minister without portfolio. Israel feels
it has no choice but to attack Egypt before it,
itself, is attacked and invaded.

CHAPTER 6

"LIFE OR DEATH," OPERATION FOCUS, 1967

June 5, 1967

At four-thirty in the morning, every pilot in the Israeli Air Force was awakened. Their planes stood ready for takeoff, fueled and armed, at the Ramat David, Hatzor, Tel Nof and Hatzerim airbases, and even at the civilian airport in Lod. In their cockpits, the pilots, barred from operating their communications systems, maintained complete radio silence; the control towers had also gone quiet. It was forbidden that anyone, anywhere, might receive even a hint of the massive takeoff. The ground crews directed the planes using signals from colored lanterns. At seven-fourteen, the first planes, French antiquated Ouragans, took flight, followed two minutes later by another takeoff of Ouragans. After they roared into the morning skies, in accordance with a timetable calculated down to the last minute, Vautours, Mystères, Super Mystères and Mirages took flight. The planes took off at a frenzied pace, from several bases, at a frequency of a plane per minute; at the Hatzor airbase, seventy-seven planes took off between seven-fourteen and eight-fifteen, an average of one every forty-eight seconds. Very quickly, there were 183 planes in the sky—in fact, Israel's entire air force. They entered formations of four and set forth, each on its own flight path. Twelve Mirages were left to guard the skies over Israel.

The planes' takeoff was the opening act of the Six Day War.

The descent into war had begun three weeks earlier, on Israel's Independence Day, May 15. Divisions of the Egyptian Army had unexpectedly thundered into the Sinai Peninsula, stationing themselves along the Israel border. Egypt's president, Gamal Abdel Nasser, expelled the UN observers from Sinai, closed the Straits of Tiran and signed military agreements with Syria and Jordan. Even Iraq announced it was joining in. The Arab street reacted with tremendous excitement, the masses dancing in the squares, waving flags and posters, and screaming slogans of rage and hatred against Israel. Nasser's image appeared across the media, smiling and confident, surrounded by Egyptian fighter pilots, young eagles clad in their G-suits, at the Bir Gifgafa airbase. Turning to the television cameras, Nasser made his historic statement, "If Israel wants war, *ahlan wa sahlan*—welcome!"

Radio and television across the Arab world reported Israel's imminent demise. Britain and the United States couldn't find a way to solve the crisis and reopen the Straits of Tiran to Israeli shipping. The president of France, Charles de Gaulle, abandoned his alliance with Israel and imposed an embargo on the delivery of arms to the IDF.

The people of Israel sensed the danger of extermination hovering overhead. Prime Minister Levi Eshkol and his government appeared hesitant, afflicted with paralysis and trying to buy time. The public forced the leadership to establish a unity government, in which Moshe Dayan, the celebrated hero of the Sinai campaign, was appointed defense minister.

On June 4, the government decided to go to war. The first step would be the air force's Operation Focus, and victory in the war would depend on its success.

Operation Focus had been designed to wipe out the Egyptian Air Force—or, if needed, all enemy air forces—on the ground. Rafi Sivron, a young captain, had prepared the original plan, which rested on a surprise attack on the enemy's airfields, the bombing of the runways to prevent landings and takeoffs, and the destruction of planes on the ground. In 1965, Sivron had been taken on by Major Yossi Sarig, a former commander of the 110 Squadron's Vautour planes, who had been appointed the head of the Attack Section within the Operations Department. The new role fit Sarig like a glove. He had previously carried out dozens of daring photo-surveillance missions, both during the day and at night, over almost every Arab airfield in Egypt, Jordan, Syria and Lebanon. He knew the fields like the back of his hand. In light of the drastic changes that had occurred in the Middle East and within the region's air forces, Sarig immersed himself in the detailed, constantly changing plan for the operation. The surprise factor would be an essential condition of the plan's success. The attack planes would need to strike the Egyptian airfields suddenly and at precisely the same moment. Consequently, they would need to take off and fly in complete radio silence, at the lowest possible altitude—below the zone covered by radar—and to reach their targets at exactly the same time. Most of the flights would need to be carried out over the Mediterranean Sea in order to reach Egypt from the north. Others, directed at the most remote airfields, would fly over Israel's Negev Desert and the Red Sea. It was necessary to lay out precise flight paths and timetables, and endless drills were conducted involving takeoffs and flights at an altitude of up to one hundred feet above sea level.

To carry out its plan, the air force would need 530 attack planes, even though it possessed just two hundred. The solution, it turned out, was born out of a remark made by David Ben-Gurion during a visit to the Ramat David airbase, when he asked the base commander, "How long does it take you to prepare a plane that has just returned for another mission?"

That vital period of time—for refueling from tankers, bringing in ammunition trucks and more—was between an hour and an hour and a half. Ben-Gurion's remark was a wake-up call for the air force staff, who decided to shorten drastically each plane's prep time before its next flight. Fueling pipelines and hoses were laid to the underground hangars where the planes were parked so that they could be refilled the moment they arrived. In each hangar, a load of munitions and bombs for one or two missions was kept at the ready, and the moment it was placed on the plane, another load was sent to the site for the next flight. Ground crews were trained to perform all the preparations and checks in record time. Their commanders stood next to the planes with stopwatches, assessing ways to cut additional minutes and seconds. Contests began among the squadrons' air crews and even among the different bases.

Each fighter plane's prep time was shortened to between five and seven minutes; as a result, the air force's power increased several times over, as the number of planes was multiplied by the number of additional missions they could now carry out. And, as the Arab Air Forces' planes spent longer periods on the ground between flights, it was possible for Israel's Air Force to launch several offensive waves with a much smaller number of aircraft.

The bombing of the airfields was now planned. At some, the runways had been paved with concrete, and with asphalt at others. Each type of runway required a different weapon. The air force had bombs weighing 110, 154, 551 and 1,102 pounds, and needed to match the types of explosives and attack planes with the airfields. Some airfields had just one runway, but Egypt's MiGs could also take off from the taxiway that ran parallel to it; it would be necessary to hit that strip as well. At other airfields, the runways intersected. Several had runways that were more than 1.85 miles long, even though the MiGs needed only a third of that distance; in those cases, it would be necessary to divide the runway into thirds and hit each part with precision strikes.

The research lab at Israel Military Industries (IMI), under the management of the engineer Avraham Makov, had overseen the development of the anti-runway penetration bomb, which would be dropped from roughly 330 feet overhead. A tiny parachute would immediately eject, directing the nose of the bomb at a sixty-degree angle toward the ground; simultaneously, a retro-rocket in its tail would activate, propelling it with great force toward the runway. The 154-pound bomb would penetrate the concrete runway and explode six seconds later, leaving a crater nearly five feet deep and more than sixteen feet in diameter. IMI had also developed a large anti-runway penetration bomb of even greater strength and, by the start of the war, had supplied the air force with sixty-six of the larger model and 187 of the smaller.

The question was how to bomb the runways. Would a plane carrying two bombs drop both during the same pass or would it need to carry out another pass? What should be done in the event of strong winds? What were the chances of strong winds in the morning? And how much damage would the bombs cause the runways?

In order to check, it was decided that the IAF would bomb Israel's Hatzor airbase. At the time, the runway had been taken out of service for repairs. The crews' families were evacuated, and at night IAF planes dived over Hatzor and bombed the runway. After the results were assessed, the air force also calculated how long it would take the Egyptians to plug the holes in their runways and restore the fields that had been bombed. The estimate was roughly forty minutes, starting from the moment the Egyptian base commander took a jeep, went to check the damage and ordered the holes filled in. But the air force wanted the repairs to last two hours and then for the second wave of planes to bomb the field again.

The solution: bombs with timed fuses that could lodge at a great depth without blowing up. The Egyptian commander would surely order that the craters be covered over, and after a predetermined amount of time, the buried bombs would explode, causing damage that would again paralyze the field. It was agreed that any formation going out on a bombing mission would have a bomb or two with a delay mechanism.

And how could Israel be defended while all its planes were in Egypt? Air Force Commander Mordechai ("Motti") Hod took a tremendous risk by placing Israel in the care of ten to twelve Mirages. The air force also decided that several Mirage formations would attack enemy airfields close to Israel so that they could return immediately and defend the country as needed.

The final question: when to attack? Some commanders preferred last light before sunset, knowing that the Egyptians didn't fly at night. But intelligence reported that Egyptian Air Force preparedness focused on first light: the pilots got up early, went out on reconnaissance missions and landed at their bases around 7:30 A.M. (6:30 A.M. Israeli time). Then they would go to drink coffee and eat breakfast. At the same time, the base commanders and General Staff officers were on their way to their offices. Hod himself explained, "When I go from my house in Tzahala to headquarters at seven forty-five A.M. and they tell me on my Motorola that there's a problem, I can't do anything."

The decision was made: the attack would be at 7:45 in the morning.

The plan was rehearsed endlessly. Everything was prepared, but no war appeared on the horizon—until, on May 15, 1967, everything changed.

Sarig had completed his role and departed for the United States to receive Skyhawk aircraft for a new squadron. But ten days later he received an urgent call telling him to come back to Israel immediately. He was driven straight from Lod airport to the so-called "Pit," the underground operational command post at IDF headquarters in Tel Aviv, where he reclaimed his former position and started receiving updates. Intelligence reported that the Egyptian Air Force was changing alert levels and its Tupolev Tu-16 bombers departed for more distant airfields, such as Luxor and Ras Banas.

Hod, Sarig and Ezer Weizman, the IDF's deputy chief of staff and a former commander of the IAF, appeared at a General Staff forum, and Sarig presented Operation Focus. General Herzel Shafir asked, "And what about Syria and Jordan?"

Sarig replied, "Three hours later, we'll carry out Focus in Syria and Jordan, too."

General Yitzhak Hofi interjected, "Look at these air force guys. Ezer Weizman and Motti Hod are bragging, as usual, but now a major is talking this way, too?"

On the night of June 4, final briefings were conducted with the base commanders. The order issued to the pilots was to maintain complete radio silence: "Even if there's a problem with your engine, if you need to come back or even abandon your plane, don't turn on your communications system." The pilots were permitted only the use of a watch, a compass and a map and could have no other aid on hand to help lead them to their targets in Egypt. They were allocated five to seven minutes to bomb the runways and to carry out three more passes over the airfields, to strafe planes and other targets in the area.

The pilots were sent to bed early so that they would be fresh by morning. Many couldn't get to sleep. At stake was a tremendous operation whose goal was the destruction of the entire Egyptian Air Force. The outcome of the war, and even the existence of Israel, depended on it.

One of the pilots, Yair Neuman, wrote in his squadron's log, "June 5, 1967. A day before the great fall of Egypt and its satellites. My hand is shaking!" (Neuman was killed on the first day of the war.) Another pilot wrote, "We felt as though the fate of the entire people of Israel were placed on our shoulders." Another penned, "The eyes of all the world's Jews are on us, in deep anxiety," and his friend added, "God is with the Jews—the burning bush and the burning tanks are in Sinai."

At seven-fourteen, the first plane rocketed skyward, followed by 182 more.

Radio silence was maintained, but to keep the Egyptians from suspecting that something was afoot, several Fouga training jets took off, their pilots speaking by radio while mimicking Mystère and Mirage squadrons carrying out routine practice drills over Israel. If the Egyptians were listening, they could rest assured that this was just another day in the Israeli Air Force.

As the planes neared the skies of Egypt, the IAF electronic combat systems were activated, silencing or disrupting Egypt's transmission networks and radar systems. At the Pit, a nerve-wracking wait began.

At 7:45 A.M., the planes were over their targets. A hundred and eighty-three aircraft dived toward the Egyptian airfields. The meticulous preparations, planning, calculations and training bore fruit. The radio silence was suddenly broken, and the air force's communications networks filled with excited reports from the skies over Egypt. The Egyptians' surprise was total, and the result was better than expected. One after another, eleven Egyptian airfields were blown up, pillars of smoke and fire rising above them. A hundred and seventy-three planes attacked the airfields of El Arish, El Sir, Bir Gifgafa, Bir Tamada, Kibrit, Fayed, Abu Suwayr, Inshas, Cairo International, West Cairo and Beni Suef. The ten other planes carried out patrol and photo-reconnaissance missions.

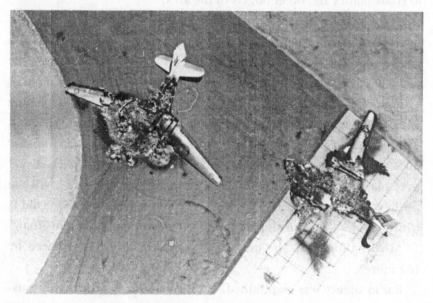

Egyptian bombers destroyed on the ground. *(GPO)*

The first anti-runway penetration bombs landed on the Kibrit airfield. The pilots spared the runways at El Arish so that they could serve the IAF when the Armored Corps captured it. At Bir Gifgafa, five MiGs were destroyed, with one managing to get away. At Cairo West, fifteen Tupolev Tu-16 bombers, among others, were destroyed. At Inshas, every MiG was wiped out, even though the morning mist made it hard to see. One of the Israeli formations accidentally arrived at Cairo International Airport, but when it spotted fighter planes among the commercial jets, struck many of them. The Abu Suwayr airfield put up exceptional resistance, and several of its MiGs managed to take off and attack Israel's planes. Twenty-seven passes over the field were carried out, dropping 102 bombs.Captain Ben-Zion Zohar stood out during the battle, his Vautour engaging with MiGs, returning to bomb the field, and, on its way back to Israel, even attacking a surface-to-air missile battery, landing on its final drops of fuel. He would later be decorated.

Immediately after, the second wave took to the air—164 sorties over sixteen airfields, some of them not attacked during the first wave, like Luxor, where some of the Egyptian planes had escaped. Then came the third, fourth and fifth waves, the last reaching even the remote airfields of Ghardaqa and Ras Banas.

During the third wave, it became clear that Syrian MiGs and Jordanian Hawker Hunters were attempting to attack Israel. Hod ordered a group of planes to change direction and carry out Operation Focus in Jordan and Syria too. The air force destroyed the entire Jordanian Air Force and eliminated most of Syria's planes.

A few errors occurred during the operation, the most bitter being the attack on H-3 airfield in Iraq. MiGs, Hunters and even Tupolev bombers had set out from the field to try attacking targets in Israel. The field wasn't well known, and it hadn't occurred to anyone that it might serve as a departure base against Israel. Air force pilots carried out three attacks on the Iraqi field, achieving success during the first two. But the Iraqis recovered, and when Israeli planes appeared for a third time, they fell into an ambush. Two Vautours and a Mirage crashed after getting hit and one of the pilots who ejected was taken captive; the three remaining planes returned to Israel with their tails between their legs.

But that failure couldn't overshadow Operation Focus's enormous success. Within a few hours, the enemy's air forces were wiped out. The operation would be the decisive component of Israel's victory in the Six Day War. "The pride surrounding this story," one air force leader wrote, "was simply inexhaustible. There are those who will claim that this was the crowning achievement of all the IDF missions ever."

During the Six Day War the IDF had destroyed 327 Egyptian planes, 30 Jordanian planes, 65 Syrian planes, 23 Iraqi planes and one Lebanese plane. But the price was heavy: during the war, the air force lost 46 aircraft and mourned 24 of its pilots.

MAJOR GENERAL AVIHU BEN-NUN, A FORMER COMMANDER-IN-CHIEF OF THE AIR FORCE

"Before Operation Focus, the IDF chief of staff Yitzhak Rabin visited the squadron base. He met with the pilots and said to us that this mission was 'life or death.' The existence of Israel depended on it. Rabin and Ezer [Weizman] instilled in us the sense that everything depended on us, that if we didn't succeed at our task, there was no future for this country.

"I led a formation of four Mystères to the Fayeed airfield. Every plane carried two bombs, each weighing seven hundred ninety-four pounds. On the way, over the sea, the number four plane disappeared on me, and I felt a stone in my heart. At Bardawil, on Sinai's shore, clouds appeared at an altitude of one thousand feet, and another stone was added. But when we reached Fayeed, I saw a bit of blue sky—and we attacked. I dropped the bombs on the runway and, on the next pass, strafed two MiGs at the edge of the runway, which went up in flames.

"An Antonov An-12 transport plane suddenly appeared in front of me, turned and started fleeing southward. I had a dilemma. It would take ten seconds to bring it down, but perhaps I'd miss the main objective, which was destroying the planes on the ground. Ultimately, I decided to focus on the MiGs. We destroyed sixteen MiGs and also blew up an SA-2 battery across the canal. We even found our number four eventually—he had gone back because of a problem with his fueling system. When I landed, I was told that the squadron commander, Yonatan Shachar, had been hit and had ejected, and I was appointed squadron commander in his place.

"Years later, Cairo's daily *Al-Ahram* published an article about the most decorated pilot in the Egyptian Air Force, who, on June fifth, 1967, had managed to escape the planes chasing him in his Antonov. The entire Egyptian General Staff had been on that Antonov that I hadn't brought down. That didn't bring me much pleasure.

"On the third day of the war, we flew over Jerusalem, and the radio played 'Jerusalem of Gold.' It was the only time I've cried during a flight."

The conquest of East Jerusalem has not been one of the Six Day War Israeli goals. Its main offensive is in Sinai. But when Jordanian artillery starts firing on Israel, the IDF counterattacks and conquers the West Bank. Two cabinet ministers exert heavy pressure on Prime Minister Eshkol to liberate Jerusalem. At first Eshkol hesitates. So does Moshe Dayan. Finally, on the third day of the war, he gives the IDF its green light.

CHAPTER 7

"THE TEMPLE MOUNT IS IN OUR HANDS!"
1967

"R ed Sheet! I repeat, Red Sheet!"

In the early morning of June 5, 1967, shortly after the IAF destroyed most of the Egyptian aircraft on the ground, the order "Red Sheet" echoed in the transceivers of the land forces massed on Egypt's border. Thousands of tanks, troop carriers, self-propelled guns, jeeps and trucks crossed the border and charged the Egyptian positions in Sinai.

The Six Day War had started.

Israel didn't want to be drawn into a war with Jordan as well. Foreign Minister Abba Eban alerted General Odd Bull, chief of staff of the United Nation Truce Supervision Organization in Jerusalem, and asked him to convey an urgent message to King Hussein of Jordan: "Israel will not, repeat, not, attack Jordan if Jordan maintains the quiet. But if Jordan opens hostilities, Israel will respond with all of its might." The message was delivered to the king, but in vain. On May 30, Hussein had signed a military pact with Nasser and was convinced that this time the Arabs would crush the Jews. The Jordanian Army was ordered to attack Israel.

At 10:45 A.M., the Jordanian Legion opened fire all along the armistice lines with Israel; Netanya, Kfar Saba, Jerusalem, Ramat David, were shelled. "Long Tom" cannon positioned close to Qalkiliya and Jenin, on the West Bank, fired on Israel's populated centers. Jordanian jets headed for Israeli targets. The legion threw in the battle land forces as well, and occupied Government House, Odd Bull's headquarters in Jerusalem. The IDF Jerusalem brigade, reinforced by tanks, counterattacked and retook the building; it then tried to establish a connection with the Israeli enclave in Mount Scopus, a hill overlooking Jerusalem, where a small unit was guarding a hospital and the old campus of Hebrew University.

Commander of the Central Military District General Uzi Narkiss decided to send the paratroopers to Jerusalem. Their legendary commander, Arik Sharon, was not at their head anymore. Finally promoted to general by Chief of Staff Yitzhak Rabin, he now commanded a division in Sinai. Narkiss dispatched to Jerusalem the newly created 55th Brigade, composed of reserve paratroopers. Its commander was a veteran warrior, Colonel Motta Gur.

Motta was a strange hybrid of an intellectual and a born fighter. He was eighteen during the Independence War, when his training at the Officers Academy had been interrupted and he had been sent with his comrades to conquer Be'er Sheva and fight the Egyptians in the Negev. He liked to describe his baptism by fire to his soldiers. During his first battle, he said, he was just a scared young man, and while the bullets were buzzing around him he suddenly felt an expanding wetness in his pants. He was overwhelmed with shame. Had he peed in his pants? Was he such a coward? As soon as the battle was over he had run to a secluded corner and checked his clothes, then breathed in relief. An Egyptian bullet had pierced his water canteen, and the water had spilled over his pants. . . . He wasn't a coward after all.

After harsh and bloody combats where he had lost some of his best friends, he left the army and enrolled in Hebrew University. There he met Arik Sharon but was not impressed. He heard about the creation of 101, but chose to continue his studies of Middle East history and culture until the day in 1955 when he met Aharon Davidi, an old comrade in arms from the Negev combats.

"I am with the paratroopers now," Davidi said.

"What do you do there?"

Davidi told him about the unit missions; in his soft, matter-of-fact manner, he described the reprisal raids, the incursions deep into enemy territory and the new spirit motivating "the guys with the red boots." Motta was excited. "I am coming!" he said and joined the paratroopers.

As commander of Company D he fought at most of the reprisal raids. He was wounded at a battle in the Gaza Strip and was decorated for bravery by Dayan. Yet, he became the most outspoken critic of Sharon, delivered scathing accusations of his commander after the Mitla Pass battle, and used to say that "I never saw Sharon's back when we were charging the enemy," meaning that the paratroopers' legendary chief was not a hero at all. Nevertheless, he stayed in the paratrooper corps and performed brilliantly. After the Sinai campaign, where he fought at Mitla, he was sent to high-level studies at the Ecole Militaire in Paris. There, beside his martial studies, he and his wife, Rita, discovered French culture: the theaters, the museums, the books of Camus, Sartre, Giraudoux. After his return, he filled several positions in the army. In the evenings he had to tell stories to his four children, and he preferred to write them. His children's books, about "Azit, the paratrooper dog," were best-sellers in Israel and even became a kids' movie.

And on June 5 he was to lead the brigade of war-hardened veterans at the battle for Jerusalem.

I n the afternoon of that day, Cabinet Ministers Yigal Allon and Menachem Begin entered the office of Prime Minister Levi Eshkol. Allon, the legendary former commander of the Palmach, was a leader of the left-wing Ahdut HaAvoda party; Begin was the charismatic head of the right-wing Herut. But both of them were political hawks and they urged Eshkol to liberate the Old City. Yet a formidable obstacle stood in their way: Defense Minister Moshe Dayan, who worried about possible damage to the world's holiest places and the international reaction to the conquest of the Old City. He feared that any fighting inside Jerusalem might result in foreign pressure on Israel that would also influence the campaign against Egypt and prevent Israel from completing its war goals. Dayan knew, however, that the fall of Mount Scopus into the hands of the Jordanians would be considered a severe blow to Israel's prestige. He therefore authorized the IDF only to conquer the road to Scopus, in northeast Jerusalem.

Following Dayan's order, Motta assigned the missions of his three battalions that would attack East Jerusalem: Yossi Yaffe's Battalion 66 would storm the Jordanian Police Academy, conquer it and the nearby Ammunition Hill and Hotel Ambassador. The two other battalions would take the Rockefeller Museum in a pincer attack. Uzi Eilam, the hero of Black Arrow, would lead his Battalion 71 through several Arab neighborhoods and the American Colony and approach the Rockefeller Museum; Yossi Fradkin's Battalion 28 would advance farther up along Salah a-Din Street, a major artery in Arab Jerusalem, conquer the museum and the area adjacent to the Old City Wall. The paratroopers would be supported by tanks and artillery. At the outcome of these attacks the paratroopers would control the road to Mount Scopus. All the objectives of the paratrooper assault were in Arab Jerusalem, but none was inside the Old City.

The last briefing of the company commanders was held in the Cohen Family shelter, in the Beit HaKerem neighborhood. During the briefing the house owner's elderly mother entered the shelter. She handed an old, threadbare Israeli flag to Captain Yoram Zamosh. Her voice was breaking when she told the paratroopers that the flag had been floating over her house in the Old City during the War of Independence. She had taken it when she had been forced to abandon her home. She now asked the officers to raise the flag over the Western Wall. Her plea electrified the soldiers; unwittingly, the elderly lady had determined the goal of their mission, even though it hadn't been formulated in any official document.

At 2:30 A.M., Uzi Eilam led his battalion to Arab Jerusalem, crossed the border fences and after bitter fighting, conquered the American Colony and approached the Rockefeller Museum. But the other operations didn't turn out the way they were planned. The paratroopers were not familiar with Jerusalem, and the intelligence reports about the legion's positions and firepower were far from adequate. Battalion 28, which was to perform the second part of the pincer movement, crossed the no-man's-land, followed by several tanks, and headed for the Rockefeller Museum. But at the crossroads by the wall it missed the turn, and instead of advancing through Salah a-Din Street, the battalion entered the Nablus Road. This turned into a death trap.

The dark Nablus Road and the Old City Wall were fortified with elite Jordanian troops manning heavy-machine-gun nests and riflemen positions, equipped with mortars, bazookas and recoilless guns. The Jordanians opened a murderous crossfire on the approaching paratroopers, inflicting heavy casualties upon them. The medic Shlomo Epstein, who was dressing the wounds of Yossef Hagoel, heard the hiss of an approaching shell and threw himself on Hagoel to protect him. The shell crushed his body. Hagoel survived. Lieutenant Mordechai Friedman raised his hand to throw a hand grenade on a spitting-fire position in a dark alley and was mown down by a machine-gun burst. He collapsed and the grenade exploded in his hand.

The battalion commander called for help and several tanks joined the fighting. Some of them were hit, others got stuck. Only after seven hours of fighting did the paratroopers succeed in clearing the entire road, which was less than a mile long. They reached the hotels Columbia, facing the Nablus Gate, and Rivoli, by Herod's Gate. The legionnaires, barricaded on top of the wall, focused their heavy fire on Rivoli. Haim Russak tried to rescue a wounded comrade and succumbed to the fire of a Jordanian machine gun. The medic Nathan Shechter tried to save him, in vain. Shechter, himself, would soon be killed at Rockefeller Museum.

While the battle was raging on Nablus Road, Battalion 66 was engaged in terrible combat. The paratroopers broke into the Arab city and stormed the Police Academy. At their head was Giora Ashkenazi's company, which advanced using bangalores—long pipe-shaped explosive charges that blew up both the barbwire fences and blazed paths across the minefields. Giora was followed by the company of Dodik Rotenberg, which invaded the fortified trenches and the academy building. The companies of Gabi Magal and Dedi Yaakobi mopped the building, and paused, seeing the sinister outline of Ammunition Hill.

The hill was a formidable bastion, a fortified compound that used to be the armory of the Police Academy during the British mandate. The Jordanians had transformed it into an impregnable fortress. The hill was surrounded by fences, scarred by narrow, winding, stone-plated trenches that some writers later described as a bundle of tangled bowels. Most positions were covered, and between them rose concrete bunkers, cunningly positioned. Every inch of the hill was covered by crisscross fire from several sources. The hill was defended by crack troops, the best of the legionnaires. They were excellent, indomitable warriors who knew they had no way out of the hill and had to fight to their death.

Dedi Yaakobi led his paratroopers to conquer the hill, but his men soon realized that they were trapped in a deadly inferno, exposed to heavy and murderous fire from all over. The night thundered with machine-gun bursts, bomb and grenade explosions, shouts of the wounded and death rattles. The paratroopers advanced in the narrow trenches but were easy prey for the heavy fire of the bunker positions. The company broke into several units that all encountered a grim fate. Corporal Meir Malmudi's squad was decimated in a crossfire trap in an open stretch. Yoram Eliashiv, quiet and calm, was slain at the head of his platoon. A bullet pierced the forehead of Yirmi Eshkol, Dedi's deputy. Soon after the battle began, most of Dedi's men were killed or wounded. He called Dodik for help but even before reinforcements arrived, his remaining soldiers, some of them severely wounded, kept running forward in the treacherous trenches, often bumping against the bodies of fallen legionnaires.

A similar fate awaited Dodik's soldiers. Platoon commander Yoav Tzuri led his men through the exposed stretch where Malmudi's soldiers had been killed. He was hit on his turn and fell, dead. Dodik's deputy, Nir Nitzan, led another platoon to the western part of the peripheral trench. He called Eitan Nava, a tough moshav boy, to get out of the trench and run ahead of the paratroopers, shooting at the enemy with his mini–machine gun. Nava knew that this was a suicide mission but didn't hesitate. He jumped out of the trench and ran forward, spraying the Jordanians with continuous fire while also attracting fire from all over. His comrades shouted at him, "Jump in the trench, you'll be killed!" but he kept running, hitting thirty legionnaires before he was slain.

Another fighter, Israel Zuriel, immediately leapt out of the trench and took Nava's place. He survived against all odds.

Most of the medics running in the trenches between scores of wounded were injured or killed. Didier Guttal crouched in one of the trenches, his arm torn from his body. Another medic, Yigal Arad, ran like mad between the wounded of the two companies, dressed wounds, tied tourniquets and firmly fixed broken limbs.

From different directions, the surviving soldiers approached the main bunker. Zvi Magen, a platoon deputy commander, charged ahead of his soldiers and tried to throw a hand grenade on the position; he was killed by a burst of machine-gun fire. In the meantime the sun rose in the east and exposed the paratroopers to the accurate fire of snipers and machine gunners. Yet they kept fighting, advancing inch after inch to the monstrous bunker. It was a double bunker, protected with eighteen-inch-thick concrete plates. Three paratroopers approached the bunker from both sides—Yaki Hetz, David Shalom and Yehuda Kendel. All their efforts to destroy it by automatic fire, bazooka shells and hand grenades failed. Their commander ordered them to bring over bags of explosives, which they piled up by the bunker's walls. A formidable explosion blew up the bunker, yet the soldiers had to confront and kill five legionnaires who had miraculously survived.

The battle ended at six-fifteen in the morning. Thirty-six paratroopers and seventy legionnaires died on Ammunition Hill.

Some legionnaires were captured, and their first task was to bury their fallen comrades. A paratrooper stuck an improvised sign by their grave: HERE ARE BURIED 28 LEGIONNAIRES. Another fighter corrected the sign to read, " . . . 28 *brave* legionnaires."

Ammunition Hill was in the paratroopers' hands, but at what price! Only a few survivors remained of the two companies. An Israeli poet, Yoram Taharlev, wrote a chilling poem about the battle:

Seven came back into the city
And smoke was rising from the hill
The sun was high up in the east
On Ammunition Hill.

On all the concrete bunkers there
On all our dear comrades in arms
Left behind, forever young
On Ammunition Hill.

The paratroopers now held the Police Academy, Ammunition Hill and the Rockefeller Museum, which had been captured by Eilam's 71st Battalion and A Company of the 28th. The road to Mount Scopus was open; that very morning Dayan and several senior officers visited the Israeli enclave. The paratroopers and the other units fighting in that sector were now ordered to encircle the Old City from all over till it fell "like a ripe fruit." The Jerusalem brigade completed the conquest of the Abu Tor neighborhood, south of the Old City; Colonel Uri Ben-Ari, commanding an armored brigade, captured the Mivtar Hill and the French Hill, on the northeastern approaches to the city. The Jordanian high command hurriedly dispatched a task force of forty-two superior Patton tanks to Jerusalem, but Israeli jets destroyed them on the road before they even approached.

At nightfall, Motta Gur dispatched a unit of tanks and Micha Kapusta's paratrooper commando to the last hill rising in the north of Jerusalem—the Mount of Olives and the Augusta Victoria compound. Once again, the Israelis took the wrong turn; the tanks got stuck on a bridge over the Kidron creek, facing the legion's positions. They were met by a stunning volley of shells and machine-gun fire. The commando fighters were hit: some were killed, some fell into the creek and a few of their jeeps overturned or caught fire. Micha Kapusta ran down to the dried-up creek to try to save some of his men. He was joined by the legendary Meir Har-Zion, who was not on active duty but had rushed to Jerusalem to be with his comrades. The slaughter in the Kidron creek was very hard on Motta Gur, who followed it from his new command post at the Rockefeller Museum; beside his troubles with the Kidron creek, he was now subjected to a fierce shelling by the Jordanians. He almost lost his voice shouting at his men to take cover. He sat on the ground among them, dejected and pained by the thought of all these fine soldiers who had died. But he soon regained his composure; on the evening of June 6, it seemed that the Jordanians were breaking down.

At 4:00 A.M., Menachem Begin heard a news broadcast on BBC radio, claiming that the combats in Sinai were coming to an end, and the UN Security Council was about to declare a cease-fire. Begin conveyed the news item to Eshkol and Dayan. They took it very seriously; if they didn't act immediately, the Old City might remain as a Jordanian enclave in Israeli-occupied territory. They therefore overcame their hesitations and gave the order to conquer the Old City.

Motta Gur and his officers watch the Old City from the Mount of Olives, minutes before the final attack. *(GPO)*

At dawn, Motta's paratroopers and several tanks conquered Augusta Victoria and the Mount of Olives. One of the casualties at Augusta Victoria was Giora Ashkenazi, the company commander who had led his men in the storming of the Police Academy the previous night. The advanced command post of Motta settled on the Mount of Olives, close to the InterContinental Hotel. Before them lay, in all its beauty, the fairy-tale scenery of the Old City.

"Jerusalem" was like a magic word that reignited the fighting spirit in the mutilated brigade's soldiers. The 71st Battalion reorganized on the Mount of Olives; the 66th on Scopus, and the 28th by the Old City Wall, also reported they were ready for battle.

The moment had come. Motta radioed an order to his men and the tanks supporting them: "Storm the Old City!"

Motta jumped into his half-track and darted toward the Lions' Gate in the Old City Wall. On the way he bypassed the tanks and emerged at the head of the column. His driver, a huge soldier named Bentzur, accelerated like mad, yet Motta kept shouting at him, words that would become famous in Israeli lore: "Go, Bentzur, go!"

The half-track broke into the Lions' Gate. Perhaps the gate was booby-trapped; perhaps the legionnaires were waiting in the narrow, crooked alleys; perhaps a mine was concealed in the motorcycle lying in the middle of the street, blocking Motta's way. He didn't think of all that. He ordered his driver to run over the motorcycle and head for the Temple Mount, where Solomon's temple had stood thousands of years ago. "Go, Bentzur, go!" he repeated, his mind obsessed by a single thought: what will his little daughter Ruthy say when she hears that he conquered the Temple Mount? The half-truck climbed the narrow streets and suddenly emerged in the large concourse on top of the mount. The golden dome of Omar Mosque glistened in front of him.

Motta's voice echoed hoarsely in the radios and walkie-talkies of the army, soon to be repeated over the Israelis' and the world's radios: "The Temple Mount is in our hands!"

Motta's deputy and close friend Moshe ("Stempa'le") Stempel ran with Yoram Zamosh and a few other paratroopers to the Western Wall, the last vestige of Solomon's Temple. Zamosh drew a folded flag from his pouch. It was the flag old Mrs. Cohen had brought over in 1948 from the Jewish Quarter in Old Jerusalem and given to him a few hours before the battle of Jerusalem began. Zamosh and his comrades raised it over the wall.

The Jewish people in Israel and the Diaspora felt like they were dreaming. The prayer of thousands of years had come true.

One hundred and eighty-two soldiers, ninety-eight of them paratroopers, fell in the battle of Jerusalem.

Three days later, the Six Day War ended. Israel had conquered Jerusalem, the West Bank, the Sinai Peninsula and the Golan Heights.

Was peace any nearer?

GENERAL MORDECHAI ("MOTTA") GUR—FORMER 55TH BRIGADE COMMANDER

[Translated from his speech at the paratroopers' victory ceremony on the Temple Mount, December 6, 1967]

"To the paratroopers, conquerors of Jerusalem:

"When the Temple Mount was occupied by the Greeks, the Maccabees liberated it; Bar-Kochva and the zealots fought the Second Temple's destroyers. For two thousand years, the Temple Mount was barred to the Jews.

"Until you came—you, the paratroopers—and brought it back into the heart of the nation. The Western Wall, every heart beating toward it, is again in our hands.

"Many Jews put their lives in danger, throughout our long history, to reach Jerusalem and live there. Countless songs of yearning expressed the profound longing for Jerusalem beating in the Jewish heart.

"During the War of Independence, tremendous efforts were made to restore the nation's heart—the Old City and the Western Wall.

"The great privilege of closing the circle, of returning to our people our capital and center of holiness, fell to you.

"Many paratroopers, among our best and most experienced comrades, fell during the cruel combat. It was an intense, hard-fought battle, and you acted as one body, storming forward, crushing all the obstacles without paying attention to its wounds.

"You didn't argue. You didn't complain. You didn't file claims. You simply pressed onward—and you conquered.

"Jerusalem is yours—forever."

PART FOUR

The War of
Attrition

The conquest of Sinai, the West Bank,
Jerusalem and the Golan Heights have put an end
to the Six Day War. Israel now expects her Arab
neighbors to engage in peace talks in order to recover
their lost territories, but the Arab leaders stubbornly
stick to their former positions: no to negotiations,
no to reconnaissance and no to peace with Israel.
Egypt starts a "war of attrition" against Israel.

Some of the main players on the Israeli side
have changed. Eshkol has died, in February 1969,
and been replaced by Golda Meir. Yitzhak Rabin is now
ambassador to Washington and been succeeded as chief
of staff by General Haim Bar-Lev, whose cool, soft-spoken
behavior hides nerves of steel and an inclination for bold
commando operations. He is supported by
Defense Minister Moshe Dayan.

CHAPTER 8

"I FELT I WAS SUFFOCATING": THE RAID ON GREEN ISLAND, 1969

"I heard members of Sayeret Matkal getting closer, and I called out for them to get into position. Suddenly a grenade exploded beside me. I stopped feeling my right side. My arm was fine, but a warm object had pierced my neck, and I felt I was suffocating. It was an impossible thing to endure. Suddenly, I heard a death rattle coming out of my throat, a terrible sound I remembered hearing from Egyptian soldiers who'd been hit moments earlier," recalled Ami Ayalon, a naval commando who took part in the battle for Green Island, was severely wounded and later received a Medal of Valor.

It was the summer of 1969, during the war of attrition with Egypt. In an attempt to exhaust Israel, the Egyptians had been attacking IDF forces in Sinai, causing heavy losses. A week before the raid on Green Island, the Egyptians had assaulted an Israeli position facing Port Tewfik. Seven IDF soldiers had been killed, with five wounded, one taken captive and three tanks destroyed. A gloomy atmosphere reigned within the General Staff. In order to recover the IDF's confidence, they decided to launch an effective deterrence operation.

The commander of Shayetet 13 naval commando unit, Ze'ev Almog, devised a plan for a raid on Green Island, submitting it to the General Staff's chief operations officer, David ("Dado") Elazar. Green Island was a formidable fortress located in the northern Gulf of Suez and was originally intended to defend the southern entrance to the Suez Canal. There were roughly a hundred Egyptian soldiers stationed on the island, with six dual-purpose guns on the roof of the fortress, antiaircraft fire-control radar, and twenty positions for heavy and medium machine guns and light artillery. It was also within the range of Egyptian 130-millimeter cannon batteries located on the coast.

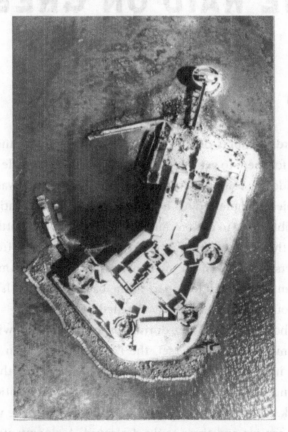

Green Island, a fortress in the Red Sea. *(IDF Spokesman)*

The goal of the operation was to undermine Egyptian confidence with a strike deep in the country's territory, where its soldiers felt safe and secure. Moreover, the mission was simultaneously intended to raise IDF soldiers' morale, which was at a nadir because of the growing number of casualties at the canal. The attack could persuade the Egyptians to respect the cease-fire with Israel. The destruction of the Green Island radar would also disrupt the early-warning system of the Egyptian Air Force and facilitate the task of the IAF aircraft on their frequent sorties over Egyptian territory.

The task of seizing the island was assigned to Shayetet 13 and Sayeret Matkal under the command of Menachem Digli. The chief paratroopers' officer, Raful Eitan, was in command of the operation. Raful, who had led his paratroopers on the jump in Sinai in 1956, as a major, had distinguished himself during the Six Day War and was now a general. He realized that forty soldiers would be needed, as it was clear that a raid on the fortified island would require an amphibious landing, face-to-face combat and a high risk of the loss of life.

According to the plan, the raid force would sail in twelve rubber boats. Twenty Shayetet commandos, constituting the penetration force and the first to land, would be in the first five, and the rest of the boats would carry the twenty soldiers of Sayeret Matkal. The Shayetet fighters were instructed to get within just under three thousand feet of the island, and from there to move forward by swimming and diving toward it. The moment they managed to break through the fences and gain a foothold on the island, they would alert the rest of the boats, which would be waiting just under a mile away. The Shayetet soldiers were to swim and dive while equipped with personal weapons and other combat gear weighing just over eighty-eight pounds, and would be linked by rope to the lead commander—not a simple task, as would become clear.

After a model of Green Island was built and the teams had practiced the raid, it was decided that the operation would be carried out on the night of July 19, between 1:30 and 2:30 A.M.

Shortly before H-Hour, Chief of Staff Haim Bar-Lev arrived at the gathering point. Slight of build, always wearing a black armored-corps beret, Bar-Lev had a slow manner of speaking, and his calm, matter-of-fact elocution inspired confidence in his listeners. In a conversation with the soldiers, Bar-Lev emphasized the subject of losses, commenting that if there were more than ten casualties, the mission would be considered a failure. The remarks were delivered against the backdrop of heavy recent IDF losses at the canal; to the chief of staff, a mission with a high human toll was dangerous to morale and outweighed the benefits of capturing the target.

At 8:00 P.M. on July 19, the rubber boats and a small submersible nicknamed "Pig" were lowered into the water, and the soldiers sailed toward their destination. The Shayetet fighters were ready to dive, clad in wetsuits and in Dacron uniforms, wearing sneakers with flippers attached, combat vests outfitted with significant battle gear, as well as life jackets, oxygen tanks, submachine guns, grenades and magazines. At 11:00 P.M., they reached the dive point, three thousand feet from their objective, and started swimming toward the island. Then the complications began: the twenty Shayetet soldiers were situated along two ropes, led by two officers, each pulling ten men carrying nearly ninety pounds of gear apiece. The equipment was too heavy and the number of soldiers too large; the currents were much stronger than they had thought. They lost stability, some men got bogged down and the force struggled to move forward. Dov Bar, the commander of the first wave, decided to transition to diving earlier than planned—but that, too, turned out to be less than easy. The force was carried off course by the current, and half an hour later, Captain Bar rose to the surface and discovered that they were almost two thousand feet from their objective. It was 12:30 A.M.; Eitan and Almog were waiting for updates and calling on the radio, expecting to hear that the fence had already been breached, allowing the Sayeret soldiers to be brought in for battle—but the force hadn't even reached the island.

Bar made a decision on his own: "I decided that I'm getting to the target, no matter what," he later said. He signaled to everyone else to rise to the surface and to continue forward by swimming, contrary to the accepted plan, and only to submerge again just before reaching the target.

The moonlight threatened to expose them, but Bar remained calm. After another half hour of swimming, they reached the island.

It was 1:38 by the time they stripped off their diving gear, eight minutes past the operation's start last deadline. The penetration team cut the first fence with ease but found two more, which would have taken too much time to get through. From an earlier observation, the planners concluded that there should be another opening in a fence nearby. The soldiers, who had surreptitiously taken cover under a small bridge, could make out three Egyptian guards, one with a lit cigarette in his hand. They could spot the fence in question, but it was directly below the Egyptian position. The head of the penetration team feared that the force would be discovered and decided to surprise the Egyptians by opening fire on the guard, and, in doing so, delivering the opening shot of the operation. The battle had started.

The Egyptians, caught very much off guard, responded immediately with gunfire, which passed over the commandos' heads. In less than a minute, they had sent up flares that illuminated the entire island. The Israeli diversion force began firing bazookas at the target.

Almog, Digli and Eitan were waiting with twenty Sayeret fighters for the agreed-upon signal to enter the target. The signal didn't come. But the moment they heard echoes from the shooting and saw flashes of light, Almog decided not to wait any longer and ordered the boats to advance toward the island.

All the same, for ten long minutes the Shayetet commandos fought alone on the island, even though the Sayeret fighters were already supposed to be battling at their side. After crossing through the fence, the Shayetet members had begun advancing while throwing grenades and shooting Egyptian soldiers who crossed their path. This was how they reached the central building. One team went up in the direction of the roof and another turned toward the rooms, with the objective of mopping them. A tall, broad, strong soldier named Jacob Pundik stood under the roof and served as a ladder, earning the nickname "Jacob's Ladder."

First Lieutenant Ami Ayalon climbed onto his shoulders and reached the roof. His team had been assigned to destroy the cannon and machine-gun positions on the fortress roof; he had studied the positions of the different weapons during the rehearsals for the mission. The moment he got on the roof, he was wounded by shrapnel to his forehead. "I threw a smoke grenade to get a little cover," he recounted, "and I shouted to Zali [Zalman Rot], who had gone up, too, to charge the enemy with me, but the grenade didn't explode. I threw an explosive grenade toward the position the shooting was coming from, but it didn't blow up either. Zali threw a grenade at the position from the left side and then, with a long burst of gunfire, I rushed into the Egyptian Position Two. Gunfire came again from Position Ten, which had shot at me earlier. We fired back. The Egyptian, who was shooting with an automatic weapon, fell, and the position started to burn."

As Ayalon and Rot charged the cannon position, the Egyptians opened machine-gun fire. Rot shouted that his fingers had been cut off but went on fighting anyway. Yedidya ("Didi") Ya'ari joined the commandos on the roof to hit the third cannon but was immediately wounded: "I took a bullet in the leg and was laid out like a rabbit. . . . They carried me to the side and I was hit again, in the face and body, by grenade shrapnel that made me deaf and blind. . . . My face was burning and I was half-conscious, and I didn't understand what was happening."

In the meantime the Sayeret fighters landed on the island and joined the fighting. The Shayetet's ammunition started to run out; nevertheless, Bar pressed on with the charge, sending two fighters to Position 5. They were hit by a grenade and killed on the spot. A grenade was thrown at Ayalon, too, badly injuring his neck. He heard himself gurgling like the dying Egyptians and thought that perhaps now was his turn. He crawled back and evacuated to the boats under his own steam.

A detail of Sayeret soldiers joined the fighting on the roof. A team commander, Captain Ehud Ram, advanced, crouching, along the roof; as he was receiving a report from one of his men, a bullet pierced his forehead, and he was killed. After Ram was hit, two teams came down to clear out the internal courtyard; one of the men was hit and later died from his injuries.

It was already 2:15 A.M.. Almog reported to the command post that the Egyptian gunfire was dying down, and that his forces had suffered deaths and injuries. The fighters now set off 176 pounds of explosives in the northern section of the fortress. A tremendous explosion shook the small island, and its cannons and machine guns were destroyed. Minutes later, Eitan ordered the start of the evacuation. Now that the outcome of the battle was becoming clear, Egyptian cannon, positioned on the mainland, opened heavy fire on the island and blasted one of the Shayetet boats.

"When the evacuation began, I already knew the whole truth," said Dani Avinun, one of the wounded. "The dead and injured came past by me. We threw Yedidya Ya'ari—later the commander-in-chief of the navy—into a boat because we were convinced he was dead, and we told headquarters as much on the radio. Later it turned out that he was only wounded."

Close to 3:00 A.M., at the end of the battle, the boats headed back, carrying the exhausted fighters, six dead and eleven wounded. The Egyptian death toll was more than thirty.

Debriefings conducted after the operation revealed more than a few failures. The intelligence data had not been sufficient in regard to the water currents; the identity of the Egyptian soldiers on the island, who proved to be commandos prepared for a raid; or the radar, which turned out to be a dummy; and the cannons, revealed as heavy, outdated machine guns.

Yet, despite it all, the raid on Green Island is considered one of the IDF's shining successes. Some regard it as a historic turning point in terms of planning, preparation and implementation in the field. Eitan later commented, "The execution of the Green Island raid was exceptional in its inordinate success. The achievement was the operation itself, in which we paved the way for a new method of fighting that strengthened our security. The Egyptians, in their worst nightmares, had never dreamed of such a daring operation. During the action, we demonstrated a capability and performance level that served as a milestone for many years to come."

The day after the operation, the newspapers went out of their way to sing its praises: "An event that will be remembered for generations . . . A story that will become a legend . . . A raid on a steep-walled fortress built on stone and coral . . . An event comparable to the story about the British raid on the island of Navarone in the Aegean Sea, during World War Two. 'The Guns of Navarone' is a myth invented in the writer's imagination, but the guns of Green Island are a real-life legend whose story will one day be told."

The Egyptians also treated the operation with gravity. Dr. Mustafa Kabha, in his study "The War of Attrition as Reflected in Egyptian Sources," wrote that "this operation constituted a turning point in the war of attrition. It symbolized the start of a new phase in the war that most Egyptian researchers called 'the counter-attrition stage,' in which the military initiative passed from Egyptian hands to Israel's."

ADMIRAL AMI AYALON, LATER COMMANDER IN CHIEF OF THE NAVY

"I get to the roof and it becomes clear that, in contrast to what we prepared for, there's no cover, and I'm completely exposed to continuous Egyptian gunfire. I raise my head and the bullets are whistling over me, the ricochets are grazing my forehead, and I realize that I'm in a life-or-death situation. . . . I decide to charge, my friend Zali charges after me, and both of us burst into the position. I eliminate two Egyptian soldiers and Zali another two, . . . From there we continued fighting toward the other positions. . . .

"In today's terms, there's a big question mark about whether this operation should have been carried out. I don't think it brought about a reversal in the war of attrition, nor did it demonstrate a professional capacity or special level of performance, as was said after the mission.

"But, in those days, the operation had a dramatic impact on the IDF, on our faith in ourselves, on the morale of Israeli society and also on the Egyptian forces along the canal.

"I have to admit that, from the Shayetet's point of view, this exposed our professional shortcomings, because it was the first operation of its type in the world, the first time in the history of war that a force of divers used the cloak of diving to reach an enemy target underwater, and to start a gun battle the moment it pulled its head out of the water."

Israel's relations with the United States dramatically improved after the Six Day War. Under Presidents Johnson and Nixon the U.S. has become the main supplier of weapons to Israel after De Gaulle's embargo. That embargo is tightened further by De Gaulle's successor, Georges Pompidou.

CHAPTER 9

THE FRENCH DEFENSE MINISTER: "BOMB THE ISRAELIS!" 1969

December 24, 1969

The owner of the Café de Paris in the French port city of Cherbourg was tossing anxious glances at the entrance. The numerous clients visiting the restaurant this evening had eaten, drunk and sung, but fourteen guests who reserved a table for the Christmas meal had lagged in coming, and now it was after midnight. Foie gras, roasted turkey and champagne had been left orphaned. The unhappy restaurateur didn't know that these same fourteen men, along with 106 of their friends, were spending the evening in the belly of five state-of-the-art missile boats in the city's civil port, attuned to the howls of the raging storm outside and praying to the God of Israel that it would pass quickly. The tremendous storm threatened to sink one of the Israeli Navy's most important missions, officially called Operation Noa but later seared into the public lore as the "Boats of Cherbourg."

The affair had begun two and a half years earlier, in June 1967. On the eve of the SixDay War, the president of France, Charles de Gaulle, had abandoned his pro-Israel policy and imposed an embargo—a total ban—on the sale of weapons to Israel. Emissaries of Israel's defense ministry, along with their allies in the French Army, were laboring night and day to smuggle vital arms from France to Israel. But several orders at French factories remained incomplete, including an order of fifty Mirage fighter jets and one of twelve fast missile boats at the Cherbourg shipyards. The shipyards were managed by a friend of Israel, Felix Amiot. About two hundred Israelis had settled in Cherbourg, including naval personnel and their families; they had been received with affection, unsurprising given that the boats' construction provided a livelihood to a thousand French families.

There were still a few cracks in the French embargo, and through them, Israel had received five of the twelve boats immediately after their construction was completed. But on December 28, 1968, the situation changed completely. Following an attempted attack on an El Al plane in Athens by terrorists coming from Lebanon, Raful Eitan and his paratroopers landed at Beirut airport and blew up thirteen planes belonging to Middle East Airlines, stoking de Gaulle's fury because the paratroopers used French-made Super Frelon helicopters. Telegrams were immediately wired to all the French factories building weapons ordered by Israel, principally in Cherbourg. French friends of Admiral Mordechai ("Moka") Limon, the head of the Israeli Defense Ministry delegation in Paris, informed him of the telegram to Cherbourg, and he ordered the officer responsible for the missile boat project, Colonel Hadar Kimchi, to immediately send a recently completed boat, the *Akko*, to Israel. Another boat, the *Tempest* ("*Sa'ar*"), was still in the final stages of construction, but Limon, a former commander in chief of the Israeli Navy, ordered that it be loaded with fifty tons of fuel. Lieutenant Colonel Moshe Tabak outfitted the ship with everything required and "went out for drills in the ocean." A few days later, the *Akko* and the *Tempest* arrived in Israel.

The missile boats had a special status: they had been paid for almost in full (except for the five vessels which had not yet been completed), and they effectively belonged to Israel; nevertheless, their departure despite the embargo enraged de Gaulle. Cherbourg's French officers decided to punish the Israeli Navy by banishing it from the port's military section to the civilian area. It also became clear beyond any doubt that the embargo would be applied to the five remaining boats, which were in advanced stages of construction. This policy would continue even into the days of de Gaulle's successor, President Pompidou.

The missile boats in Haifa Port. *(Moshe Milner, GPO)*

Israel's war of attrition with Egypt, then at its peak, had increased the urgency of supplying the navy with state-of-the-art weaponry, and pressure grew for the acquisition of the five missile boats. Limon, a calm, composed man, flew to Israel and presented the heads of the defense establishment with three ways to bring them over. The first: to wait patiently, perhaps for years, for the embargo to be lifted. The second: to smuggle the boats out of Cherbourg illegally. And the third: to formulate a legal plan to deceive the French government and get the boats to Israel, namely through Israel's theoretical surrender of the boats and their sale to a third party—who would then send them to Israel.

Defense Minister Moshe Dayan and his deputy, Tzvi Tzur, were inclined to take the third route, to avoid breaking the law. The commander in chief of the Navy, General Avraham ("Cheetah") Botzer, and his deputy, Brigadier General Benjamin ("Bini") Telem, dealt with the planning. It would be necessary to wait until all the boats were ready before bringing them out. Zim, the Israeli shipping company, put two boats, the *Dan* and the *Leah*, at the operation's disposal. Large fuel tanks were installed in the belly of both ships, and they performed fueling drills at sea with the navy's missile boats. The refueling ships would meet the flotilla of missile boats during its voyage from Cherbourg to Israel; one boat would wait next to Gibraltar, and the other south of Malta. Zim made two more ships, the *Netanya* and the *Tiberias*, available for the operation in case of a serious accident at sea: one had been outfitted to tow a damaged missile boat, and the second, to aid in the getaway of naval crews.

By the end of August 1969, construction on four of the five boats was complete: the *Storm* ("*Sufa*"), the *Spear* ("*Hanit*"), the *Volcano* ("*Ga'ash*"), and the *Sword* ("*Herev*"). The fifth boat, the *Arrow* ("*Hetz*"), was going to be delivered in November.

In September, Limon met with his friend Mordechai Friedman, the CEO of Netivei Neft, an Israeli state company that pumped oil in Abu Rudeis, in Sinai. Limon and Friedman were looking for an intermediary who would buy the boats from France and focused their attention on Akers, a Norwegian firm that searched for oil. At its head stood Martin Siem, an engineer and World War II hero who had led the anti-Nazi underground in Norway and was a good friend of Friedman's.

Limon had reached the conclusion that the best date for taking the boats would be Christmas Eve, 1969. That night, the French would be celebrating, and their level of vigilance would be low. By then, the *Arrow* would be ready to sail.

In October, Limon and Friedman met with Siem in Copenhagen, where the Norwegian gave his approval to the fictional purchase of the missile boats. However, he wouldn't be able to conduct the acquisition via Akers but through a subsidiary under his control, Starboat, which was registered in Panama.

Operation Noa was under way. Starboat contacted Amiot and expressed interest in acquiring between four and six fast boats that could be used in the search for oil in the North Sea. "Purely by chance," Limon later told us with a wink, "Starboat's requirements matched the specifications and performance capacities of the boats of Cherbourg."

Amiot replied that he had a customer for whom he was building such boats, but if the customer relinquished the vessels, Amiot would sell them to Starboat. The French Defense Ministry was enthusiastic. If Israel would agree to give up the boats and they were sold to a third party, the bothersome issue would be solved. Limon, for his part, pretended to be dubious about the desirability of the deal, and only three weeks later did he accede to the French request. The deal was completed and the papers signed. Wood signs bearing the name STARBOAT were placed next to the missile boats, and with considerable generosity, Limon agreed that Israeli crews would man the boats for the time being. In secret, Limon and Siem had signed an agreement that voided the entire deal with the French.

According to Kimchi, the operation's commander, the contract was long and detailed but noted that the boats' final destination was "a company that dealt with the search for oil in the Gulf of Suez"—in point of fact, Israel. Consequently, before the contract could be investigated in depth by the French bureaucracy, it would be necessary to speed things along and get the boats out of France.

In total secrecy, eighty of the Israeli Navy's best officers and sailors were brought to Cherbourg, flying to Paris in civilian attire and arriving in the port city, in pairs, by train. Barred from speaking Hebrew or attracting attention, they lodged in Cherbourg in private apartments and in the boats themselves. Each crew numbered twenty-four, so the total would be 120 sailors for the five missile boats. Forty additional sailors, beside the eighty who came from Israel, were selected among the IDF Navy personnel already in Cherbourg. As their D Day approached, the sailors discreetly purchased great quantities of food at various locations—1,200 days' worth, based on an expectation of 120 sailors at sea for 10 days. Because the boats' communications systems hadn't been completed, the Israelis spread in the city, trying to acquire walkie-talkies with a three-quarter-mile range. They finally found them in toy stores. The sailors also began turning on the boats' engines each night, claiming that there was a power shortage in the shipyard, and the city grew accustomed to hearing the constantly booming engines. Meanwhile, the Zim ships set sail, placing themselves at predetermined positions at sea.

By Christmas Eve, everything was ready. The teams had settled onto the boats. Admiral Limon, Hadar Kimchi, his deputy, Ezra ("Shark") Kedem, and the commanders of the five boats sat in the *Sword*'s commander's quarters. The French were fulfilling the role that had been "assigned" to them, sitting down for the holiday meal at exactly the appointed hour.

Only one variable wasn't playing its part: the weather.

A terrible storm was raging in the open sea, with huge waves rising from the west; naval personnel rated the water as "sea 7 to 9," fraught with lethal danger to anyone who struggled against it.

The hours passed and the officers collected any bits of information they could about the storm's location and movement. Limon was determined to set sail that night; otherwise, the entire plan might collapse. But the final decision belonged, of course, to Kimchi. Ten P.M., 11:00 P.M., midnight. . . . The storm raged on, and the tension grew. Kimchi decided to delay his final decision until 2:00 A.M. After one o'clock, an updated forecast arrived that inspired hope among the sailors. The direction of the wind was going to change; the storm was turning toward Scotland and Scandinavia. Ten minutes later, another forecast: the wind had indeed shifted course.

The crews feverishly prepared the boats for departure. The boats' engines broke out in a tremendous roar and, at two-thirty, the order was given to sail. First the *Sword*, then the four remaining ships set out toward the open sea. As they disappeared into the darkness, the Israeli defense delegation's vehicles blocked the entrance to the port, in order to frustrate any sudden check by the police. At the Hotel Atlantique, overlooking the sea, lights in the windows turned on and off intermittently, as the families of some of the crew members that had been living there bade farewell to their loved ones.

The docks remained empty. Limon was the last to leave the port. At three-thirty, he awakened Amiot and informed him that the boats had sailed for Israel. Amiot embraced him and burst out crying. Limon handed him a check for $5 million, the final payment for the boats' construction.

The five boats sailed into a stormy sea, fighting hard against the waves. Their connection to naval headquarters in Israel was lost again and again, and the engines didn't function properly. Nevertheless, the original plan was executed; the rendezvous with the *Leah* took place on the night of December 26, and the boats were refueled, if terribly slowly because of unexpected complications. The second refueling took place south of Malta. The most severe difficulty cropped up when water seeped into the *Arrow's* engine; in the absence of appropriate gauges, the sailors were forced to taste the fuel to see whether it had been contaminated with seawater, which could have damaged the engines. After several rounds of tasting, the problem was fixed and the boat continued on its way.

The storm in the Mediterranean subsided, but it erupted in a new location: the international press. Nearly two days had passed between Christmas Eve and the world's discovery that the boats had vanished from Cherbourg. "Where are they?" reporters asked the staff at the Israeli embassy in Paris; the diplomats nonchalantly answered, "The boats are no longer ours, presumably they're sailing to Norway." But a Spanish helicopter and later a light BBC aircraft discovered the boats at sea, and the global media reported that the "Boats of Cherbourg" had escaped out from under the noses of the French. Front-page headlines and huge articles with aerial photos filled papers around the world. France was ridiculed, while Israel gained fame for the sophisticated operation. When the press revealed that the boats were sailing through the Mediterranean toward Israel, a massive uproar broke out in Oslo, where Siem was forced to respond to difficult, embarrassing questions, and in Paris, where the French government saw itself tricked and humiliated. The French defense minister, Michel Debré, a former staunch supporter of Israel, now demanded that the army chief of staff use any means necessary to stop the boats, even by bombing them from the air. Prime Minister Jacques Chaban-Delmas rejected the idea.

The boats, two limping behind because of glitches and three leading the flotilla, sailed toward Israel, where the entire country awaited their arrival. In the end, they docked in Haifa, where they were received by the defense minister, the chief of staff, and the navy's commander in chief.

Operation Noa had worked out according to plan. Several French generals paid the price by losing their jobs, Siem was exiled to a secondary post in the United States and Limon was forced to leave France.

Despite sharp condemnations in France, the operation generated a wave of admiration for Israel, although Paris's official policy remained chilly and distant for many more years.

HADAR KIMCHI, DEPUTY COMMANDER IN CHIEF OF THE NAVY

"The most difficult moment, for me, was making the decision to get under way. Initially, I had determined that the departure would be at eight P.M., but the terrible storm was raging, and I delayed setting sail. The boats were new, the crews were young and inexperienced with these boats, and there was a lack of standard communications equipment and radar on most of the vessels. I couldn't take the risk. I delayed until ten o'clock, then to midnight, and later to two A.M.

"At one A.M., reports came in by radio that the storm was turning northward. I informed everyone: We're leaving at two-thirty. This was a difficult decision. We struggled with the waves for more than twelve hours. The boats were shuddering; everyone got seasick. At a certain moment, planes appeared above us, taking pictures. I announced on the radio, 'Everyone, comb your hair! They're snapping photos!' Several engines were inoperative during the trip, and when we reached the Aegean Sea I requested over the radio that Israeli ships in the area be ready to tow us. The first captain who answered told me, 'I'm willing—this is for our country, and I'll do it for free.'

I was elated. I asked him, 'Where are you?' He replied, 'Near Copenhagen . . .'

"After him, similar offers came in from six more boats.

"In the end, we arrived safely at the Kishon port. Five years later, I visited Cherbourg again, and I received a warm welcome. The French said, 'You fled, but you got us amazing publicity. Because of you, the Greeks and the Iranians bought missile boats from us, and the engine company got lots of orders too.'"

The war of attrition along the Suez Canal claims
many casualties on both sides. The Soviet Union,
determined to regain her lost prestige in the Arab world,
supplies Egypt with state-of-the-art military equipment—
tanks, aircraft, missiles and electronic installations.

CHAPTER 10

"WHY BOMB IF WE CAN TAKE?" 1969

O n the night of December 26, 1969, three IAF Super Frelon helicopters crossed the Gulf of Suez into Egypt and landed on the sands of Ras Gharib. After setting down behind enemy lines, a company of paratroopers set out, in total silence, for its destination, launching one of the most imaginative operations ever conceived by the IDF.

These were the days of the war of attrition, which had broken out following the Six Day War. Israel controlled Sinai, and the core of the conflict was an endless duel between the IDF and the Egyptian Army along the length of the Suez Canal: artillery bombardments, commando raids, operations deep in Egypt, aerial battles, ambushes and planting of mines. The number of Israeli losses constantly grew. The Egyptians had replaced the military equipment destroyed in the war with a massive supply of sophisticated Soviet weaponry. New tanks and troop carriers, MiG aircraft, ground-to-air missiles and sophisticated radar stations had all arrived from the USSR. Over and over again, the Israeli Air Force attacked the radar stations, which disrupted its planes' freedom of action in the skies over Egypt.

In particular, the air force was troubled by a P-12 radar station that was among the most sophisticated ever built by the Soviet Union, capable of detecting aircraft flying at very low altitudes. The station was spotted in Ras Gharib, at a secure, protected site, and was attacked by the IAF in mid-October. The attack was successful, and the station was completely destroyed. But a few days later, to the Israelis' surprise, it turned out that the station continued to operate; air force experts realized that they had blown up a dummy station built to deceive them, and that the real station was in fact operating at another site hidden in the desert.

On December 22, the IAF conducted a photo-reconnaissance mission in the area. Two sergeants from the Technical Services Unit of the intelligence department were charged with deciphering the images. Sergeant Rami Shalev, who reviewed the photo sequences, recounted, "Suddenly, as I was going through them, I found it! I locked in on the real Ras Gharib radar station. I said to myself, You have a radar station here." The facility was very well camouflaged, resembling two Bedouin tents in the heart of the desert. They were, in fact, two huge containers installed on Russian ZiL trucks. The station was neither defended nor secured; an Egyptian military installation containing a mortar battery was located just a few kilometers to the north. Antiaircraft guns had not been placed in the area around the station, apparently in order not to draw attention. By contrast, a force of roughly fifty Egyptian soldiers was positioned around the decoy station that had been bombed, equipped with machine guns and antiaircraft artillery.

First Lieutenant Yechiel Haleor, from the Technical Services Unit, brought the images to Colonel Yeshayahu Barkat, the head of the aerial-intelligence department. The head of IAF operations, Colonel David Ivry, was also present at the meeting. Barkat instructed Haleor to prepare an "objectives sheet," including the geographical coordinates for bombing the station.

Haleor asked, "Why bomb if we can take?"

Haleor's remark fired up his commanders' imaginations. "To take"—to swipe an entire radar station from under the nose of the Egyptians and bring it to Israel! But would it be possible to transport an entire station over the Gulf of Suez—two heavy containers and a tall antenna? The station was a fifteen-minute helicopter ride from Sinai, then under Israeli control. Ivry called for an assessment of whether helicopters could carry out the task. On December 24, Major Nehemiah Dagan, the commander of the Sikorsky ("Yassour") wing in the helicopter squadron, informed him that it was feasible. At the time, there were only three Yassours that could carry out the operation—new Sikorsky helicopters that had just arrived in Israel. Dagan estimated that if the radar station's two containers were separated, it would be possible to lift them with the helicopters and bring them to Israeli territory. According to early estimates, the weight of the main container, the "heart" of the station, was approximately four tons. Going by the book, the Yassour was capable of lifting roughly three. The weight of the second container was lower, about two and a half tons.

Air Force Commander Motti Hod transmitted the proposal to Chief of Staff Haim Bar-Lev, who assigned the ground operation to the paratroopers. A computer spit out its name: Operation Rooster 53. The head of the 50th Battalion, Lieutenant Colonel Arieh ("Tzidon") Tzimmel, was appointed the operation's commander.

Tzimmel assembled the raid force using two types of fighters: those with battle experience, the majority of them officers, and soldiers with technical skills who would be able to detach the radar station's two containers from the truck platforms on which they were placed, break the connections between them and take down the antenna.

Eliezer ("Cheetah") Cohen, one of the air force's most senior helicopter pilots, turned to First Sergeant Ezra, a radar expert, and told him that he was looking for a model that the helicopter pilots could use for training.

"Why do you need a model when you have a Russian radar at the ready?" Ezra asked. Located at the Tzrifin base among Israel's captured enemy equipment was a Russian radar container taken during the Six Day War; although its parts were out of date, its size and shape were identical to those of a P-12. Cohen, Ezra and the paratroopers' deputy commander, Levi Hofesh, hurried to Tzrifin. Instead of turning to the quartermaster general of the IDF and getting tangled up in bureaucracy, as well as the potential leak of the secret, the three called a tow truck and "stole" the container. It was transported to an air force base, and two Yassour pilots, Nehemiah Dagan and Ze'ev Matas, along with their crews, trained at tethering it to the helicopters and lifting it up.

At the same time, the paratroopers were practicing the capture and dismantling of the radar station. They received wrenches that fit the Russian standards, technical scissors for cutting the cables and connections, oxygen tanks and welding devices in the event that the scissors didn't work. Martin Leibovich, a company sergeant major for the 50th Battalion, was called by his company commander, who blindfolded him and drove him by jeep to one of the airfield's most distant runways. When the blindfold was removed, Leibovich saw before him a soldier from the Ordnance Corps standing next to large oxygen tanks. The soldier kept loudly declaring that he wouldn't be going on the mission because he was a *jobnik*, or pencil pusher. Leibovich took on the role. "I became the locksmith of the operation," he said later. In addition to Ezra and Leibovich, several technical experts were also attached to the mission, as well as a young man who knew how to drive a Russian ZiL truck, in case it was decided to move the trucks with the containers to the canal shore. All these preparations were completed in twenty-four hours.

The following night, three Super Frelons crossed the Gulf of Suez and unloaded their cargo—sixty-six commandos—close to the radar station. There was a full moon out, and so the paratroopers wore light-colored clothes and wrapped their weapons in light-colored fabric, in order to blend into the sand. They spotted the station site close to an oil rig nearby and reached it at a brisk walk, and later by crawling. They split into a blocking force and an attacking force, and charged at the station. An Egyptian guard opened automatic gunfire on them, and a second joined in. After a brief battle, the paratroopers took control of the installation, killing two soldiers and capturing four; three other Egyptians got away. In the bunker and tent next to the station, the paratroopers found detailed files and guidebooks about how to operate the electronic equipment.

They then began dismantling the installation, but the work stretched on. The wrenches didn't fit; the scissors proved completely useless. Eventually, the welding devices were used, but the cables connecting the two caravans needed to be taken apart one at a time. The antenna, held in place on a sturdy steel base, reached a height of almost seventy feet, and it refused to move from its place until several paratroopers climbed on top and used the weight of their bodies to bring it down. The dismantling process, which was supposed to take thirty minutes, lasted more than an hour. At the same time, IAF Skyhawks were attacking Egyptian targets in the Gulf of Suez as a diversionary tactic. The work finally ended, and, at 2:45 A.M., the first Yassour appeared, flown by Dagan. The main container was then tied on with a "hammock," a special sling, and Dagan slowly rose up above the site. At that moment, he realized that the precise weight of the container was beyond expectations: 4.1 tons. The Yassour was built to carry a weight of up to just three tons. But the helicopter lifted off anyway, and the soldiers on the ground cheered with excitement.

The battle is over; the radar is in the paratroopers' hands.
(Zvi Malik, IDF Archive)

The enthusiasm spread to the senior commanders waiting on the other side of the gulf, but that feeling faded away quickly and was replaced by deep anxiety. Inside the helicopter's cockpit, red lights started blinking and sirens wailing. Dagan reported that one of the two hydraulic systems installed on the helicopter had become completely inoperable. It appeared that the cables harnessing the load had become too tightly strung because of the excess weight and had crushed the oil tube, which had spilled oil that damaged the helicopter's hydraulic drive system. According to the operating manual, Dagan had to dump the cargo immediately; otherwise he was risking a fatal accident. But Dagan decided to carry on. From the command post on the Israeli beach in Sinai, the commanders followed him with bated breath. They understood the risk he was taking on, continuing to fly with a load much heavier than the Yassour was capable of carrying, and with just one functioning hydraulic system. "The aircraft was shaking," Dagan recounted. "But we crossed the Gulf of Suez, and we immediately landed on the sand."

Simultaneously, Matas was reaching his destination, loading the second container which was lighter—and the antenna, and starting on his way. Over the Gulf, the Yassour bounced around violently, but Matas kept control and he, too, arrived safely. The three Super Frelons landed next to the defunct radar station and returned the commandos to Israeli territory.

Upon their return, the paratroopers were received by Raful Eitan, who told them about a similar mission carried out by British commandos during the Second World War. The soldiers had landed on a German base in France but brought back only a few components of a radar station, and many were killed. Israel's air force and paratroopers had obtained an intact radar station, without losses—the only operation of its kind in the world. Defense Minister Moshe Dayan sent two bottles of champagne to the commander of the helicopter squadron, a gift to the team.

The secret surrounding the mission was kept for a few days, until it was published by London's *Daily Express*. In the Israeli newspapers, which were submitted to strict military censorship, cartoons appeared showing Israeli helicopters transporting the pyramids and the Sphinx.

IAF experts analyzed the radar systems and learned the principles of the Soviet methods. On the basis of their findings, they then developed new methods of electronic combat. The radar secrets were also revealed to the Americans.

Dagan was honored with a Medal of Distinguished Service, and Chief of Staff Bar-Lev told the paratroopers who had participated in the missions, "You performed one of the most complicated, daring, impressive actions the IDF has ever carried out."

NEHEMIAH DAGAN, COMBAT PILOT

"The first two Yassours arrived from America in September, and within a month we were deeply immersed in the war of attrition. We trained there—four pilots and fifty mechanics. I was appointed commander of the Yassour wing within the Frelon squadron.

"They called me from headquarters and talked to me about lifting a radar container. Officially, I could have lifted two-point-nine tons with a Yassour. We trained only for one day, Ze'evik Matas and me, at lifting a radar container. They told me, 'A radar container weighs three-point-two tons.' I said, 'Look, guys, this is heavier.' They replied, 'Nehemiah, don't wear us out with your problems.'

"We didn't have night-vision devices, so we needed moonlight, and we came in flying low. I feared that there would be problems with tying up the container, that it would be installed too high on the truck bed. But we discovered that the truck had been dug into the ground, and I could hover practically at surface level.

"I lifted the container and saw that it weighed four-point-one tons—one-point-two more than the permitted load. The instant I lifted off, a row of warning lights came on. I said,

'The hydraulic system has gone out on me.' Typically in such a situation, you land and turn everything off immediately.

"I decided that I'd keep going. I told the copilot, Tron, a top expert in the aircraft's mechanics, 'Let's shorten the flight path.' I reached the Red Sea and ordered the aircraft mechanic to look out the window to see whether a fire had broken out in the engines. I landed on the other side of the gulf. The moment that Ze'evik Matas unloaded the second container on our side, they immediately sent him to take my container, which had shaken so hard during the passage. I received a medal, but believe me, I've been in much more dangerous operations."

In 1970 the Soviets heavily increase their involvement in
the Middle East conflict, to the point where it may degenerate
into an armed confrontation with the United States.

CHAPTER 11

"THE ENEMY SPEAKS RUSSIAN!" 1970

O n April 18, 1970, at the height of the war of attrition, two Israeli Phantom pilots, Eitan Ben Eliyahu and Rami Harpaz, were on their way back from a photo-reconnaissance mission over Egypt. The war of attrition had broken out a short time after the Six Day War. Initially, the fighting had focused mostly on the area around the Suez Canal, but it spread incrementally, and the IAF had been carrying out audacious sorties deep in Egyptian territory.

That morning, as Ben Eliyahu and Harpaz flew toward Israel, several Egyptian MiG-21s appeared at high altitude. There was nothing special about this encounter, but this time, listening devices belonging to the IDF's 515th Intelligence Service Unit (later Unit 8200) recorded strange voices speaking an unfamiliar language. The person who understood the language was a young man named David, who was serving at the Umm Hashiba base, in Sinai. He immediately called his commander, Major Tuvia Feinman, and excitedly reported, "We've recorded transmissions between Soviet fighter pilots."

Feinman responded with a colorful curse. He knew that Russian technicians, trainers and advisers—not pilots—were working in Egypt, and he surmised that the soldier and his friends had recorded a conversation between them.

"No, Tuvia," David responded. "This is something else."

Feinman immediately sent a Bell helicopter to Umm Hashiba, which returned with the recording reels containing the conversations. Feinman, who knew Russian fluently, listened to the tapes and rushed to the head of military intelligence, General Aharon Yariv. At 8.00 P.M., Yariv held a crash meeting with Minister Golda Meir, and that night she passed along the recordings to U.S. president Richard Nixon.

The recordings were definitive proof: not only were the Soviets supplying weapons to the Egyptians, they were secretly sending military troops and fighter squadrons. The planes were adorned with the logos of the Egyptian Air Force, but they were being flown by Soviet pilots!

This marked a dangerous turn of events. Israel didn't want to get entangled in a conflict with a superior power. The Soviet Union had been the main weapons supplier to Egypt and Syria (and later to Iraq) from the mid-fifties onward, and again after the Egyptian Army was defeated by the IDF in 1967. Moscow responded to the Egyptian president's request by sending military experts, advisors, air controllers and pilots. These facts had been kept secret until Israel's discovery.

Thirty-four Israeli soldiers of Russian background reported the Soviet presence. They were serving in the top-secret Masrega ("Knitting Needle") unit, commanded by Major Feinman. In addition to training in intelligence, the soldiers had received a refresher course in Russian. They had formed a special subculture for themselves, with Russian underground songs and Pushkin poems, vodka drinking and stories in Russian, and were nicknamed the "Grechkos," after the Soviet defense minister. As the reports of Soviet involvement in Egypt grew, they were dispatched to the 515th, in Sinai. Bit by bit, they gained mastery of the military terms used by the Russians; however, until April 18, they had only recorded conversations between technical crews. Suddenly, that day, the voices emerging from their radio devices belonged to Soviet pilots.

This raised the latent conflict between Israel and the Soviet Union to a dangerous level. Israel tried not to escalate it. Defense Minister Moshe Dayan instructed the head of the air force, Motti Hod, to halt the attacks deep in Egypt. The United States also advised caution; after all, they said, Israel wouldn't want a confrontation with a superpower. But the Soviets's self-confidence only grew; they moved their missile batteries to the shores of the Suez Canal, and their planes pursued Israeli jets on photo-reconnaissance and bombing missions, trying to engage them in combat. On one occasion, they even hit the tail of a Skyhawk with an air-to-air missile; the pilot managed to land at the Refidim airbase, in Sinai.

Meir and Dayan still hesitated. But on July 25, when Israeli Skyhawks attacked Egyptian positions on the Suez Canal, Soviet MiGs appeared in the sky and chased them into Sinai. "Superpower or not," Meir grumbled to herself, and ordered that Israel strike back at the Russians, as they deserved.

Hod decided to devise an operation against the Russians: an aerial ambush of the sort his pilots had pulled off more than once in the region. David Porat, who had designed ambushes in the past, was chosen to put together something special.

But how does one lay an ambush in the clear blue sky?

Hod established an elite team of the air force's best pilots and on July 30, 1970, ordered it to spring the trap. The area chosen as the site of battle was a third of the way between Cairo and the city of Suez, close to the Katameya airbase, where the Russian squadrons kept their planes. Israel's opening shot in the operation—code-named Rimon 20—was the takeoff of four Phantoms guided by Ben Eliyahu from the Ramat David airbase. The planes crossed the Gulf of Suez and started attacking the Egyptian positions next to Adabiya. The Phantoms mimicked Skyhawks fighter jets with bombing capacities but inferior to the Soviet MiGs. The Phantoms kept flying in an "Indian circle" over their targets—imitating American Indians circling cowboys on horseback—with one pilot at a time diving toward his objective, dropping his bombs and returning to the formation. This was a classic Skyhawk tactic. At their radar stations, the Egyptians and the Russians saw four dots circling above Adabiya, and it seemed clear to the ground controllers that they were Skyhawks.

Simultaneously, a dot of light appeared on their screens, passing from north to south at an altitude of twenty thousand feet. The controllers identified the dot as a lone Mirage jet, apparently on a reconnaissance mission. The Israelis were misleading them here as well. The "lone" dot was in fact comprised of four Mirages, which were flying in a tightly compact formation that was made to look like a single plane. The Mirage pilots even reported via radio on the progress of a reconnaissance mission. Together, they were the bait—what appeared to be an unarmed reconnaissance plane and four antiquated Skyhawks. The commander of the Russian squadrons fell for it and decided to unleash his pilots on the easy prey.

The Russians didn't know that an additional quartet of Mirages had taken off from Ramat David and was flying at low altitude in Sinai, below the mountain ridges, so that their radar stations wouldn't see them. Meanwhile, four more Mirages, engines thundering, were ready on the runways of the Bir Gifgafa airfield, in Sinai. As Ehud Yonay wrote in his book *No Margin for Error: The Making of the Israeli Air Force*, Porat succeeded, through this trickery, in "hiding four Mirages and four Phantoms in the blue summer sky, and another eight Mirages not far away."

The Russians dispatched four quartets of MiGs from the Beni Sueif and Kom Osheim airfields. The first, lead by Captain Kamenev, flew northward, in the direction of the "solo" reconnaissance Mirage, in order to confront it on its journey. The second, led by the squadron commander, Captain Nikolai Yurchenko, was meant to close in on the Mirage with a forceps maneuver from the south. A third quartet, under the command of Captain Saranin, had been directed to strike it from the west. Another formation of four MiGs turned toward the "Skyhawks"; four more MiGs took off a few minutes later. At the air force Pit, Hod pressed a button on his stopwatch and ordered his pilots to attack.

The Soviets were stunned. The "lone" Mirage suddenly became four, which dropped their detachable fuel tanks and turned toward the MiGs. The four Skyhawks suddenly climbed skyward and revealed themselves to be state-of-the-art Phantoms swooping down on the Soviets from on high. Then the four Mirages that had been flying below the Sinai mountaintops burst out, with the quartet that had been waiting on the runways at Bir Gifgafa following in their wake. The voices of the Soviet ground controllers suddenly went silent, as the electronic wizards of the Israeli Air Force blocked their radio channels. The Soviet pilots, accustomed to a constant flow of instructions from their ground controllers, were left disoriented, at a loss for what to do.

An ambush in the clear blue sky. *(AF Journal)*

The Mirage pilot Asher Snir brought down the first MiG. Its pilot ejected, and the canopy of his parachute fanned out amid the aerial battlefield, where thirty-six planes were clashing. Avihu Bin-Nun and Aviem Sella also shot down two planes, and Avraham Salmon and If-tach Spector brought down two more.

The Russian pilots weren't used to wild aerial battles in which their customary formations came apart, and there was no ground controller to guide them. Initially, their voices on the radio stayed calm, but as the battle went on, they sounded increasingly frightened, and some shouted, "Abort!" The Russian ground controllers also lost their cool, trying to contact their pilots and calling them by their names. A number of the pilots broke away and escaped toward their bases; others also tried to get away from the Israelis, however, the Israeli planes pursued them. Two and a half minutes into the battle, Hod glanced at his stopwatch and ordered a halt. The Israeli ground controller's voice emerged from the radio, instructing, "Everyone, cut off contact. Disconnect at once and get out of there!"

The skies indeed cleared at once, and the Israeli jets turned toward their bases. They left behind five burning MiGs in the Egyptian desert; three of the Soviet pilots had managed to parachute, and two were killed.

Moscow was in shock. The next day, Marshal Pavel Stepanovich Kutakhov, the Soviet Air Force commander, arrived in Egypt to ascertain the reasons for his pilots' failure. While grim inquiries were held in Egypt, modest parties were held on airbases in Israel. Air force commanders didn't forget the Grechkos and sent them bottles of champagne. The celebrations' secret participants, of all people, were the Egyptian Air Force pilots, who had been the butt of numerous insults from the Soviet pilots; the Russians had mocked their inability to take on the Israeli Air Force. This was, for the humiliated Egyptians, a moment of sweet revenge on their Soviet allies.

Within days, the news was leaked to the foreign press, and the story of Operation Rimon 20 exploded in dramatic headlines around the world.

GENERAL AMIR ESHEL, COMMANDER IN CHIEF OF THE AIR FORCE

"Bringing down the Soviet jets calls to mind one of the events of the War of Independence, when the first members of the air force took down five British planes that had infiltrated southern Israel. There are those who tell us that the Israeli Air Force is good, but only against other air forces in the region, which aren't at its level. And suddenly we're battling a superpower—a rival from an entirely different league—and we can handle it. And you achieve a result that is exceptional both in absolute terms and against the backdrop of that time. During that same period, the Americans were fighting the Vietnam War and in other conflicts, and weren't managing to achieve results like these. Meanwhile, here we are, in one battle—boom!

"Cynics will say, 'You ambushed mediocre pilots.' That isn't true. The Russians flying in Egypt knew what they were doing. They weren't suckers and knew that failure was forbidden. But our action brought out the Israeli air force's professional ability, acuity and determination.

"The state of Israel puts the best of its resources into the air force. We're able to get to places that no one else can—and to get the job done there. An air force plane knows how to attack in Tehran and to do so in Gaza, and it's in the hands of excellent people.

"Operation Rimon brought together our best attributes, talents and abilities—and is a sort of milestone, a sort of beacon."

After the debacle of the Arab armies in 1967, several terrorist organizations have stepped into the vacuum and try to harm Israel by a succession of hijackings, bombings and assassinations. The major terrorist group is Yasser Arafat's Palestine Liberation Organization, and its secret striking force is named Black September.

CHAPTER 12

WHITE ANGELS ON JACOB'S LADDER, 1972

Reginald Levy, the pilot of Sabena Airlines' Boeing 707 flying from Brussels to Tel Aviv, felt a surge of pleasant anticipation. Today was May 8, 1972, his fiftieth birthday, and he was going to celebrate it with his wife, Deborah, presently sitting in first class behind him. Levy, a former RAF pilot, born in Blackpool to a Jewish father, felt a special bond to the land of Israel, and Jerusalem was undoubtedly the best setting for marking this significant milestone in his life.

The Boeing was flying high over Yugoslavia when he suddenly felt the brutal thrust of a gun barrel against his neck. He couldn't see his aggressor, but glancing sideways, he noticed his copilot, Jean-Pierre Arins, slumped in his seat, a mustached man pointing a gun at his head. They were being hijacked.

As he soon realized, his plane had been taken over by four Palestinian terrorists who had boarded in Brussels with forged Israeli passports. The other passengers couldn't guess that "Zeharia Greid" was actually Abd Aziz el Atrash, "Sara Bitton" was Rima Tannous, and "Miriam Hasson" was Theresa Halsa. Their commander, who would soon introduce himself as "Captain Rif'at," was Ali Taha Abu-Sneina. The four hijackers were members of Black September, the new, deadly terrorist organization secretly created by Yasser Arafat. This was their first operation against Israel.

Before taking over the plane, the four hijackers had successively used the plane's bathrooms to take out the weapons they had concealed on their bodies: two handguns, two hand grenades, two explosive belts weighing two kilograms each, detonators and batteries.

Now Rif'at and Atrash were standing in the cockpit, their guns pointed at the pilots. "You will fly to Tel Aviv," Rif'at ordered Levy, his voice clipped, heavy with emotion. "No tricks! We've got explosives and hand grenades."

"But I am flying to Tel Aviv," Levy stammered.

"Yes, you are. But now you'll be following my orders."

In tourist class, a pretty black-haired girl in a flower-patterned mini-dress gracefully slipped into an aisle seat beside the elderly Hershel and Ida Norbert, who were on their way to meet their relatives in Israel after twenty years of separation. They gaped in bafflement at the young woman, who held a round black box tied to her wrist by a length of wire.

In the cockpit, Rif'at grabbed the microphone. "Attention! Attention, all passengers! Stay in your places and don't move. I am Captain Kamal Rif'at, of Black September. We represent the Palestinian people. The plane is now in our command. You must obey orders!"

Shouts and crying echoed throughout the plane. Hershel Norbert stared in horror at the girl in the flowered dress, who jumped from her seat, brandishing her box over her head. "God, a disaster!" Ida moaned. Behind her, a middle-aged Israeli woman fainted in her seat. Another woman, Breindel Friedman from Jerusalem, shrieked in fear as she saw two figures emerge from the cockpit. One of them, wearing a nylon stocking over his head, looked to her like a monster. He held a handgun and a grenade in his hands. The other hijacker was shorter, narrow-shouldered, with sallow skin and a black mop of hair that Breindel decided was definitely a wig.

Another female hijacker appeared in the aisle, wearing a light-colored pantsuit; she collected the passengers' passports in a large bag. She suddenly picked up the flight attendant's microphone and shouted, "If the Israelis don't give us what we demand—we shall blow up the plane. Everybody will die—everybody!" Some of the passengers burst into tears. "Help us, God!" a woman shouted in Hebrew. "This is the end!"

The news of the hijacking reached Defense Minister Moshe Dayan while he was on a helicopter tour of Israeli positions along the Suez Canal. "Fly straight to Lod!" he said to the pilot. But the first one to reach Lod airport (later named Ben-Gurion) was the commander of the Central Military District, General Rehavam ("Gandhi") Ze'evi.

Like Yitzhak Rabin, Haim Bar-Lev and many other senior officers, Ze'evi was a former member of the Palmach, the paramilitary underground during the British Mandate that became the elite corps of the IDF during the Independence War. Skinny to the point of looking like a skeleton, he appeared one Friday night in the dining room of his kibbutz, head shaved, torso naked and a towel wrapped around his waist; the resemblance to the Mahatma was striking, and he won the nickname "Gandhi" for the rest of his life. He had an odd sense of greatness; on becoming commander of the Central Military District, whose emblem was a lion, he brought to his compound two lion cubs that he kept in a cage at the entrance to his office.

And yet, he was an excellent soldier, daring, smart and resourceful. Two years before, several terrorists had hijacked four American airliners, landed them in Jordan and Egypt and blown them up. Gandhi had gathered his staff officers, and amid their smirks and ironical grins had asked them for a response to the hypothetical landing of terrorists in Lod aboard a plane and the taking of hostages. Undeterred by his officers' attitude he had devised a plan, Isotope, to stop the plane and later overpower the hijackers. When Moshe Dayan and Transport Minister Shimon Peres reached the airport, Isotope was already partly implemented. Commando units were in place and orders had been given to direct the plane to Runway 26, "the silent runway," which was situated far from the main terminal.

Several senior IDF officers arrived in haste and crowded the tiny third-floor room that had turned into an improvised command head-quarters. Beside the new chief of staff Dado Elazar stood the Head of Operations Israel Tal, IAF Commander Motti Hod, Head of Intelligence Aharon Yariv and a few members of Shabak, the Internal Security Service, in civilian clothes. Dayan maintained permanent contact with Prime Minister Golda Meir and kept her informed of the developments.

The plane landed at 7:05 P.M. The hijackers' scheme was a daring gamble. The very landing in Lod, in the lion's mouth, was a challenge to Israel's formidable might. By threatening to blow up the plane with its innocent passengers, the terrorists were placing a gun at Israel's head that should force her to accede to their demands. But their smart and daring plan had one flaw: they did not realize that Moshe Dayan and his colleagues could not afford to be defeated by terrorists who challenged Israel on its very soil, with the whole world watching.

Using the plane radio, Captain Rif'at stated his demands: Israel would release 317 Palestinian terrorists held in its jails; they would be flown to Cairo immediately. The Sabena plane would wait in Lod airport until the Palestinians landed in Cairo. Then it would fly to Cairo, and there the hijackers would free the hostages.

Dayan, cold and cynical, assumed control of the operation. His main goal was to draw out the negotiations and wear down the terrorists; a military operation should be planned, but only as a last resort. General Yariv was charged with the negotiation with Rif'at. Soon he was joined by Victor Cohen, the head of the Shabak Investigation Department, who spoke fluent Arabic. Yariv politely asked Rif'at, "How much time do you give us to satisfy your demands?"

"Two hours," Rif'at snapped. "If you don't comply in two hours—we shall blow up the plane."

"But in two hours I could barely get fifteen people over here," Yariv protested.

Actually, the IDF had gotten more than fifteen people over, but they were not the people Rif'at had in mind. The newcomers were the members of the legendary Sayeret Matkal (Unit 269)—the best commando team of the IDF, a unit where only the most qualified and the most daring soldiers could serve. The Sayeret had been created in 1957. Its members and commanders were never identified, its missions never disclosed, and its very existence was protected by rigid censorship. The soldiers serving in the Sayeret were discreetly handpicked, subjected to a variety of tests, then trained at a secret base. The Sayeret was a rumor, a mirage. At its head, in 1972, was a daredevil, Colonel Ehud Barak.

Raised in kibbutz Mishmar HaSharon, the young soldier had soon been noticed for his creative mind and his bravery. He was a gifted piano player, known for his passion for taking apart and assembling clocks and watches. He had soon become the most decorated soldier in the IDF, for his courage and military feats, some of which remain secret to this very day. He left the army to study physics and mathematics at Hebrew University, earned another degree at Stanford University, in the U.S., worked for a while at the Weizmann Institute and finally reenlisted. In 1971, he was appointed commander of the Sayeret.

On the night of May 8, while Yariv and Cohen were negotiating with Rif'at, the Sayeret was at a remote area of the airport rehearsing a surprise attack on a Boeing 707, placed at their disposal by Israel Aircraft Industries. Under the dazzling light of powerful arc lamps, the commandos were rehearsing a simultaneous penetration into the plane through the pilot's cockpit and the emergency exits. In the shootout that would ensue, the terrorists would be neutralized before they had time to trigger their explosive charges.

As night fell, Dayan's major concern was to immobilize the hijacked aircraft on the ground and prevent it from taking off. Benyamin Toledo, an El Al veteran mechanic, escorted by Barak and another soldier, sneaked to the back of the plane. Toledo crawled to the aircraft's belly and expertly removed the valve controlling the hydraulic system of the landing gear. The oil immediately started to spill on the runway. A few moments later Toledo quietly laid the valve in front of Dayan.

Still, Dayan was not fully satisfied. Five minutes later, Toledo and another mechanic, Arieli, were crawling under the Boeing again. This time their objective was the plane tires. As the compressed air started hissing its way out, the plane sank down a few inches without anybody noticing. Only Captain Levy saw the hydraulic oil warning light engage. He called the control tower and reported the problem. A moment later he reported trouble with the tires.

"Tell those guys," Dayan told Levy, "that they can't take off."

"I already have," Levy said, and asked that somebody come to repair the hydraulic gear. Dayan answered that this would take time, as the airport authorities would have to bring over an expert from Tel Aviv. Captain Rif'at tacitly agreed to wait, but now he demanded to talk immediately with the Red Cross representatives in Israel. Their arrival was also delayed. At 1:30 A.M., Rif'at lost patience and threatened the Israelis that if the plane was not repaired in one hour, he would blow it up; to which Cohen calmly answered that the aircraft could not be repaired during the night. Finally, Rif'at agreed to wait until 8:00 A.M.

Under the cover of darkness, the Sayeret fighters surreptitiously approached the plane. They felt they were ready to attack it right then, but Dayan chose to wait a little longer. Yet, he told General Elazar, "Starting from now, you must be ready for action."

At about 3:00 A.M., a momentary lull descended upon the airport, and several of the Israeli officers fell asleep in their chairs. Dayan had found refuge in the air controllers' room, but was soon driven out by the flushing and gurgling of a nearby toilet. He finally stretched out on a sofa in the children's playroom, flanked by a plastic-foam giraffe and a rubber effigy of Popeye.

With sunrise the Red Cross officials arrived and were allowed to visit the plane. At 9:00 A.M., they were back at the terminal and told Moshe Dayan that the situation in the plane was unbearable. The food and water had run out, the air-conditioning didn't work, the passengers were exhausted and the hijackers were tense and nervous. "Will you release the prisoners?" the Red Cross envoys asked Dayan, but he stuck to his delaying tactics. "We agreed to negotiate," he said.

There was something absurd in the situation. It was a glorious sunny day, and Lod airport was carrying on its routine activity: planes were taking off and landing, crowds of passengers filled the terminal halls, arriving and departing. And in full sight of all, at the distant end of a runway, a hundred hostages were held in an explosive-rigged plane that could blow up any moment.

Captain Levy was alone in the cockpit when one of the hijackers, Atrash, walked in. Levy felt it was now or never. He threw himself on the Palestinian, grabbed his gun, aimed it at him and pulled the trigger.

Nothing happened.

He pulled the trigger again. Nothing.

Only now did he realize that the safety catch was on.

Atrash jumped him and wrung the gun out of his hand. He then released the safety catch and aimed the weapon at Levy's head.

Levy begged for his life. "Don't shoot!" he managed. "Don't! If you kill me, that would be the end of everything!"

To his great surprise, a lopsided grin spread on Atrash's face. "I should have killed you," he slowly said, "but you might be right, and we'll still need you to get out of here."

Captain Rif'at entered the cockpit. He suspected that the Israelis were delaying the negotiation because they didn't believe he could blow up the plane. He stuck a small plastic bag in Levy's hands that contained some of the explosive he had brought on board. He ordered him to get off the plane and meet "the people in the control tower." He didn't mince words. "Tell them that the plane is rigged with this stuff, and that we have enough of it to blow up not one but five planes. If you return with a negative answer or do not return at all, we'll blow up the plane."

A Red Cross car took Levy to Dayan. The pilot carried out his mission calmly. A quick examination by two officers proved that the contents of the plastic bag were indeed a powerful explosive. In the meantime word came from Shabak analysts who had discovered Rif'at's true identity. The man was a serial plane hijacker. He had hijacked an El Al plane to Algeria in 1968 and a Lufthansa plane to Aden in February 1972.

When facing Dayan and the generals, Levy gave them a clear and succinct report about the situation aboard the plane, the terrorists and their positions. The two female hijackers had placed their explosive belts in the front and the rear of the plane cabin, and carried hand grenades. The pilot's report was to be of great help to the Sayeret fighters later. While he was speaking, an observer positioned on the terminal's roof reported that he had identified one of the female hijackers and she could be easily recognized by her dress's color.

Dayan was cheered when Levy described to him his confrontation with Atrash in the cockpit and the Palestinian's decision not to kill him. That confirmed Dayan's motive in delaying the negotiation and wearing down the terrorists. Dayan had been right: the terrorists did not want to commit suicide; they wanted to live, that was why they had spared Levy's life.

Dayan reached his decision. "Go back," he told Levy, "and tell those guys that we agree to release the prisoners. We'll bring them to the airport so they can see them with their own eyes. We'll repair the plane and you will fly it to Cairo."

Levy seemed relieved, but he took Dayan aside. "I have a last wish," he said. "If we don't get out of this alive, will you make sure that Israel takes care of the education of my daughters?"

Dayan promised. Before Levy left, Dayan asked him, "Are there any sick people aboard?"

"No."

"Any pregnant women?"

Levy chuckled. "Not yet." Even in those fateful moments, the guy's sense of humor had not evaporated.

Dayan was deeply moved by the pilot's courage. But when he turned to Dado Elazar, he was his old cynical self. "Dado," he quipped, "you have until four P.M. to free the passengers. I must be back at the office by five. I have an appointment."

Levy returned to the hijacked plane. Shortly before four, the terrorists saw a magnificent sight: a TWA Boeing was being towed by a small tractor to the vicinity of their plane. That was the plane that would take the released terrorists to Cairo! Rif'at and his comrades also saw buses carrying handcuffed prisoners dressed in sweatsuits; it was clear that these were the terrorists, soon to be released. Rif'at and his three friends burst into wild shouting, "The Zionists have surrendered!" They jumped with joy, hugging and embracing each other.

They were wrong. The "prisoners" in the buses were Colonel Yitzhak Mordechai's paratrooper recruits, who had been dressed and cuffed and brought over as a deception. As for the Boeing, it was a wreck, recently purchased by the Israel Aircraft Industries; it even had been stripped of its engines.

The operational plan was ready. According to an agreement with the terrorists, a convoy of small service vehicles was to approach the Sabena plane, carrying the mechanics who were about to repair the aircraft. But actually the "mechanics" were sixteen Sayeret fighters. Barak had divided his men into attack details. Among their commanders were Uzi Dayan, Moshe Dayan's nephew and a future commander of the Sayeret, who had been home sick with rubella, but hurried to volunteer for the mission; Dany Yatom, a future head of the Mossad; Mordechai Rahamim and Benyamin ("Bibi") Netanyahu.

At the last moment an argument had set the two Netanyahu brothers, Yoni and Bibi, against each other. They were members of the Sayeret (and their third brother, Iddo, who was studying in the U.S., would join the Sayeret the following year). Sons of a famous Israeli scholar of right-wing convictions, Professor Benzion Netanyahu, the two young men, raised in Israel and America, were known for their courage. Both of them wanted to participate in the Sabena mission. Barak was willing to take only one of them. Yoni pulled rank and seniority on his younger brother, but Barak finally opted for Bibi.

In order to make the deception work, the commandos donned white overalls, urgently brought from the nearby Tel Hashomer hospital. They got on their service vehicles but were intercepted by Gandhi, who had noticed that their overalls were too white, too immaculate. That was not the way mechanics were supposed to look. The terrorists might see through the ruse, Gandhi said, and the entire plan would be doomed. Gandhi ordered the soldiers to crumple and soil their overalls and roll about on the runways, so they would look as mechanics should after a long day's work. He also added some older, real mechanics to the team, lest the youthful faces of the commandos arouse suspicion.

An important challenge facing the Sayeret was the use of handguns. The attack should be carried out with handguns, but the fighters had trained in the use of all sorts of firearms except handguns. "That was the first time in my life that I held a gun," Netanyahu later admitted. In order to overcome that obstacle it was decided to bring over several reserve fighters of the Sayeret who were employed as security guards in the El Al planes. Those men had been extensively trained in the use of handguns and were considered experts. One of them, Mordechai Rahamim, even had become a hero when he'd single-handedly pounced on four terrorists armed with Kalashnikov submachine guns and hand grenades who had attacked an El Al plane in Zurich. Athletic, Kurdistan-born Rahamim had jumped out of the plane, killed one of the terrorists and kept firing at the other three, until the Swiss security forces arrived. The world press sang the praise of this young man who'd held at bay three Kalashnikov-armed terrorists with nothing but his handgun. Rahamim was covered with glory, and his gun, a Beretta 0.22, became very popular in Israel.

Rahamim was called at the last moment to join the Sabena commando. Some Sayeret members lay in wait by the terminal, and as soon as an El Al plane landed, they would snatch the security guards and embed them in the team.

The major concern was the explosives. The mission commanders knew that if the charges exploded, the aircraft would turn into a death trap. The first task of the rescue team, therefore, was to neutralize the explosive belts. A minute before the mission was launched, Chief of Staff Elazar pulled Rahamim aside. "Morduch," he said emotionally, using Rahamim's nickname, "break into the plane and find the charges!"

Finally, the small convoy got on its way and slowly approached the plane. The terrorists ordered the "mechanics" to pass, each one in his turn, before the cockpit, where Captain Rif'at stood with a gun in his hand and watched them. On the ground, beside the "mechanics," stood the Red Cross representatives. Every fighter had to open his overalls when passing in front of the plane to show he was not armed. Actually, all of them had stuck their handguns in the backs of their belts. The Red Cross men noticed the soldiers' guns but didn't do or say anything.

The soldiers started moving around the plane, equipped with tool-boxes and other instruments. They secretly assembled the ladders they would use to climb into the plane. "I was certain I was not going to come out of this plane alive," Rahamim recalled. He whispered to his friends what to tell his family after his death.

And then, suddenly—a new problem. One of the security guards, Yaakov Tzur, who had just arrived with a long El Al flight from abroad, declared that he could not function. "I must relieve myself," he said. "I held back all the way to Israel, and you kidnapped me right from the plane. I have to bend down and do my thing." The incident was both embarrassing and comic, but nobody was in the mood for laughing. Every minute counted. Tzur's comrades tried to convince him that the mission would be very short, and later he would have as much time as he wanted. Netanyahu, the head of his detail, asked him, "Yaakov, you need a small one or a big one?" But Tzur didn't wait, pulled down his trousers and crouched under the plane. And all the Sayeret, and all the generals and all the people of Israel had to wait patiently until Tzur got up and buttoned his pants.

Now, finally, the commandos positioned their ladders. At 4:24 P.M., they heard Barak's shrill whistle. That was the signal. In seconds they climbed to the exit doors and the cockpit entrance. The first to break into the plane from the front left exit door were Mordechai Rahamim and Danny Arditi. Mordechai found himself face-to-face with Atrash, who fired at him. Mordechai fired back but missed. At the same moment Bibi and Arik broke in by the front right exit door, while Omer Eran and Danny Brunner got in by the back left exit door. Omer saw Atrash and shot him.

Danny Yatom failed to enter by the front door, which got stuck after Captain Rif'at fired at the commandos. Meanwhile Uzi and his detail broke in by the back door. Uzi saw in front of him a swarthy man and fired, thinking he was one of the terrorists. The man was actually a diamond merchant from Belgium, who was severely wounded but survived. Less lucky was an Israeli passenger, Mary Holtzberg-Anderson, who was caught in the crossfire and fatally wounded. Uzi's task was to find Rima Tannous, the female hijacker who was somewhere in the back of the cabin with her explosive belt. He moved from the back toward the center of the cabin and suddenly a passenger, Marcelle Eini, pointed at a woman crouching in the aisle, holding an armed hand grenade. "Don't shoot!" Rima begged. "Don't shoot!"

Uzi grabbed her hand and very cautiously pulled the live grenade from her stiff fingers, "finger after finger." He threw the explosive charges out of the plane and had Rima taken outside.

In the meantime, Mordechai Rahamim was slowly moving forward. Rif'at fired at him from the cockpit door. Rahamim fired back till he emptied his magazine, then crouched behind a seat to reload. While doing so, he tried to calm down a frightened woman sitting next to him: "Don't worry," he mumbled in English, "it will be all right." He did not know that the lady was Reginald Levy's wife. During the exchange of fire, Rif'at escaped to the toilet and Rahamim pursued him there and shot him dead.

On the plane wing, after the rescue. Ehud Barak is in white overalls. *(Ron Ilan, GPO)*

Bibi and Marko Eshkenazi also moved toward the front, looking for Theresa Halsa. Bibi caught her at the left side of the cabin. Marko found in her clothes a battery for the activation of her explosive charge. She violently objected to being taken out of the plane and Marko slapped her; his gun went off and the bullet wounded both her and Bibi.

And then it was over.

The takeover had lasted ninety seconds. The two male hijackers were dead. The women were captured. The passengers were jumping with joy, kissing each other.

Dayan and his staff joined the rejoicing. He congratulated his men and got into his car. When he arrived at his office in Tel Aviv, he glanced at his watch. It was 5:05 P.M. He was on time for his appointment.

Hershel and Ida Norbert were almost smothered with love by their family. But Norbert couldn't forget the sight he had glimpsed by the plane window when the Sayeret attack started. He had seen white figures climbing up and down ladders on the wing of the plane. That reminded him of the book of Genesis in the Bible, describing Jacob's ladder and the angels ascending and descending upon it.

For him and a hundred other passengers, they were angels indeed.

BENYAMIN NETANYAHU, SAYERET MATKAL FIGHTER AND LATER PRIME MINISTER

"What is seared deep into my memory is the moment before the raid, as we stood in white mechanics' overalls on the plane's wing and waited to receive permission to break in. Everyone who has gone through the experience of waiting before a raid involving opposition gunfire knows that, in these moments, every fighter withdraws into himself.

"I had reached the unit before dawn, and there was no one there. We realized that something was happening at the airport, went there and quickly organized in teams. My brother Yoni came and told me, 'I need to be there.' He explained that he was the most experienced fighter in the unit, a claim that was hard to argue with because it was true. I told him that I had to lead my soldiers, and he persisted in taking over my command. I refused. He said, 'Then the two of us will take part in the mission.' I asked him, 'What will we tell our parents if something happens to one of us?' Eventually we turned to Ehud Barak to decide, and Ehud determined that I should go with my soldiers.

"When the signal was given to break in, we pounded on the emergency door over the wing; it let loose, and we threw it onto the runway. Terrorist bullets were whistling around us and hit the hostage Miriam Holtzberg-Anderson. This, too, was a moment seared into my memory until today.

"As we were looking for the terrorists, one of the passengers pointed at a woman crouching between the seats and shouted, 'She's a terrorist.' I pulled her hair, and it turned out that she was wearing a wig. I pulled again and asked her where the explosives are. Marko Ashkenazi ran toward us and said, 'Bibi, I'll deal with her.' I saw that the pistol in his hand was cocked. Because the terrorist wasn't armed, I called at him, 'Marko, no!' But it was too late. The pistol had already discharged the bullet, which hit her and, in a two-for-one, me, too.

"The great significance of Operation Sabena was strengthening the principle that when there is a military option, we execute! Operation Sabena was a groundbreaking operation from the standpoint of resisting hijackings and fighting terror without compromise. Since then, the terrorists' methods have changed, and with them the painful price of hits by suicide bombers, missiles and more. But terror won't stop unless we fight it, and the danger won't disappear if we don't address it."

The IDF code of ethics states that no Israeli soldier
can ever be left behind enemy lines and abandoned,
be it on the battlefield or in captivity.

CHAPTER 13

"STOP! HALT! HANDS UP!" 1972

O
n June 21, 1972, Sayeret Matkal embarked on Operation Crate 3, whose objective was the abduction of senior Syrian Army officers from Lebanese territory, in order to trade them for three Israeli pilots held captive over the previous two years in Syria.

"The Crate operations were born after we submitted several crazy plans to the General Staff about how it might be possible to free the pilots, and all were rejected," recounted General (Res.) Uzi Dayan, the operation's deputy commander and later the head of Sayeret Matkal. "One day, I got angry and went to the defense minister and told him, 'Maybe you're too old to understand this, but the captives are our friends. We're hoping that if the situation were reversed, they would also be doing everything to free us.'"

The defense minister was Moshe Dayan, Uzi Dayan's uncle. Chief of Staff David Elazar was also troubled by the plight of the pilots—Gideon Magen, Pinchas Nachmani and Boaz Eitan—who had undergone severe torture in Syrian prisons. The chief of staff had been looking for a way to speed up negotiations over the prisoner exchange and ordered the submission of operational proposals for the abduction of Syrian officers. The Sayeret's idea had fallen on receptive ears and would also be approved by Prime Minister Golda Meir.

The thinking was that, in exchange for such a valuable bargaining chip, senior members of the Syrian intelligence establishment would agree to free the Israeli pilots, as well as influence their Egyptian allies to release ten captives jailed in Egypt.

Operation Crate 1 got under way after several observation missions conducted by Sayeret commanders from the Mount Dov sector, next to the Lebanese border. The location selected as suitable for the abduction was a dirt road in Lebanon, ascending the mountain from the north, at a point where vehicles had to slow down. The Sayeret commandos penetrated into Lebanon in the dead of night and reached the target area. The mountain slopes were covered with dense vegetation. The Sayeret set an ambush with Ehud Barak serving as commander of the raid team and Benyamin Netanyahu as head of the blocking team. They lay in wait for hours, but the Syrians never came, and the mission was called off.

A second attempted abduction, Operation Crate 2, was scheduled for June 19 in the Rosh Hanikra sector, in upper Galilee. This time, the ambush was set on a different route within Lebanese territory. Again, Barak commanded the operation and Netanyahu headed the blocking team. Both of Bibi Netanyahu's brothers, Yoni and Iddo, also took part in the mission. "This was the only operation that Bibi, Yoni and I all participated in together," said Iddo Netanyahu. "Actually, we did something which was not allowed in the IDF." Indeed, the IDF did not allow several brothers to participate in the same mission for fear that they could be all killed or wounded.

The role of the blocking team was to prevent reinforcements from reaching the zone of action and to trap anyone attempting to flee the encounter with Barak's unit. As they lay in wait, a Lebanese shepherd appeared and spotted the border fence barbwire that had been flattened down by one of the teams. He and his flock nearly stumbled onto the hiding men; Bibi Netanyahu radioed Barak, and he instructed his men to capture the shepherd immediately. The commandos grabbed him and laid him down next to them. The shepherd was scared to death, certain he was going to die. "To shut him up, I told him, *'Uskut!'*- 'Shut up!' in Arabic—and signaled with my hand that we would slit his throat if he didn't keep quiet," Iddo Netanyahu said. The shepherd got the message.

But then a new issue arose: a Lebanese armored car armed with a cannon, as well as an additional vehicle, were following the officers' convoy at a distance of roughly 1.25 miles. The two vehicles positioned themselves next to Bibi Netanyahu's concealed detail, and the convoy continued toward the mountain ridge. Netanyahu whispered the news into his radio, informing Barak, who instructed him to keep hiding. Barak reported to General Motta Gur, now commander of the Northern District, and to the chief of staff, who instructed him to halt the operation immediately and withdraw back to Israel.

Barak tried to argue, attempting to persuade the senior command that it would be possible to carry out the assignment without risk, but the response was total refusal. A disappointed Bibi Netanyahu instructed his men to prepare to go. This was his last mission before his discharge from the army, and he had so much wanted it to succeed.

"In the end, the convoy passed mere meters from us," Uzi Dayan said, "and we looked at them longingly." Later they found out that among the Syrian and Lebanese senior officers in the convoy was no other than the chief of staff of the Lebanese Army.

When the Israeli troops returned to the assembly area next to kibbutz Hanita, the debate continued. "Why did you stop us?" Barak asked the chief of staff and the senior officers who were with him. "We were so close to them, we could have carried out the assignment without any trouble. They were in our hands, and we let them go."

Elazar tried to calm him down. "I didn't want to endanger the troops at the ambush—the Lebanese armored car would have discovered them."

Barak countered, "You're forcing us not to tell the truth. If I had known that the mission would be called off, I wouldn't have reported the Lebanese vehicle to you. You could have trusted my opinion. I'm telling you that we could have carried out the assignment successfully. In the future, I'm not going to tell you about any armored cars!"

Two days later, on June 21, authorization was given for Operation Crate 3. Bibi Netanyahu had already been a civilian for twenty-four hours; Yoni Netanyahu was appointed the operation commander, and Uzi Dayan, his deputy.

This time, to avoid yet another aborted mission and retreat, Barak decided to stay at the forward command post, together with General Gur and his later successor, Yitzhak Hofi, so that the operation would be completed.

The group this time was much larger. The Sayeret Matkal force was accompanied by a covering team of paratroopers, an armored unit and members of the Egoz commando unit. In addition, tanks and anti-tank cannons were allocated to provide cover as well. It appeared that no-body wanted to take any chances this time.

"In the lead-up to the mission," Iddo Netanyahu recounted, "we trained a lot for the abduction under Yoni's command—how to grab them, how to pull someone out of a moving vehicle and more. Yoni decided to demonstrate how to do it and chose one of the team members, the poor guy! During the demo, Yoni sprinted unexpectedly at the soldier, who was sitting in a vehicle, grabbed his hair and pulled him out. The guy was thrown from the vehicle onto the ground, and the maneuver was deemed a success—except that the boy was still suffering from scalp pain days later."

At daybreak, the forces breached the border fence and penetrated into Lebanon. Yoni Netanyahu went forth and checked that the path leading to the road was clear of mines. At 11:00 A.M., the Syrian officers' convoy came into view, accompanied by two armored cars and two Land Rovers. The convoy moved in the direction of the village of Rameish and stopped less than a mile to the north.

At 11:25, the Sayeret commandos left their hideout in two vehicles, approaching the breach and stopping next to it. The soldiers pretended to fix a broken-down vehicle; meanwhile, the Syrian convoy started to move forward.

At noon, the convoy passed the village of Ramia. Yoni Netanyahu received the order to enter the ambush site on the road. Uzi Dayan's team took up positions by the vehicle, and the rest of the unit spread out along the road in the direction from which the Syrian officers would arrive.

Then something unexpected happened: some Lebanese villagers had seen the Israelis. They stopped a Volkswagen that was driving ahead of the convoy, warning the driver of the Israeli soldiers waiting in the area. The surprised driver continued a few feet, quickly turned around and started fleeing eastward. The soldiers lying ready at the front of the ambush position, awaiting the convoy, saw the Volkswagen turning around, swiftly getting away. One of the commandos ran to Netanyahu and reported what he had seen, just as Netanyahu was receiving word from the command post that the convoy was also starting to turn and head back.

"We realized that they were starting to turn around," Dayan said. "We immediately started running toward them. Yoni's jeep also got there, half a minute later. Initially, they didn't really understand what was happening—they might have thought we were a different Lebanese unit. I shouted at them in Arabic, 'Stop! Halt! Hands up!'"

This was the critical moment: who would pull the trigger first? Dayan fired warning shots at the feet of the Syrians and Lebanese. They were in shock but, after a moment, opened fire as well. The exchange was short but left four Lebanese escort troops dead, among them an officer. A Syrian officer and an Israeli commando were wounded.

Amid the tumult, two officers, one Syrian and one Lebanese, fled north and vanished into the vegetation. The rest of the officers were captured: an intelligence officer at the rank of brigadier general; two armored corps colonels, who served in the operations wing of the Syrian Army; and two pilots with the rank of lieutenant colonel who belonged to the Syrian Air Force intelligence. The Syrian officer who managed to escape was the head of Syrian field intelligence.

The teams of Yoni Netanyahu, Dayan and Muki Betzer conducted wide sweeps in search of the escaped Syrian and Lebanese, but without success. In addition to the officers, a green Mercedes had also gotten away. The blocking team to the east was alerted by radio and gave chase to the Mercedes. The car was later found abandoned, riddled with bullets, next to Ramia. It turned out that the Volkswagen and the Mercedes had happened upon the combat zone by chance, without any connection to the officers' convoy.

The battle scene, minutes after the shooting was over.
(Courtesy of Aviram Halevi & "Israel Defense")

The mission concluded shortly before 1:00 P.M. The soldiers, who had spent just ninety-three minutes in Lebanon, returned to Israel in euphoria. Dayan later remembered, "On the way back to Israel, we already heard the newscast on the radio that there had been an operation in Lebanon. I was driving back in a Chevrolet Impala, and I remember that we worried about filling the holes that the bullets had left in the Land Rovers and the Impala, the latter of which stayed in the service of the intelligence wing for years to come."

The next morning, the Jordanian newspaper *Al Ra'i* commented, "This was the greatest victory for Israeli intelligence in the history of the Arab-Israeli conflict. Israel landed a heavy intelligence blow to the Syrian Army."

Following the abduction, Syria demanded that Israel return its officers without conditions because they weren't prisoners of war. A year later, the two sides agreed to an exchange of captives, and on June 3, 1973, the three members of the air crew returned to Israel. In return, Israel released the abducted officers, as well as forty-one additional Syrian and Lebanese captives. Israel agreed to grant clemency to Kamal Kanji, a Druze leader from Majdal Shams, in the northern Golan Heights, who the previous month had been sentenced to twenty-three years in prison for spying for Syria.

UZI DAYAN, LATER THE DEPUTY CHIEF OF STAFF

"I personally knew the captive pilots, whom we wanted to free following the abduction of the Syrian officers. "Pini" Nachmani had grown up on the moshava of Yokneam, and his mother knew mine. He had also trained in the air force academy with my cousin. He had been a leading navigator in the Sikorsky helicopters of the 114 Squadron, and had participated in many of the operations that his unit had carried out. Through him, I knew Gideon Magen, a Phantom squadron commander, who had also fallen captive.

"When the pilots were released, we met them at the Ramat David airbase, and Nachmani's first words were 'I knew you'd eventually get us out.' It turned out that he had been updated by his wife, Rochaleh, who had written him a letter that had reached him via the Red Cross, and in it she had told him, 'We went fishing in the Kfar Baruch lake and came back with five particularly fat fish.' Nachmani, who knew his wife didn't like fishing, asked the Red Cross representative about operations conducted recently, and he brought him a newspaper clipping about the operation. . . ."

"The greatness of this mission was in our devotion to the task, that we didn't give up. We went back three times before the operation succeeded. Its uniqueness was that it wasn't a mission to bring back intelligence or to strike the enemy—it was intended to save our pilots jailed in a Syrian prison."

After the massacre of the Israeli athletes at the
Munich Olympics, Golda Meir's anti-terrorism adviser,
Aharon Yariv, and the head of the Mossad, Zvi Zamir,
have told the prime minister that if Israel assassinates the
Black September leaders, their organization will cease to exist.
Several Mossad operations in Europe have resulted in the
deaths of Black September commanders. But the major figures
still live with total impunity in the Lebanese capital, Beirut.

CHAPTER 14
THAT LADY MEANS TROUBLE, 1973

The night of April 9, 1973, the moon was full in Beirut, capital of Lebanon.

It was long after midnight when a couple of lovers appeared, walking along Verdun Street. The man was tall, athletic, clad in a fashionable suit. The woman, small, black-haired, wore a black dress clinging to her slight frame and large breasts. As two gendarmes approached on the same sidewalk, the couple tenderly embraced, their sweet hug lasting until the gendarmes disappeared from sight. The couple then continued walking till they reached a posh apartment building; at this point the two separated. The man, together with some other guys and a blond girl who had emerged from the dark, swiftly entered the building; the woman in the black dress stayed in the street, where she was joined by another, auburn-haired girl.

Across the street was parked a red Dauphine. A huge sentry got out of the car, suspiciously watching the two ladies. He drew his gun and started across the street. But he was in for his life's surprise. The two women suddenly flung off their vests, drew Uzi submachine guns from between their curves and sprayed him with fire. The sentry jumped for cover and dived behind a low fence. A bullet hit the Dauphine's steering wheel and the shrill wail of the car horn tore the stillness of the night.

Operation Spring of Youth was on its way.

The couple the gendarmes had crossed on the street were not a couple of lovers. The tall man was Muki Betzer, one of the best Sayeret fighters. His girlfriend was none other than Ehud Barak, the Sayeret commander. Barak was wearing a black wig, his face was heavily made up and his brassiere was stuffed with hand grenades and old socks. Under his vest he carried weapons and a walkie-talkie. The "other girl" was Amiram Levin, a future Sayeret commander and IDF general. They both had chosen female disguises because they were short and slight; so was "the blond girl," Loni Rafaeli, who got in the building with the men, all of them Sayeret fighters.

Operation Spring of Youth was born at the height of the secret war that Israel waged against the terrorist group Black September. The group had been created by Palestine Liberation Organization leader Yasser Arafat after King Hussein of Jordan had massacred many thousands of PLO members in Jordan, in September 1970; hence "Black September."

At first, the new terrorist organization attacked Jordanian targets, leaders and secret agents; but soon it turned against Israel, hijacked the Sabena Boeing 707 (see Chapter 12) and slaughtered eleven Israeli athletes at the 1972 Munich Olympics. Following the advice of Mossad head Zvi Zamir and the prime minister's adviser on terrorism Aharon Yariv, Golda Meir unleashed the operational team of the Mossad against Black September's leaders, operating undercover in Europe. Zamir and Yariv believed that the elimination of the organization leaders would cause the demise of the entire group and put an end to its terrorist actions. In quick, ruthless Mossad operations in Rome, Paris, Athens and Cyprus, several Black September leaders were killed. But the Mossad and the IDF believed this was not enough, that it was necessary to hit the organization leaders in their very bastion—Beirut. The Lebanese capital had become the base of myriad terrorist groups and organiza-

tions that carried out their activities with total impunity. It was time
to prove to the terrorist leaders that there was no place under the sun
where Israel's long arm wouldn't reach them.

The goal of the operation was to kill three major leaders of Black September and the PLO: Kamal Nasser, the main PLO spokesman; Kamal
Adwan, the PLO operations commander, in charge of the activities in the
territories occupied by Israel; and the chief commander of Black September himself, Muhammad al-Najar (Abu Yussuf). All three of them lived
in a tall apartment building on Verdun Street—Nasser on the third floor,
Adwan on the second and Abu Yussuf on the sixth floor at the northern
wing of the house. The original idea was to launch a large-scale IDF operation, with the landing of big elite units in Beirut, blockage of the streets
around the building, an elaborate attack on the house—but Ehud Barak
cancelled that plan. Such a plan, he said to his superiors, means losing
the most important factor on which its success depends—surprise. The
Sayeret could carry out the mission with fourteen fighters, who would
quietly penetrate into Beirut, sneak into the house and break into the terrorists' apartments like a bolt from the blue sky.

Spring of Youth commanders, from right: Amnon Lipkin-Shahak, Shaul Ziv,
Emanuel Shaked, Ehud Barak. *(GPO)*

Moshe Dayan accepted the plan but decided to enlarge it. We don't land in Beirut every day, he said; this mission will be quite unique—so let's get the best out of it and hit several enemy targets simultaneously. Chief of Staff Dado Elazar and Chief Paratroop Officer Colonel Mano Shaked decided that while the Sayeret dealt with the three PLO leaders, another team of paratroopers from Airborne Battalion 50 would attack the headquarters of Nayef Hawatmeh's Popular Democratic Front for the Liberation of Palestine (PDFLP), a Maoist, left-leaning terrorist organization. The Battalion 50 team would be led by lieutenant-colonel Amnon Lipkin-Shahak, a lanky, cool-headed officer decorated for "leadership and courage under fire" in a 1968 attack on a PLO base, codenamed Operation Inferno.

The plan was that Lipkin's paratroopers would kill the guards at the entrance of the terrorist headquarters on Khartoum Street and blow up the building with two hundred kilos of explosives (about 440 pounds), killing everybody inside. At the same time other paratrooper units would land outside Beirut and carry out smaller diversion operations.

The Sayeret and the Battalion 50 team would approach the Lebanese coast in navy missile boats and land on Beirut's beach in Zodiac rubber dinghies. A small team of Mossad agents, who would fly to Beirut from several European cities, would be waiting for them on the beach. The agents would arrive a few days before the operation with false passports; they would rent cars, tour the city and get familiar with its streets and avenues. On the night of the mission they would drive the soldiers to their targets and back to the beach after the operation was over. Barak asked for three American cars into which he could squeeze his fourteen men.

The IDF computer supplied the mission's code name: Spring of Youth.

The intensive training of the units started right away. Mano Shaked and Chief of Staff Elazar spent a lot of time with the fighters. Shaked personally wanted to make sure that his paratroopers were becoming familiar with Beirut's streets. He would show one of them air photographs and maps, then place the man with his back to the maps and ask him, "What is on your right? What is on your left?" He believed that his boys should achieve a sense of orientation "with eyes closed" in the neighborhoods where they would operate.

The paratroopers and the Sayeret trained for landing from the sea, moving to their targets by foot or civilian cars, then retreating to the beach and departing aboard their Zodiacs. A model of the house that the Sayeret would attack was built of wood and fabric in a remote army base, and the commandos stormed the apartments using live ammo; they also trained in an abandoned police barracks in Samaria. The Battalion 50 team used the Lamed neighborhood in Tel Aviv as a "model" of Beirut. Some of the houses in that area were still in the building stage and could be used for training purposes without raising the neighbors' suspicion.

Or so their commanders thought.

One night in March 1973, a Lamed resident, sitting by his window, saw some suspect characters sneak between the houses, and heard heavy footsteps and short calls. He alerted the police, who arrived promptly, and Mano Shaked had a lot of trouble convincing them to go. Another doubt was voiced by the owner of a men's store on Disengoff Street. One after the other, young guys came to his store and each asked to buy a suit, one size larger than what he needed. The store owner did not know that these were paratroopers who were supposed to set out for Beirut wearing civilian suits and needed the extra size in order to conceal their weapons under their jackets. The merchant started asking questions, and the paratroopers persuaded him to forget what he heard, what he sold and who bought it.

But the civilians were not the only ones asking questions. One night, after hours of rehearsing the landing in the north of Tel Aviv, the weary paratroopers crouched on the beach, awaiting the rubber boats. One of them, Lieutenant Avida Shor, approached the chief of staff. "May I talk to you, sir?" In no other army in the world would a junior officer dare to approach the chief of staff, but Israel was different.

"Shoot!" Elazar said to the young man.

Avida, member of kibbutz Shoval, was one of the finest paratroop fighters. He had proven his courage in the Tripoli raid, when his unit had landed on a desert beach 133 miles beyond the Israeli border, attacked and blown up four terrorist bases and returned practically unscathed. Avida was also known for his high moral principles. He now drew a small notebook out of his pocket and said to Elazar, "We plan to blow up the PDFLP headquarters with two hundred kilos of explosives. But I made my own calculations and found out that we can bring down the house with only one hundred and twenty kilos."

"What difference does this make?" General Elazar asked.

"The difference is," Avida said forcefully, "that there is another building next to the PDFLP headquarters. It is a seven-story house, inhabited by scores of civilian families. I believe that we should use fewer explosives and avoid casualties among the civilians." Then he added, "The terrorists should know that we were there and could carry out the mission, but that we would not harm women and children."

There was a moment of silence. Finally Elazar nodded. "I'll buy that," he said. "One hundred and twenty kilos it will be."

From April 1 to April 6, several tourists arrived in Beirut: Gilbert Rimbaud, Dieter Altnuder, Andrew Whichelaw, Charles Boussard, George Elder and Andrew Macy. Most of them carried British or Belgian passports and were later identified by foreign sources as Mossad agents. They checked into various hotels and rented cars from Avis and Lena Car. At least three of the cars were American-made, as Barak had requested: a Buick Skylark, a Plymouth and a Valiant.

On April 5, nine missile boats and "Dabur" fast patrol boats took to sea from Haifa port, carrying the Sayeret, the Battalion 50 team and Flotilla 13—the IDF Navy SEALs. Before departing, the soldiers were shown the latest aerial photographs of Beirut, the landing beach and the targeted buildings. The Sayeret fighters received photographs of the three terrorist leaders they had to kill. Some of the men were given silenced Beretta handguns. The targets were designated with women's names: Aviva, Gila, Varda, Tzila and Judith.

After nightfall the boats approached Beirut; the city was bathed in light, its nightclubs and restaurants bustling with activity. At the same time, on the Israeli boats, navy soldiers covered the fighters with large, transparent plastic sleeves to prevent their civilian clothes and the makeup some of them were wearing from getting wet. They boarded twelve rubber boats, and shortly before midnight reached the two landing areas—Ramlet Al-Baida and Dove beaches. The beaches were deserted, and the last couple of lovers had left the sandy stretches. In total silence, like ghostly apparitions, the dinghies emerged from the black sea.

Barak's Sayeret and Lipkin-Shahak's team quietly disembarked. Simultaneously, other paratrooper teams prepared to land at some secondary targets. A Flotilla 13 team would land at the Al-Uzai neighborhood, and head for a sea-mines plant and a terrorist base. Another paratrooper team would attack and blow up a warehouse in Beirut port, while the paratrooper commando unit targeted a weapons workshop north of Sidon. The floating headquarters of the mission, headed by Mano Shaked, and a paratrooper rescue unit approached Beirut's beach in two missile boats. Everything was in place.

On the beach, the rented cars and their Mossad drivers were waiting. The soldiers jumped from the Zodiacs and ran to the cars. One of the fighters in Barak's team was Yoni Netanyahu. Barak felt he owed Yoni compensation, after having preferred his younger brother, Bibi, for the Sabena hostage mission. The Sayeret soldiers piled up in the American cars, which drove to Verdun Street and parked in the neighboring Ibn el Walid Street, close to the target building. The men got out and walked in small groups to the big house. The other three cars carried Lipkin-Shahak's paratroopers to Ghana Street, and they surreptitiously moved toward the PDFLP headquarters at the neighboring Khartoum Street. By 1:29 A.M., both teams were in place.

When the odd couple—Ehud Barak and Muki Betzer—reached the house on Verdun Street, they found out that the building's gate was not locked and the guard wasn't there; there would be no problem entering the building. The intelligence reports they had received specified that some security guards would be sitting in a gray Mercedes parked across the street, but there was no Mercedes in sight. The Sayeret teams entered the building and climbed the stairs to the terrorists' apartments. Only

Barak and Levin, who had remained outside, suddenly discovered that the security guards were sitting in the red Dauphine and engaged in a shooting fight with the man who got out of the car. The strident blare of the Dauphine's horn, whichwas hit by a bullet, echoed in the sleeping neighborhood, and the surprise effect was lost.

Muki Betzer, Yoni Netanyahu and two other soldiers reached Abu Yussuf's apartment and blew open the door with an explosive charge. For Betzer, the two seconds between the activating of the charge and its explosion seemed an eternity. The door blew off its hinges, and the commandos hurled themselves into the apartment. They stumbled upon Abu Yussuf's sixteen-year-old son. "Where's your father?" one of them asked in Arabic. The teenager stared in horror at the strangers wearing nylon stockings over their heads, then ran to his room and slipped down the drainpipe to a friend's apartment on the fifth floor. Abu Yussuf's remaining four children were in the apartment, but nobody touched them. Suddenly, a bedroom door opened before the soldiers and there was Black September's chief, Abu Yussuf, in his pajamas. He jumped back into the bedroom and slammed the door. His wife, Maha, tried to get her husband's handgun from the wardrobe. The fighters fired at the door, and Muki kicked it open. Several bursts of gunfire hit Abu Yussuf and Maha, who stood behind him. Yoni and another soldier shot him dead. Abu Yussuf, the man responsible for the Munich Massacre, lay dead on the floor.

Muki left the apartment and ran down the stairs, followed by his men.

In the other wing of the house the two other Sayeret teams approached the apartments of Adwan and Nasser. A few fighters, led by Amitai Nahmani, reached Adwan's apartment and one of them kicked the door open. Adwan stood in front of them, a Kalashnikov submachine gun in his hands. He hesitated for a split second before diving behind a curtain, simultaneously firing at the Israelis and wounding one of them. A soldier who had climbed the water pipe outside the building jumped into the room. At that moment Nahmani shot Adwan. The soldiers searched the apartment, refraining from harming Adwan's wife and two children; they stuffed files and documents into two suitcases and rushed out.

At the same moment the third team, led by Zvi Livne, blew up Kamal Nasser's door. The soldiers broke into the bedroom, where two women lay in their beds. Nasser was not there; the men fired under the beds, searched the closet and finally found the PLO spokesman in the kitchen, where they shot him. As they came out, the door of the apartment across the landing suddenly opened. One of the men fired instinctively and mortally wounded an elderly Italian woman who had been awakened by the shooting.

In the meantime a firefight had erupted in the street. A base of the Lebanese gendarmerie was located at a nearby corner; minutes after the exchange of fire with the security guard started, a Land Rover jeep from the gendarmerie arrived at the scene. Barak and Levin fired at the approaching jeep and hit the driver. The jeep crashed into the cars parked in the street. All its passengers were hit by Barak and Levin, soon joined by the fighters who came out of the building. Another gendarmerie jeep rushed up the street. The soldiers opened intense fire and stopped it as well. Barak ordered his men to get into the cars—and then a third jeep appeared. It was also met by heavy fire and a grenade thrown by Betzer. The gendarmes jumped off the burning vehicle and escaped to the entrance of a neighboring house.

The soldiers ran to the cars, and Yoni was the last to jump into the third car. The entire operation had lasted half an hour. The cars sped toward the beach, but as they approached the beach promenade, two gendarmerie jeeps appeared in front of them, moving slowly and inspecting the area. The American cars crawled behind the Land Rovers in perfect order, till the jeeps turned the corner. The Sayeret team safely arrived at the beach.

At the same time, in another part of Beirut, Lipkin-Shahak's paratroopers stealthily approached the headquarters of the PDFLP. They were fourteen, too—four details of two paratroopers each; Lipkin-Shahak; the unit physician; a Flotilla 13 fighter and the three drivers. The attack would start after two paratroopers would approach the building guards and kill them with silenced Berettas. The two paratroopers chosen for that task were Avida Shor—the one who had convinced Elazar to use fewer explosives—and his friend, Hagai Maayan from kibbutz Magen.

They strolled in a leisurely way up Khartoum Street and stopped by the entrance to the terrorists' building to light their cigarettes. The guards stood there. "Excuse me," Shor said to one of them in English. When the guards turned toward the Israelis, Shor and Maayan drew their handguns and shot them. As he fell down, one of the terrorists groaned, "Allah!"

Nobody noticed the two other guards sitting in a Fiat jeep armed with a "Dushka" Russian-made machine gun that was parked across the street. They suddenly opened fire and riddled the two paratroopers with bullets. Avida Shor was killed on the spot; Maayan was to succumb later. Yigal Pressler, another paratrooper who followed the two, was wounded. Lipkin called Shor and Maayan by radio but there was no answer. For Lipkin-Shahak, "this was a moment of real trouble. Shor doesn't answer, Maayan lies wounded in the street, Igal is bleeding—and we still have to blow up the building!"

From porches, windows and even from the street, the terrorists opened heavy fire on the paratroopers with rifles, Kalashnikovs and machine guns. For Lipkin-Shahak this was "real hell." He radioed to Mano Shaked that there was "a complication."

"Do you need help?" Shaked asked.

"Not for the moment," Lipkin-Shahak said. Shaked immediately launched the diversionary operations, in order to pin down the Lebanese Army forces that might try to interfere in the fighting. The rubber boats, laden with soldiers, darted toward the beaches. The attack was advanced by three minutes, but these were precious minutes.

In Khartoum Street, a full-scale battle was raging between the paratroopers and the terrorists. A soldier tried to haul the wounded Igal to safety; one of the terrorists thought that Igal was one of them and tried to drag him to a nearby courtyard. He let go only after a fierce struggle with Avishai, a Flotilla 13 frogman. The explosions and the bursts of gunfire were accompanied by the terrorists' shouts: *"Yahood! Yahood!"* ("Jews!") To the Israelis' amazement, in the heat of the battle, while the street trembled with the fusillade, local civilians calmly kept going in and out of the neighboring buildings or stood on their porches and watched the combat with interest.

Under the heavy fire four paratroopers managed to enter the building lobby. Firing long bursts with their automatic weapons and throwing hand grenades, they repeatedly hit terrorists who came down the stairs. They now controlled the lobby. One of the paratroopers, Aharon Sabbag, suddenly noticed the lights on the elevator screen blinking in quick succession as the elevator descended to street level. He watched the numbers as if hypnotized. Four . . . three . . . two . . . one . . . As the elevator stopped, he emptied his whole magazine into the cabin. Nobody came out alive.

At that moment the car carrying the explosives broke into the lobby, and the sappers rapidly placed the charges by four of the supporting columns. The soldiers set the fuses for a 180-second delay, then retreated, while their comrades covered them by firing RPGs, bazookas, eighty-one-millimeter mortar shells and tear gas grenades on their way out. The paratroopers loaded the body of Avida Shor, and the still breathing Hagai Maayan, into one of the cars. The driver ignored Lipkin-Shahak's order to wait for the others and rushed down to the beach. The fighters tossed iron nails on the street, to delay any pursuing vehicles, then piled up in the two remaining cars and sped madly toward the beach. The entire operation had lasted twenty-four minutes.

Israeli helicopters emerged over Ramlet Al-Baida beach and evacuated the wounded, while the other men boarded the rubber boats and headed toward the missile boats. The six Mossad agents neatly parked the cars on the beach, leaving the keys in the ignitions, then jumped into the Zodiacs. The car rental bills would be paid in a few days through American Express. In the meantime the diversionary operations of the paratroopers and Flotilla 13 were completed as well, and the soldiers returned to the mother ships from other beaches.

Amnon Lipkin-Shahak turned back—and was petrified. He felt "like Lot's wife" from the Bible, as he saw a huge smoke mushroom rise over the PDFLP building.

In Haifa port Dayan and Elazar were waiting for the commandos. The mission was crowned with total success. The PDFLP headquarters had been destroyed and scores of high-ranking terrorists were buried beneath the ruins. Three of the top leaders of Fatah and Black September were dead. The world press described the IDF's amazing feat on its front pages. In the days to come, following the deaths of Black September's top leaders, the organization crumbled and then simply ceased to exist.

Mano Shaked, impressed with Lipkin-Shahak's calm under fire, awarded him his second medal. Ehud Barak and three other fighters were also decorated.

Less than six months after Spring of Youth, the Yom Kippur War exploded on the banks of the Suez Canal and the peaks of the Golan Heights.

EHUD BARAK, SAYERET MATKAL COMMANDER, LATER DEFENSE MINISTER AND PRIME MINISTER

"About four months earlier, Head of Operations General Kuti Adam had told us that several Fatah leaders were living in these buildings in Beirut, and asked if we could act. We said that we might. We passed on questions to the Mossad, received answers, but the issue calmed down. We made other plans—a raid on an officers' club in Syria and freeing pilots from a prison next to Damascus.

"I was with my wife on a weekend in Eilat when I was summoned to the chief of staff's office. Dado showed me some photographs and told me, 'Here, these buildings.' The chief infantry and paratroopers' officer Mano Shaked proposed that we attack with a task force from the Thirty-fifth Brigade. To me, this looked like an assault on a fortified target—you arrive with forty guys, set down roadblocks, raid every house. . . . I said, 'It's impossible with such a large force. We need the element of surprise. We need to do this with fourteen or fifteen people, to come in civilian attire with American cars and kill them.' This was approved.

"I told my people, 'We'll kill them in bed.' But two of the team commanders said to me, 'What do you mean, kill them in bed? We kill people in bed? What have they done that makes killing them justified? Does that square with our principle of "purity of arms"?'

I said, 'They are bad, dangerous people, working with Arafat.' They said, 'That's nice, but you don't have authority. We want to know that the chief of staff thinks this is legitimate.' I said fine, but I brushed it off. They reminded me of what I had said again and again, and eventually I brought in the chief of staff—and he explained it to them.

"They carried out the task very well. Both were killed in the Yom Kippur War."

AMNON LIPKIN-SHAHAK, COMMANDER OF A PARATROOPER BATTALION, LATER THE CHIEF OF STAFF

"During the battle, we loaded Yigal Pressler, who was wounded, and the body of Avida Shor into one of our cars. But suddenly we saw that the car had disappeared, along with the driver, an older man from the Mossad. We all managed to get into two cars, and we sped off toward the beach. We found the driver there with the third car. I asked what had happened. He told me that, during the War of Independence, he had fought at the Koach fortress, in Galilee, and his commanders had told him, 'You don't move from here.' He didn't move, and fought, even when his friends retreated, until the Arabs won. He hid under the corpses, and that was how he survived. He later crawled out of there and managed to get away.

"Now, during the battle against the terrorists, he recalled that during the War of Independence, he had nearly been killed because he had stayed until the end. 'I thought that you wouldn't get out of there,' he told me, 'and I decided to drive to the beach where we landed, hoping that someone would save me.'

"He had simply fled."

PART FIVE

The Yom Kippur War

Since the 1967 Six Day War, Egypt and Syria have been planning their revenge. On October 6, 1973, Yom Kippur, they attack Israel simultaneously. Israel has its same leaders, and the chief of staff is David Elazar. The Arab leaders have changed: Egypt's Nasser has died and been replaced by Anwar Sadat. Syria's Salah el Jadid is in prison, after a coup by his defense minister, Hafez al-Assad. King Hussein is not a member of the Sadat-Assad alliance; on the contrary, he has secretly warned Israel's leaders of the forthcoming attack. Unfortunately, his warnings have not been taken seriously.

CHAPTER 15
THE BRAVEHEARTS
LAND IN AFRICA,
1973

A t 4:30 P.M., on October 15, 1973, the paratroopers of the 247th Reserve Brigade climbed into their half-tracks. The last-minute briefing had just ended, and harried staff sergeants ran to the commanders' half-tracks, carrying the operational maps. A soldier pressed an open tin of cold goulash in his comrade's hand, one of the authors of this book. "Eat something," he cracked, "you'll get your next meal only in Africa."

Africa. For nine days thousands of IDF soldiers and officers were expecting that mission: the moment when their battered army would break through the Egyptian lines that had been established in Sinai, would cross the Suez Canal and emerge at the enemy's rear. They knew that this mission would tip the scales of the war. They also believed that they were taking part in a crazy gamble—penetrating through a gap in the Egyptian lines, advancing between two huge Egyptian concentrations and reaching the canal. But exactly because of the mission's daring and tremendous risk taking it had great chances to be crowned with success. The Egyptians certainly wouldn't even imagine that the IDF would take such a risky gamble before it had succeeded in crushing their forces entrenched on the eastern bank of the canal.

The war had started on October 6, 1973, Yom Kippur—the Jewish Day of Atonement. At 2:00 P.M., the armies of Syria and Egypt simultaneously attacked Israel on two fronts—in the Golan Heights and along the Suez Canal. In the Golan Heights, the Syrians were stopped only because of the desperate courage and the resolve of a few. In the south, the Egyptians crossed the Suez Canal to Israeli-occupied Sinai, conquered most of the IDF forts along the canal and entrenched themselves strongly in a five-mile-deep strip of land in Sinai, causing painful losses to Israel. Defense Minister Moshe Dayan seemed to waver, as he expressed fear for the possible collapse of "the Third Temple" symbolizing the state of Israel; the pretentious declaration of Chief of Staff Elazar that "we'll break their bones" turned out to be just a bubble of hot air.

The counteroffensive of Division 162, under the command of General Avraham ("Bren") Adan, was launched on October 8 and ended in failure. He confronted the Egyptian army and tried to cross the canal, but was repelled. The mission was reluctantly handed over to General Arik Sharon, whose Division 143 also included the famous 247th (former 55th), the reserve Paratroopers Brigade that had conquered Jerusalem in the Six Day War.

At forty-five, Sharon was back in the saddle. After several years in minor positions, he finally had been brought back from the cold by Chief of Staff Yitzhak Rabin, who appreciated his military talent. Ben-Gurion himself had asked Rabin to "take care" of Sharon, whom he loved, in spite of the flaws in his character. Sharon had been promoted to general, and had performed brilliantly in the Six Day War; his combined assault on Abu Ageila fortress in Sinai was being taught in military academies around the world. He had left the army in 1973 after serving as commander of the Southern District and had turned to politics, joining the Likud party, but when the Yom Kippur War broke out he returned as commander of Division 143. In the meantime, Sharon had been hit by two tragedies: his wife, Margalit, had been killed in a car crash, and their eleven-year-old son, Gur, died in an accident, playing with an old rifle. Sharon, though, found solace in the arms of Gali's younger sister, Lily, who married him, gave him two sons and became a wonderful support for him for the rest of her life.

Sharon's superiors in the IDF didn't really want him to cross the canal. Sharon was a maverick, undisciplined, arrogant and a lover of publicity. Besides, he had just become a right-wing political leader, while most of his superiors, including Chief of Staff Elazar, were former members of the left-leaning Palmach. But after Adan's failure of October 8, and Dayan's intervention in favor of the 101 founder, they had no choice but to turn to Sharon.

Sharon, determined that it would be him who'd cross the canal, conceived a plan that seemed absolutely insane. On a patrol in enemy territory, the reconnaissance battalion of his division discovered an intriguing fact. The Egyptian forces that had crossed the canal and occupied a five-mile strip along it were divided into two armies—the Second and the Third. The reconnaissance battalion found out that there was no land continuity between the two armies, but a kind of narrow no-man's-land was separating them. This gave Sharon the idea to send a brigade along the "seam" between the two armies. After reaching and crossing the canal, it would establish a bridgehead in the rear of the Egyptians, lay bridges over Suez and bring the war to the Egyptian heartland. The idea was insane indeed—so insane that nobody in a normal state of mind would believe it could be carried out.

Michael Bar-Zohar, one of the authors of this book, accompanied Sharon and Colonel Amnon Reshef, the commander of an armored brigade, on their climb to the top of an arid hill, and Sharon ordered Reshef's artillery to fire phosphorus shells at five-hundred-meter intervals along the "seam" between the two Egyptian armies. When the firing started, Sharon watched through his binoculars the white smoke mushrooms that sprouted along the "seam" to the very canal; the lack of any movement in the no-man's-land between the two armies proved that there were no Egyptian units there. Still, no crossing was possible as long as the bulk of the Egyptian armor was deployed on the African side of the canal; it could easily destroy the bridgehead and eradicate any IDF unit that had crossed the waterway. Sharon had to wait for the elite Egyptian armored units to cross the canal and engage the Israeli armor. And the Israeli armor was ready.

He didn't have to wait long. On October 14, hundreds of Egyptian tanks, including a large part of the crack 4th Armored Division, crossed the canal. A formidable battle ensued, and after a few hours the burning carcasses of 250 Egyptian tanks were strewn in the sands of Sinai. The IDF lost only twenty-five tanks. The time had come to launch Sharon's plan, code name Bravehearts.

. And bravehearts they were indeed, all those reserve paratroopers who had fought in most of Israel battles, their feats crowned with the conquest of Jerusalem. Motta Gur wasn't their commander anymore—he had been appointed IDF attaché to the Israeli embassy in Washington. The leader of Brigade 247 was another legendary commander—Danny Matt.

Born in Cologne, Germany, raised in a religious moshav on the coastal plain, Danny—barely sixteen—had joined the British Coast Guard, then enlisted in the British Army and participated in the last stages of World War II. Back in Israel he joined the Palmach and settled in kibbutz Ein Zurim, in a cluster of agricultural villages south of Jerusalem, called Bloc Etzion. On May 12, 1948, two days before Israel was created, a huge mass of Arab irregulars attacked the bloc, massacring scores of its inhabitants. Danny, manning a position close to Ein Zurim, found himself facing thousands of Arabs, who were yelling; waving rifles, axes, and knives; and submerging the area. Feverishly, he attached thirteen grenades to his belt, grabbed a machine gun and started firing at the advancing crowd. The first wave of attackers collapsed, but they were replaced by hundreds of others, all of them screaming and charging his isolated position. He knew that if they reached him they'd tear him to pieces, and so he kept firing, mowing down line after line of attackers. He started pulling hand grenades with his right hand, removing the triggering pin with his teeth, while firing the machine gun with his left. Scores of dead attackers piled in front of him. As he ran out of ammunition he threw away the machine gun, removed the pin of his last grenade, raised the grenade above his head and ran toward kibbutz Revadim. The mass of Arabs parted before that crazy bearded man waving an armed hand grenade. He reached the kibbutz, followed by a fierce crowd of enemies; somebody dragged him into a house, another guy sheared his beard with a pair of scissors, a third shaved his stubble with an old razor, without water or shaving cream, tearing pieces of skin from his face, while outside the Arab crowd kept yelling, "Where is the bearded one? Where is the murderer? Give us the murderer!"

Fortunately, at that moment the Jordanian Legion arrived and took all the kibbutz men prisoner. Danny put on large sunglasses and joined his comrades. He was not recognized. He spent a year as a prisoner of war in Jordan. Upon returning he grew his beard again, joined the paratroopers, commanded an elite company, participated in all the reprisal raids and was severely wounded in the Mitla battle. He spent two years at the War College in Paris, later distinguished himself in the Six Day War—and finally assumed command over the famous 247th Brigade.

On October 15, at sunset, several units carried a diversionary attack on the Egyptian forces, while Danny's brigade, riding on half-tracks, moved toward the Suez Canal on a narrow asphalt road, code-named Spider. One battalion of the 247th was late arriving to the assembly area, but Danny refused to delay the mission and moved forward with the two remaining battalions. The plan was that at 8:00 P.M., the paratroopers would reach the canal, board rubber boats and cross the waterway in proximity to Deversoir, where the canal flows into the Great Bitter Lake. Sharon, on the commanding half-track, was not far behind them.

The crossing, however, almost failed because of a traffic jam. The paratroopers' half-tracks got stuck in the middle of a nightmarish tangle of hundreds of vehicles. Heavy trucks, jeeps, pickups, and even private cars surrounded by crowds of reserve soldiers were massed along several miles on the narrow road, blocking Danny Matt's convoy. Once in a while, the paratroopers' vehicles would break through and advance a couple of hundred yards, then become immobilized again. The troubled voices of Sharon and his deputy echoed in the brigade commander's radio over and over again. The most crucial mission of the war could end in failure because the IDF could not overcome traffic congestion.

The Israeli tanks cross the Suez Canal on the pontoon bridge.
(Bamachane, IDF Archive)

The road cleared only after midnight. Headlights off, the convoy sped on the Spider route toward the red flashes and the smoke mushrooms hovering over the nearby hills and across the canal. At a road crossing a naval unit loaded a score of rubber boats on the half-tracks. The IDF artillery shelled the crossing areas in order to drive away the Egyptian soldiers that might be positioned there. A tank battalion and a commando on half-tracks from another brigade emerged at the head of the convoy to protect it on its way to the canal.

But the escort was the first to be hit. Darting forward before the paratroopers, the tank battalion fell into an Egyptian ambush. Most of the tanks and the commando half-tracks were hit and burst into flames. The losses were heavy, but Danny Matt's convoy bypassed the burning armor and continued its advance toward the canal. Miraculously, the Egyptians did not notice the advance unit and it easily reached the canal bank. But when the bulk of the convoy approached, with the brigade commander's half-track at its head, it was met with heavy, sustained fire. Egyptian soldiers of the Second and Third armies, stationed in the sandy flatlands by the canal, sighted Matt's half-track, which signaled with its headlights to Sharon, who watched the convoy from a nearby hill. The sheaf of antennae, protruding from the canvas top of the vehicle, was another sign that this was the commander's half-track. The Egyptians attacked the convoy with bazookas, machine guns and other weapons. Missiles whooshed beside the vehicles and the paratroopers returned fire. Yet, the Egyptians were too far away, as Sharon had surmised, and most of their fire was ineffective.

After several turns of the road the enemy fire weakened. The convoy stopped in a kind of courtyard, surrounded by steep sand ramparts. The soldiers climbed up the western rampart and descended on its other side. At their feet glistened a calm, silvery stripe—the Suez Canal. The rubber boats were unloaded and swiftly brought to the water. The paratroopers jumped into them, and one after the other the boats ploughed the Suez waters, heading for the African bank. At 1:25 Danny Matt radioed the word "Aquarium," meaning the boats were in the water. He then boarded one of the first boats. Bar-Zohar crouched beside him. A few shells exploded by the fast moving boats. Most of the fighters were excited, feeling they were experiencing a dramatic moment, a game-changing event that could seal the outcome of the war.

Danny Matt's outward calm concealed tremendous tension. Never in his life had he felt such crushing responsibility. "We were carrying out a mission that could change the war's outcome. I felt that the entire nation of Israel was raising its eyes toward us," he later said.

The boats coasted by a low stone jetty. The paratroopers crossed a sandy strip, covered with low shrubs. Danny, never departing from his cool, radioed the code word for the landing on the African bank of the canal: "Acapulco; repeat, Acapulco!"

While excited senior officers radioed congratulations to Matt, the paratroopers scouted the area. They had landed in the very middle of a fortified Egyptian compound: sand ramparts, stone and concrete walls, reinforced positions, underground bunkers. A terrible fight could have taken place here if the Egyptians had stayed and confronted the para- troopers, but they had escaped from the heavy artillery shelling. In later years historians and writers would express their amazement that the paratrooper force that had established the bridgehead was so small and vulnerable—barely 760 men.

A grove of firs, eucalyptuses and young palms stretched out behind the compound. Small units of paratroopers took position on top of the ramparts.

Arik Achmon, one of Matt's two deputies, stopped by to see a friend. "To be in the first half-track that entered the Old City of Jerusalem," he cracked, smiling, "and in one of the first boats to cross into Africa— that's quite something in a man's life, isn't it?"

Thundering explosions were heard from the eastern bank of the canal. The paratroopers didn't know that a formidable battle was rag- ing between Reshef's armored brigade and large Egyptian forces. The fighting took place around the Tirtur ("Rattle") route that ran parallel to the Spider road that Matt's men had used to reach the canal. The fierce combat spread to the "Chinese Farm." It also delayed the crossing of the canal by large Israeli forces, because the Cylinder Bridge, a prefabricated Israeli invention, dragged by eighteen tanks, wouldn't reach the Canal before October 17.

But Sharon wouldn't give up. Two huge bulldozers arrived at the canal and breached a passage for heavy vehicles. The breaching site (the "Yard") had been prepared by Sharon long before, when he still was commander of the Southern District. He had used red bricks to mark the thinner ramparts, which could be easily breached. Now he dispatched to the breach several pontoons that should together form a floating bridge. But as some of the pontoons lagged behind, the engineers brought over the "Crocodiles," monstrous amphibious tank carriers that had been invented by a French officer and named Gillois after him; a while before, the Israeli defense ministry had bought the old Gillois from the NATO surplus stocks and refurbished them—and as dawn broke on October 16, the Crocodiles started carrying the first tanks of Hayim Erez's armored brigade across the canal.

The Yard and the bridgehead across the waterway bustled with activity. The Egyptians did not realize that an Israeli task force had landed behind their backs. It took more than two days for the Egyptian high command to find out that Israeli units had taken positions on the canal's western bank. On October 16, Egypt's President Sadat made a speech before a special session of the parliament and announced that he had ordered work to start on the Suez Canal, blocked since the Six Day War, in order to reopen it to international shipping. That same afternoon he was surprised to hear the statement of Golda Meir before the Knesset that IDF units were operating on the western bank of the canal. But even then, the Egyptians assumed that this was a limited raid of a commando unit in their territory.

During the heavy fighting against the Egyptians on the eastern bank some of the members of Sharon's advanced command unit were hurt; Sharon himself was lightly scratched, and the white dressing on his forehead became, for the soldiers, the symbol of the canal crossing. From his position in the Yard, Sharon tried to convince his superiors to allow his division to cross the canal and exploit their initial success. He pointed out that Hayim Erez had crossed with twenty-seven tanks on the Crocodiles and had darted westward; Erez had destroyed several bases of ground-to-air missiles and cleared the skies for the Israeli fighter planes. But there was more: Erez almost didn't meet any resistance, and he had the feeling that the road to Cairo was opened before him. He radioed Sharon, "I can get to the Nile!"

Shortly before the crossing of the Suez Canal, a meeting of senior IDF commanders in Sinai. From left to right: General Ariel Sharon, Division commander; General Moshe Dayan, Minister of Defense; Colonel Braun. General Adan; one of the authors of this book, Sergeant Michael Bar-Zohar; General Tal; General Tamir; General Gonen. (*Uri Dan*)

But Sharon's superiors firmly refused to let Sharon cross. First, they demanded that he lay another bridge over the water and open the roads leading to the canal. They feared an Egyptian move to block the road to the canal and to annihilate the paratrooper bridgehead, as long as the roads were not secured and the bridges not in place. They also ordered Sharon to stay in the Yard and let Adan's Division 162 cross the canal in order to encircle the Third Army. Sharon's repeated pleas to let him cross were to no avail. Some commentators insisted that Sharon had been stopped for political reasons.

But in the meantime the Egyptians understood that an Israeli task force had crossed Suez and established a base on the African side. Now a new chapter in the fighting started: desperate efforts by the Egyptian Army to annihilate the bridgehead. From the second day after the crossing and up to the cease-fire, nine days later, Matt's paratroopers in Africa and Sharon's other units in the Yard were submitted to nonstop heavy bombardment that caused large numbers of casualties. The Egyptians attacked

Sharon's fighters with artillery and mortars, their jets dived on them with bombs and missiles, their helicopters dropped napalm barrels or fired at them day and night, in the light of parachuted flares. But the crossing continued; the pontoon bridge was completed, the Cylinder Bridge finally reached the canal and was laid between its two banks. Matt's paratroopers watched, from the top of the ramparts, the never-ending convoys that crossed the bridges on their way to the African side. Arik Sharon enjoyed the enthusiastic admiration of the troops, and when he crossed the canal he was received by shouts of "Arik, King of Israel."

On October 24 the fire ceased. The Third Army was surrounded; Matt's paratroopers had occupied the fertile agricultural strip along the canal and advanced northward to Ismailia, a large Egyptian town; the paratroopers also had advanced south, to the city of Suez; the Israeli armor had stopped at the "101st kilometer," sixty-three miles from Cairo.

Time had come for Israel and Egypt to lay down their weapons and start talking. The talks, held at the 101st kilometer, would result in a separation of forces; five years later the two countries would sign the Camp David Accords, and the following year, a peace treaty.

MOSHE ("BOGIE") YA'ALON, LATER CHIEF OF STAFF AND DEFENSE MINISTER

"The Yom Kippur War is part of my DNA.

"The announcement of war hit me like thunder on a clear day. I was a civilian, a reserve sergeant, a newlywed. The commanders of the Fiftieth Airborne Battalion had wanted to send me to an officers' course, but I didn't want to sign on for permanent service, and I was discharged. On Rosh Hashanah [the Jewish New Year] eve, I was elected secretary of Kibbutz Grofit in the Negev.

"When I was told about the outbreak of the war, on October sixth at two P.M., I thought they were pulling my leg, but in the evening I was already at the Sirkin base with my comrades from the 247th Paratrooper Brigade. On October sixteenth, we crossed the canal on the floating bridge. We took shelling, secured the bridgehead and ended the war in the city of Suez. You find yourself at war, planes attacking, shellings, bombings, clashes . . . I thought that I wasn't going to survive all this.

"But, ironically, it was at war that I had time to think. Bad news arrived about the fall of the forts along the canal, about friends who had been killed or wounded. A sense of distrust in the political and military leadership grew in me. I felt powerless. Perhaps the country is going to fall! Where is the leadership? Where is the intelligence? Where are all the people we're supposed to trust?

"I told myself, if I come out of this war alive, the kibbutz will get along fine without me. I'm staying in the army, returning to permanent service as a platoon commander. I can't be at peace with myself if I go back to the kibbutz. My priorities must change.

"At the end of the war, I went looking for the Fiftieth Battalion. They were deployed at the Gidi Pass, in Sinai. Ya Ya [Colonel Yuval Yair] was the battalion commander. I told him, 'Ya Ya, I'm coming back to the army.'"

While the paratroopers are crossing the Suez Canal,
a fierce battle is taking place at the "Chinese Farm," bordering
with the roads leading to the canal. Disappointed with
the commander of the Southern District's performance,
Golda appoints former chief of staff Haim Bar-Lev
as commander of the Southern Front.

CHAPTER 16

"COMMANDER KILLED . . . DEPUTY COMMANDER KILLED . . . SECOND DEPUTY COMMANDER . . ." 1973

If the Chinese Farm could speak, it would recount the two consecutive nights of bloody battle that took place on its soil in the fall of 1973, recalling the dead, the injured, the moments of despair and the acts of heroism it left recorded in the history of the IDF and the Egyptian Army.

In the mid-fifties, a strip of land covering 5.8 square miles located on the Sinai Peninsula had been converted into an agricultural compound with the help of the Japanese government. Close to the Suez Canal, it had been crisscrossed with deep ditches dug for irrigation. The Israeli soldiers who reached it during the Six Day War in 1967 couldn't tell the difference between Chinese and Japanese characters, and had nicknamed it the "Chinese Farm."

The Chinese Farm was located north of the Great Bitter Lake. It was close to both the Spider and the Rattle routes to the canal, and to the important junction between Rattle and Lexicon—code name for a road that ran parallel to the canal. Israel's plan was to occupy the farm, so that the "corridor" to the canal remained free; that would ensure the success of the crossing (see chapter 15). In many aspects, the conquest of the Chinese Farm would be critical to the survival of the bravehearts' bridgehead.

Arik Sharon, who had been tasked with capturing the Chinese Farm and crossing the canal, said on the mission's eve, "We should not expect any surprises. There's not a living soul there [in the Chinese Farm]. Our force would move without shooting, without [doing] anything, and would enter the area. This entire territory is empty." But the reality turned out to be entirely different. Waiting for the Israelis was a big surprise—bigger than they could have imagined.

On the night of October 15, the 14th Armored Brigade, led by Colonel Amnon Reshef, moved toward the Suez Canal; its goal was to occupy the east bank of the canal, north of the two roads, and thus protect the paratroopers' crossing. Amnon Reshef was a tall, skinny guy sporting a huge mustache; tanks had always been his natural habitat. The Haifaborn officer had distinguished himself during the Six Day War, where he had fought in the Sinai and on the Golan Heights. His brigade, the only tank brigade that faced the Egyptian Army when it attacked Israel on the first day of the Yom Kippur War, had been badly mauled. After the first day of fighting Reshef had only 14 of his 56 tanks left; 90 of his soldiers had been killed.

Reshef had recovered quickly, received fresh reinforcements, reorganized his brigade, participated in a victorious battle against Egyptian armor the previous day, and that night he led his men into battle, hoping to surprise the enemy. Riding on tanks and half- tracks, the armored and infantry forces advanced without knowing what the Egyptians had in store for them. But Lieutenant Colonel Amram Mitzna, leading Battalion 79, had a bad premonition. Before the battle he wrote a farewell letter to his wife and left it with his jeep driver.

At nine-fifteen that evening, Mitzna's spearhead battalion arrived in the area where it was supposed to secure the route for crossing the Suez. But it quickly ran into Egyptian tanks, armored personnel carriers and artillery. Punishing battles unfolded, sometimes within a range of just a few feet. Mitzna later recalled, "The first encounter was on Rattle road. Suddenly hellfire came at us from all sides. There was hysteria all along the communication network. The brigade's order was to shoot anything that moved. Tanks were crashing into tanks. The 184th Tank Battalion was firing at the 79th . . ."

The Israeli battalion destroyed numerous Egyptian targets but also paid a heavy price in its own blood. A shell that struck Mitzna's tank killed the operations officer and gunner, and Mitzna was thrown from the vehicle and badly wounded.

The 184th Battalion, trailing Mitzna, began to take heavy fire, causing severe losses. Barely half of its tanks managed to cross the Lexicon–Rattle junction. The battle spilled over to the neighboring Chinese Farm, where the Egyptians had entrenched themselves with crack troops, tanks and every possible kind of weapon, including the anti-tank Sagger missile freshly arrived from the Soviet Union. The Sagger was an individual guided missile, carried in a small suitcase by a soldier. The Israelis later nicknamed the suitcase carriers "tourists." But these tourists were deadly. When an Israeli tank was in sight, the tourist would open his suitcase, produce his missile and guide it by remote control until it blew up the tank. That weapon destroyed scores of Israeli tanks in the terrible battle than engulfed the entire Chinese Farm.

Bloody battle at the Chinese Farm. *(GPO)*

Very soon, the area looked less like a farm and more like a killing field. "We felt like we were ramming a steel wall,"recalled one of the officers. "Every time we went in with tanks, Egyptian soldiers would pop out of the ditches and shoot at us with missiles. We fired back at them with machine guns and tank cannons. We cut them down, killing them by the dozen, and more always appeared in their place to strike at us. With each charge, we lost people and tanks."

Amnon Reshef fought beside his soldiers, taking hits from enemy shrapnel and shells; in a close encounter with the Egyptians his battered tank shot four out of five enemy tanks, and the fifth escaped. Reshef reported this incident on his radio, not in order to brag, but to reassure his men that their colonel was fighting beside them.

On a large area, tanks were burning and exploding. The desert battle-field was soon covered with charred and gutted vehicles by the hundreds. The carcasses of Israeli and Egyptian tanks lay beside each other. Dead and wounded lay on the sand, their uniforms crumpled and torn, their faces covered with soot from the firing; it was impossible to distinguish between the dead Egyptians and Israelis. One tank gunner tried to find Israeli wounded soldiers in an original way. He moved between the wounded, asking each one in Hebrew, "Are you a Jew?" In the middle of this living hell, surrounded by gunfire, explosions and death rattles, one of the wounded proved he had lost a lot of blood but had kept his sense of humor. Yiftah Yaakov of kibbutz Manara, a nephew of Yitzhak Rabin, blurted, "Yes, but it's hard to be a Jew in the Land of Israel. . . ."

At this stage, Colonel Reshef realized that the battalion's objective wouldn't be achievable because of the Egyptians' forceful resistance, the Israelis' heavy losses and the urgent need to reorganize the brigade, which had come apart during the fighting. "Around us," he recalled, "weapons stockpiles, hundreds of trucks, and artillery batteries abandoned by the Egyptians were blowing up. The Egyptian infantry ran among our tanks, hitting them with bazookas. Every so often, four or five Egyptian tanks would initiate assaults from a range of between six hundred fifty to just a couple feet."

At 4:00 A.M., Reshef launched a force of paratroopers and tanks into action to clear out the junction. Murderous fire suddenly burst out, and the soldiers were caught in a firetrap. The paratroopers attempted to get away, but the Egyptians gave chase, shooting at them from close range. One of the units lost most of its soldiers—twenty-four men—in an attempt to open Rattle road from west to east. The attempt to reopen Rattle failed, but most of the Egyptian tanks that participated in that battle were hit.

That night, as Danny Matt's paratroopers crossed the canal not far away, the battle for the Chinese Farm claimed the lives of 121 of Reshef's fighters; evacuating the wounded under fire lasted until the early hours of the morning. Out of Reshef's ninety-seven tanks, fifty-six had been destroyed. The Egyptians had succeeded in blocking both Rattle and Spider. The IDF's major problem remained opening the blocked routes to bring over the pontoon bridges and enabling the flow of Israeli troops to the other side of Suez. At a certain moment, Minister of Defense Moshe Dayan, shocked by the losses and the failure to reopen the roads to the canal, wanted to bring back Matt's paratroopers, lest they be slaughtered at the bridgehead. The idea was rejected by the IDF superior officers.

It was evident that new forces would be needed to reopen the roads, and the fighters of the 35th Paratroop Brigade were chosen. The 890th

Paratroop Battalion, led by Lieutenant Colonel Itzhak Mordechai, was assigned the task.

On October 16, the 890th was in Abu Rudeis, in southwestern Sinai, preparing to land by sea behind the Egyptian forces. Suddenly, Mordechai received an urgent call from Brigade Commander Uzi Yairi, who announced a change of assignment: the landing had been called off, and the battalion would be dispatched to the crossing zone in order to reinforce the units going across the canal. "The roads are blocked," Yairi said. "Not a single tank has managed to get past the Spider road. The IDF is waiting for it to be opened."

Mordechai, who was smart and confident, had been born in Kurdistan and immigrated to Israel at the age of five. After growing up in a moshav, he had joined the army and participated in many a perilous commando mission deep in Egyptian and Syrian territory. A born fighter, he had been deeply impressed by a former paratroop commander, now a general, Raful Eitan. Idling in Abu Rudeis was not to his liking; he was excited and invigorated when he got Uzi Yairi's call.

The soldiers of the 890th, as well, were excited by the news. They had been waiting for the moment when they would join the fighting, following ten days of standing by. A few hours later they were flown by Hercules aircraft from Abu Rudeis to Refidim, a large IAF base in western Sinai; buses waiting for them headed for Camp Tassa, where Sharon's advanced headquarters were located. The routes were blocked, and the battalion had to force its way through; only that evening did it reach camp. All the while, its assignment remained insufficiently clear. Mordechai was told, "The Rattle and Spider roads are blocked off—there's no way to evacuate the injured, no way to reinforce the troops. Your assignment is to clear out the roads of Egyptian anti-tank detachments."

Mordechai responded, "And what about artillery?"

Yairi told him, "It will take an hour to bring in an artillery-coordination officer, and we're squeezed for time."

This was the reason the paratroopers set out for battle without an artillery-coordination officer—and only in battle would it become clear how damaging his absence would be. Nor did the commanders receive up-to-date intelligence about the array of Egyptian forces on the Chinese Farm, which the previous night had conducted a lethal battle against Sharon's troops. The paratroopers' assignment was to clear out the roads and to prevent the Egyptians from penetrating the "corridor" and hitting Israeli troops. But the situation on the ground was completely different.

The 890th was flown by helicopter from Camp Tassa toward the Spider road. During a briefing in General Avraham Adan's tent, Yairi and Mordechai received their instructions: troops from the battalion would fan out immediately and clear the roads. The request for tanks and armored personnel carriers was rejected, as the division commander preferred a quiet night attack without tank noise. Anyway, he said, the tanks' efficiency was limited at night. Chief of Staff David Elazar, and the front commander, Haim Bar-Lev, pressured Yairi to launch the battalion immediately. "If the routes aren't open by morning," they said, "the force that has already crossed the canal will be in danger, and we'll need to bring them back." Mordechai felt that a tremendous responsibility had been put on his shoulders.

At midnight, the 890th moved in two columns from a point along the Spider road toward Rattle junction. At first, their advance was rapid and easy. But soon, they noticed the twisted and charred remains of the previous night's battle. Along the way, the soldiers passed a half-track full of dead bodies. The brigade's deputy commander, Lieutenant Colonel Amnon Lipkin-Shahak, recounted, "I was sure that these were the bodies of Egyptian soldiers, but, as I got closer, I could see that they were Israeli paratroopers. For me this was an inner earthquake, the first time I realized that there could be a situation in which Israeli soldiers could be laying, one corpse next to another, no one removing them."

At 2:45 in the morning, Yaki Levy, the commander of Company B, which moved at the head of the battalion, reported to Mordechai that he had engaged the enemy. A burst of heavy gunfire had hit the center of the group, "and suddenly everyone was writhing on the ground," remembered a medic. A few minutes later Levy was killed. His deputy, Jackie Hakim, took control and after a few minutes was also hit. The command then passed to the other deputy, Ben-Zion Atzmon.

The paratroopers tried to figure out where the shooting was originating and whom they were fighting against. "I stopped and looked through my binoculars to see the Egyptian force opposite me," recounted Lieutenant Hezi Dabash. "I was expecting to find bands of tank-hunters, but they looked more like an organized army. I ordered my men to shoot, but not a weapon was fired except for my own Uzi."

At this stage, Mordechai sent Aharon Margal's company to outflank and attack the Egyptians assaulting Levy's men. As they moved, they were fired upon, and Margal was badly wounded; he later died from his injuries. First Lieutenant Menachem Gozlan's platoon was then dispatched to outflank the Egyptians from the left. Gozlan began running with eight other soldiers and, after covering fewer than two hundred feet, was hit along with all the rest. Groans of pain and calls for help from the wounded drew more shooting. Two companies were trapped in a firing zone, and the ground seemed to boil from all the shells, smoke and shooting in every direction. It was obvious to the battalion commander that, rather than informal squads of soldiers ("tank hunters"), they were up against a well-entrenched formation, reinforced with tanks, anti-tank missiles, mortars and artillery.

Mordechai then dispatched Company H to rescue the wounded from Company B. Eli Shorek, the company commander, got on the radio and heard, "Commander killed . . . deputy commander killed . . . another deputy commander killed . . ." Soon, he himself was injured, and, for the entire night, the soldiers tried to rescue their comrades, dragging them to a little knoll that became known as Wounded Hill.

By four, the command realized that the battle at the Chinese Farm had gone very wrong. The battalion's state was catastrophic. Every attempt to locate the Egyptian core and outflank it had ended in chaos, causing additional losses. Given the situation, Mordechai gave the order to retreat. "All of us got up," one of the fighters recalled, "and ran wildly toward the canal as bullets flew around us. At the canal, we saw a terrible scene—a defeated paratrooper battalion, licking its wounds. I went into shock, and started to cry." The medevac station for the wounded filled up. Mordechai pressed for tank reinforcements and armored personnel carriers for an evacuation. The attack on the Chinese Farm seemed to have failed. Yet, while the battle raged, the pontoons were advancing on Spider road toward the canal, as the Egyptians were too busy fighting the paratrooper battalion.

A few half-tracks from the reconnaissance unit Bamba arrived and evacuated a group of the wounded. But everyone feared the sunrise, which would make it harder to evacuate. A medic remembered, "I ran four times to evacuate the wounded, and dawn lifted during the final trip. I was drained. I've never been as afraid anywhere as I was there." As the injured were evacuated, the medic spoke with the battalion commander; when he finished, he got up and was hit by a mortar shell. In an instant, he had gone from evacuator to casualty awaiting rescue.

An hour later, several tanks arrived to help the paratroopers. Their commander was Ehud Barak, who had returned from studying in the United States after hearing about the outbreak of war. He had established an improvised armored group, Unit 100. Barak arrived with tanks and armored personnel carriers, but couldn't advance at night, and even when dawn broke, failed to locate the paratroopers. Mordechai informed Barak by radio that he would set off a flare as identification, but then he would need to move fast to a new position, because all the Egyptian fire would be concentrated on the battalion's command post. Barak identified the flare and charged the Egyptian posts but en route drew the fire of Sagger missiles, which rained on his tanks, striking some of them. His Unit 100 retreated, leaving behind burning tanks and tank crews.

The situation in the area continued to worsen. Mordechai ordered all his men to enter the irrigation ditches. Suddenly, two Egyptian jets swooped in to attack. One was brought down and the second dropped altitude before turning back.

At six, the brigade commander, Yairi, asked for authorization to evacuate. But General Shmuel Gonen, the Southern District commander, refused. "We must maintain position at all cost; there is no possibility of reinforcement or replacement." Gonen believed that the paratroopers' presence in the area prevented the Egyptians from advancing toward Spider road. Only after the intervention of front commander Bar-Lev was permission given, and, at 11:00 A.M., the paratroopers' evacuation from the ditches began.

For seventeen hours, from night until the afternoon, the 890th Paratroop Battalion had fought against Egypt's 16th Division, which was reinforced by tanks, anti-tank weaponry and artillery—and against units of Egypt's Second Army. The battalion had lost forty-one dead and 120 wounded.

After more tank battles that lasted the entire day, the Egyptians, who suffered heavy losses, realized they could not continue fighting. In the early evening the Egyptian command ordered its forces to evacuate the Chinese Farm. The evacuation was carried out under cover of night; Rattle and Spider roads remained definitely open.

The heavy price paid for opening the roads was 161 dead and hundreds of wounded. But the roads were open and the crossing tipped the scales of the Yom Kippur War.

YITZHAK MORDECHAI, DECORATED WITH THE MEDAL OF COURAGE

"One of the hardest moments I've had was when dawn broke and I had to face the fact that the battalion's entire chain of command had been hit. During the nighttime battle, I had sent in new commanders to replace the officers who had been killed, to rescue fighters from burned-out tanks and to continue maintaining position, no matter the price, on the exposed dunes.

"Another difficult moment was when mortar and artillery barrages were being fired toward my position, and I say to the soldier standing to my left, 'Why aren't you shooting?' And then I raise my head and see that he has taken a bullet to the head and has been killed.

"These were seventeen of the hardest, most complicated hours of fighting that the paratroopers battalion could have come up against. We were required to stand against large enemy forces and lethal fire, to rescue the wounded, to stabilize our line of combat, and, in this way, to prevent the enemy from reaching the roads and blocking them."

In the north, the Syrians advance on the Golan Heights,
and a handful of Israelis are trying to stop them and
save northern Israel from an invasion.

CHAPTER 17

"I SEE THE LAKE OF TIBERIAS!" 1973

At a meeting of the IDF general staff at 4:45 on the morning of the third day of the Yom Kippur War, Defense Minister Moshe Dayan issued an unprecedented directive: "There will be no retreat—not even a centimeter—on the Golan Heights. Even if we lose the entire Armored Corps, we have to come to a decisive conclusion in the north. The Golan Heights is our home, and if the front collapses there, they"—the Syrians—"will be in the Jordan Valley. We need to consider every necessary action, including bombing Damascus."

In September 1973, the Syrians had begun building up their forces on the Golan Heights. By the start of the war, in October, their numbers had grown from 550 tanks to 900, in addition to a concentration of 140 artillery batteries located less than two miles from the border.

These were dark omens. It was obvious that the Syrians were planning to attack, but the scale of the assault was unknown. Syrian documents published after the war revealed that the Syrian chief of staff had planned to seize the Golan within twenty-four hours. It can now be said that they came very close but were halted in battles drenched in blood.

On October 6, General Yitzhak ("Haka") Hofi, the commander of the Northern District, summoned his senior staff and announced that war would erupt that evening. The 7th Armored Brigade had already been deployed as a reserve force. Hofi ordered that Israeli settlements on the Golan be evacuated, but many of the residents of moshav Ramat Magshimim refused to leave until that afternoon. Hofi reviewed the plans for the Golan's defense along with General Rafael Eitan, who had assumed the command of a division in the north. There was speculation that the Syrians would break through the border with an immense force from the north, coming by way of Quneitra, a town that Israel had occupied during the Six Day War. The Syrians would come that way, the IDF experts said, in part because, for the Syrians, Quneitra had become a symbol and a goal for liberation, and because this route led to the strategically valuable Daughters of Jacob Bridge, spanning the Jordan River. A secondary force would probably enter from the south by way of the Rafid Gap.

With the outbreak of war, the 7th Armored Brigade, under the command of Yanosh Ben-Gal, was rushed to the Golan's northern sector and Yitzhak Ben-Shoham's 188th, the Barak ("Lightning") Brigade, was sent south. Syria's 51st Brigade crossed the border and advanced in a three-prong offensive, passing Hushaniya, in the back of the Golan, and progressing in the direction of Camp Nafach and the Oil Road. Yitzhak Ben-Shoham took positions south of Hushaniya, spreading his tanks along a large front. At 9:30 P.M., an officer from the Northern Command's operations department, Uri Simchoni, got on the radio and informed Colonel Ben-Shoham, "This is the operations officer speaking. The Syrians keep reporting that they're behind you, that Hushaniya is in their hands, and that they're already at the junction past Hushaniya."

Ben-Shoham replied, "Negative. They intend to get there, but they seem to have gotten mixed up at the junction. . . . I'm firing at them right now and engaging them from the north."

Ben-Shoham was killed a few hours later, during the battle for Nafach, along with his deputy. The Barak Brigade was almost entirely wiped out and ceased functioning. Contrary to the IDF assessments, the Syrians had actually decided to attack through the Golan's vast, flat southern sector. They realized that, from there, it would be possible to launch a tank assault on a large front, unlike in the mountainous northern area, where the invader would be compelled to advance in a single tank column, thus giving the advantage to the defenders. The Barak Brigade, indeed, paid a dire price for this mistaken assessment.

Ben-Gal, a Holocaust survivor, later analyzed the Barak Brigade disaster: "In a routine defense situation, spreading out your forces is a good thing, but during war, that logic is a disaster. They scattered their tanks and became cannon fodder."

The Barak Brigade had fought for its life to halt the Syrian brigades, which had breached the border, the anti-tank canals and the minefields, and in the darkness were quickly swooping across the Golan. They were stopped only at Camp Nafach, where Eitan and his headquarters had been located and then forced to retreat. The surviving Barak fighters retreated as well.

The situation seemed desperate. On October 7, Israeli antennae intercepted the chilling shouts of a Syrian brigade commander on the radio, as he screamed, ecstatic, "I see the Lake of Tiberias!" His brigade indeed was fewer than ten kilometers from the Sea of Galilee (Kinneret, in Hebrew).

Everything had to be thrown into the battle, to prevent a bloody Syrian invasion of the Galilee and the Jordan Valley. On the second day of the war, Ugda Mussa, a division of reservists led by General Moshe ("Mussa") Peled was dispatched to the Golan. The performance of this combat-scarred, rugged farmer from moshav Nahalal in the battle for the Golan would deeply impress the experts at the American Armor Museum in Fort Knox, Kentucky, and earn Peled the title "One of the five greatest armor commanders in history," alongside mythological figures like General George Patton and Field Marshal Erwin Rommel.

The front commanders faced a fateful choice: should they deploy the division to prevent the Syrians from crossing the Jordan River or launch a counterattack? Under Peled's pressure they finally decided that the division would attack in the direction of the Rafid Gap, despite the large numeric advantage held by Syria's tanks.

General Hofi explained, "We opted to attack even though, during an offensive, you're risking more than during a defensive maneuver. However, you can achieve more . . . On defense, it's possible to cause losses to the enemy, to grind him down, but not to determine the outcome of the battle. . . . If we had left the attack for a later stage, we would have been forced to attack while climbing the mountain, because the Syrians would already have been on the slopes of Lake Kinneret. . . . If the Syrians had advanced a little more, the Jordan Valley and the Kinneret would have been in their hands, and the battle would have become much harder. . . . The speed of the attack was significant because it didn't leave them time to reorganize."

The Golan Heights hero, Avigdor Kahalani, with Yossi Eldar at the height of the battle. (*Uzi Keren, Bamachane, IDF Archive*)

At dawn on October 8, Peled's division entered the battle, determined to repulse the Syrians from the southern Golan. The battle proved slow and grueling, unfolding in a very narrow area with no room for maneuver or flanking actions. En route, the division liberated Ramat Magshimim, the only settlement to have fallen into Syrian hands. At the end of the first day of fighting, Peled's men had managed to split the Syrian formations and repel them ten and a half miles back.

The next day they were battling the Syrians on three fronts: from the west, against retreating forces; from the east, against attacking forces; and from the north, against forces that were under attack. The division wiped out the armored brigade it was fighting, closed the Rafid Gap and, eventually, with the capture of Hushaniya, forced the retreating Syrians out of the gap. The next day, the Syrians were pushed out of the area completely, meaning that in less than three days, Peled's division had repelled five Syrian brigades and destroyed the southern pillar of the network of armor positions established by the Syrians in Israeli territory.

Peled's offensive had been coordinated with a reservist division led by General Dan Laner, which had reached the Golan on Saturday night, within hours of the war's eruption, and had launched its attack by Sunday. A kibbutz member, Austrian-born Laner had been parachuted into Yugoslavia during World War II and had fought the Nazis with Tito's partisans. After a brilliant career in the IDF he had been recalled from retirement to lead a division headed for the Golan Heights. His men aided in halting the advance by the Syrian Army and by an Iraqi expeditionary force that had rushed to its help. Simultaneously, Eitan's division had stopped the Syrians in the Quneitra area.

In the Golan's northern region, the 7th Armored Brigade continued fighting. Avigdor Kahalani, whose fame had preceded him ever since his daring fighting in the Six Day War, led the 77th Battalion to Quneitra and Booster Ridge. Two other units were dispatched to the area, which would later be called the Valley of Tears. With the start of battle, Syria's planes bombed and Israel's air force bled; within hours, Mount Hermon had fallen, becoming an excellent observation point for shooting at Israeli forces. At nightfall, the other units evacuated the Valley of Tears. Kahalani, for his part, discovered that Syrian shooting capabilities also functioned at night; they were using Russian tanks equipped with infrared projectors that could zero in and fire at the Israeli enemy.

"My tank crews are shouting at me that they're unable to stop the

Syrians," Kahalani recounted. "Israeli tanks that had previously been considered top notch are suddenly being exposed for their weaknesses. Within our force, only the commanders and drivers have infrared goggles, but not the gunner, who needs them. I ask myself, how do we stop the Syrians? I'm the battalion commander, everyone's turning to me, and I feel that I'm not fulfilling expectations. I'm responsible for the area, and they'll accuse me of not being up to the task."

Kahalani ordered the lighting of flares, and after three went into the air, he discovered that they had been the last ones. The soldiers in the tanks were anxious, unable to see where to aim their cannons or how to advance. Meanwhile, the Syrian Air Force was flashing into view overhead—certainly not the sort of lighting Kahalani had been looking for.

"Turn off the infrared," he commanded his soldiers. "You can stick your heads slightly out of the tank turrets and navigate forward." Around them, tanks that were hit or on fire illuminated the area, but it wasn't clear whether they belonged to Israel or the enemy. "Stop and silence your engines," Kahalani instructed. "Listen for the noise of their chains and you'll be able to locate them."

The soldiers did as they were told, shutting off their engines, listening for the sound of the enemy's tanks, and shooting. The shells fired into the darkness yielded results; the Syrians were halted. In the dark, it was very difficult to identify enemy tanks until they were within a few meters of Israeli forces. A tank standing sixty-five feet from Kahalani's, with a cannon pointed toward Syria, was revealed to be a Syrian T-55, and only at the last minute did they fire at it, as well as at another Syrian tank to its side. The Syrians had come so close that they had effectively merged with the Israelis, the forces mixing one with the other.

At daybreak, Kahalani's men discovered 130 Syrian tanks one mile from the Israeli positions. The Syrians started advancing, firing two or three shells and then moving forward. Kahalani ordered the fourteen Israeli tanks that remained operable to ascend to their positions. In the following battle, most of the battalion's officers were killed as they stood, exposed, in their tanks' turrets. At the end of combat on Sunday, only seven functioning tanks remained.

On the following morning, Kahalani was ordered to move toward the Valley of Tears. Raful Eitan called him on the radio, "I trust you," he said. "Wage the battle with deliberation and calm. Don't worry—we'll get them."

On October 9, two-thirds of the Golan was in Syrian hands. Ben-Gal, the brigade commander, authorized a company fighting the Syrians to withdraw from the Valley of Tears to a line 2.5 miles away. Kahalani was called from Quneitra; during the retreat, Syrian planes circled overhead, searching for tanks to prey upon. Thousands of artillery shells were landing in the area; the earth was shaking. Eight Syrian helicopters carrying commandos landed from behind, closing off the route to kibbutz Gonen, which was serving as a resupply point and evacuation site for those wounded and killed. Kahalani and his team felt that they were trapped.

At this stage, Ben-Gal reached a new decision: he instructed Kahalani to return to the Valley of Tears and try to halt the Syrians. Kahalani sped off alone, with the seven remaining tanks left behind preparing to join him. When Kahalani arrived to his destination, he discovered a troubling picture: Israeli tanks retreating from the firing ramps. He was furious. He tried to report through the brigade's communications network, but it was overwhelmed with calls for rescue and assistance. The situation was very bleak. Only three tanks still had shells, while the Syrians had large numbers of tanks. Israel's line of defense was shrinking every few minutes. Kahalani realized that if the Syrians crossed the line of IDF positions, Israel's strategic advantage would be lost because, in flat territory, the number of Syrian tanks would prove decisive.

He decided to move forward. As he advanced, he was surprised to encounter a Syrian tank between one hundred and 130 feet to his right. Fortunately, the dust hid him from the enemy tank, and the Syrian soldiers couldn't make out who he was.

Kahalani stopped his tank and shouted at his gunner, "Shoot it fast!" The shell struck the center of the Syrian tank, and it burst into flames. They had barely exhaled in relief when another three Syrian tanks appeared. The gunner fired, setting another tank on fire, while Kahalani pointed at the second tank, which had managed, in the interim, to identify them and aim its barrel. "Fire! Fire!" Kahalani shouted at the gunner, but the tank didn't fire; the shell casing had gotten stuck. In these critical moments, two of the tank crewmen acted frantically, attempting to extract the empty shell casing, pulling at it virtually with their fingernails. At the last second, the hollow casing came out; a new shell went in and was fired straight into the front of the Syrian tank. The third tank was also destroyed.

"We must make a supreme effort to bring every possible tank to the area," Kahalani said over the radio to Brigade Commander Ben-Gal, who responded, "Starting now, you are the area commander. I'm connecting all the forces to your radio network. And Avigdor, take care of yourself!"

These were the pivotal moments in the battle for the Golan. The question was who would be first to capture the positions on a hill some sixteen hundred feet away. A hundred and fifty Syrian tanks entered the valley, with just Kahalani left to face them. He destroyed ten tanks in a nearby wadi, while calling for help from the brigade.

The picture before him was frightening, and Kahalani radioed Ben-Gal again, asking him to send every possible tank to the area to halt the Syrians. The brigade commander dispatched a battalion that was fighting a couple of miles to the north. The battalion had just eight tanks remaining but sped toward Kahalani and stopped behind him. Kahalani ordered them to close off the approach of the wadi so that he could move southward, collect the rest of the tanks and charge. While advancing toward the new positions, five of the battalion tanks were immediately hit, and its commander was killed. Kahalani assigned one of the tanks that had run out of ammunition to block the wadi entrance. He headed south with the rest of the battalion's remaining tanks; seven tanks from another company joined him.

Over the radio, suddenly, Kahalani's voice stopped in midsentence replaced by the thunder of a terrific explosion. One of the soldiers called the deputy battalion commander. Kahalani was killed, he announced. Kahalani was unable to deny the report—he was facing another tank and was more focused on the gunner than on the radio. Only minutes later did he announce by radio that everything was fine, and that he was still alive.

"A stations," he radioed. "This is Kahalani. A large Syrian force is moving against us. . . . Our goal is to capture the positions on the hill and then take control of the valley from above. . . . Move! Take the positions and destroy the Syrians." However, paralyzed by fear, the soldiers didn't charge. Kahalani grabbed his microphone again. "Watch the Syrians. See how well they're fighting. See their motivation. What do I see in our battalion? Cowards? We're Jews! We're Israelis! What, we're better than those people and not capable of repelling them? Come on, guys, I'm asking you to start moving."

Kahalani charged. A moment later another tank followed, then another, and another and another. . . .

The Syrians were sweeping over the ridge, their tanks crossing the Israeli defense line. Meir ("Tiger") Zamir, a company commander, reported the approach of enemy tanks from his front and from his back; he was left without a single shell, he said. Five Syrian tanks charged Tiger's force but a young major, Avinoam Baruchin, set two alight. "They're crushing us," Baruchin shouted. Syrian tanks approached Kahalani's force unchecked, killing and wounding dozens of Israelis.

"Nobody retreats a single step!" Ben-Gal thundered on the radio. He later recalled this fateful moment. "For twenty or thirty minutes, no one was in control of the soldiers—not the company commanders, not the battalion commander and not the brigade commander. Everyone was fighting his own war. I was planning to give instructions to retreat and had taken my microphone in hand, but told myself that we'd wait a little longer. . . . I called Raful and said that we cannot hold any longer. Raful asked that we hold 'only a little more.' "

As the battle continued, Israeli units kept collapsing under Syrian pressure. Just over thirteen hundred feet separated them from seizing the controlling positions that would determine the battle's outcome. With a tremendous effort they advanced and reached the coveted positions, opening fire on the Syrian tanks. At that very moment, eleven tanks under the command of Lieutenant Colonel Yossi Ben-Hanan arrived and joined Kahalani's forces. Kahalani recalled later that they fired "like crazy" at the Syrians, managing to hit approximately 150 of their tanks.

And all of a sudden the Syrians started pulling back!

Ben-Gal later said, "I was sure we'd lost the battle. If it had gone on another half hour, we would have lost. For whatever reason, the Syrians broke down first and decided to retreat. They apparently assumed they didn't have a chance to win. They didn't know the truth, that our situation was desperate."

The perception on the ground was that the rapport between the two fighting forces had started to reverse.

"Victory is in our hands!" Kahalani shouted excitedly over the radio. "They're retreating and we are wiping them out!"

"You're tremendous," Ben-Gal responded. "You're a hero of Israel. You're all heroes! I love you. Take care of yourself."

"Gentlemen," the voice of Division Commander Raful Eitan broke into the radio receivers, "you saved the people of Israel."

The fighting to stop the Syrians went on without pause for four days and three nights. The remnants of the IDF armor had to fight without backing from the air force, the infantry, the artillery, the engineering corps, anti-aircraft batteries; they badly lacked the necessary equipment for nighttime combat. "We felt as if the nation had abandoned us," Kahalani said, "as if we had been thrown onto the battlefield with a ratio of one Israeli tank against eight Syrian ones. For us, it was a great shock."

And yet, the Syrians were routed.

The Syrian forces retreated in a disorderly way, leaving behind 867 tanks and thousands of other vehicles. Kahalani and his comrades reconquered all of the lost territories and even penetrated into Syrian territory.

By the end of the war, the 7th Armored Brigade had lost seventy-six fighters. For Kahalani, the joy of triumph mixed with great personal sadness. His brother Emanuel had been killed in the tank battles in Sinai; also killed was his wife's brother, Ilan, another tank soldier. For his feats during the war, Kahalani would receive the Medal of Valor.

AVIGDOR KAHALANI, LATER THE DEPUTY COMMANDER OF THE FIELD CORPS

"I had several brushes with death during the war. I remember one such instance in Syrian territory. I was in the tank turret. A Syrian plane passed over my tank, shooting a burst of machine-gun fire over my head. It turned around and came at us from behind, and I didn't see it, focused as I was in running the battle. My operations officer looks back and sees the plane dropping its bombs in our direction, and then he punches me in the face and shouts, 'Get inside, fast.' I didn't understand what was happening. I got inside the tank and clung to the side. The bomb hit my tank. I heard a huge explosion and realized that I was not alive anymore. I was covered in gunpowder and passed my hands over my body to check whether I still had all my limbs. My body was shaking as if it had been jolted by an electric shock.

"I pulled my head out, saw a giant cloud of smoke and a twenty-six-foot-deep hole around me. I looked right and left and saw a terrible sight—all the tank commanders who had been next to me, standing in the turrets with their heads out in the open, had been killed.

"But there was also a happy moment that I remember: they had promised us before the war that, for every Syrian tank that was hit, we would get a crate of champagne. At the end of the fighting, I sat in my tank and tried to count how many burned-out Syrian tanks there were in the valley, but I couldn't calculate the number of champagne crates because there were so many."

As the war nears its end, the Golani Brigade makes a
tremendous effort to retake the "eyes of the nation"—
the Hermon fort with its array of antennas,
watching and listening devices.

CHAPTER 18

THE EYES OF THE NATION, 1973

I don't want to look at the Hermon mountains anymore," the disheveled, sooty Benny Massas said. "My comrades' blood was spilled here like water." Benny was a Tiberias boy, a stocky, tousled Golani fighter wearing a green army cap. He was facing a television reporter on top of Mount Hermon, a couple of hours after the terrible battle was over. He was said to be one of the heroes of the battle, relentlessly charging the Syrians till the Golani flag was raised over the place. "Why did I charge?" he repeated the reporter's question. "Because we were told that the Hermon Mount is the eyes of Israel!"

The Hermon post was a fort on top of Mount Hermon, bristling with antennae, radar sensors, bowl-shaped dishes and listening devices, and manned by Golani Brigade soldiers. Not far from it, across the border, the Syrians had erected their own post. The Israeli fort had been captured by the Syrians at the outbreak of the Yom Kippur War. The battle had been lost within two hours, with thirteen Israeli soldiers killed and thirty-one taken captive. The post, dominating the Syrian plains and laden with electronic equipment, was of crucial importance for Israel. The intelligence gathered by its sensors and antennae was priceless. Two days later, a Golani elite unit had attempted to retake the Hermon but they, too, had been defeated, losing another twenty-five fighters.

Golani's wounded pride had led their commander Amir Drori to request of the Northern District chief of staff: "Save the Hermon for me for next time!"

The next time arrived thirteen days later, on the sixteenth day of the war, October 21. General Hofi, a former deputy of Sharon's at the Mitla battle and now the commander of the Northern District, decided to exploit the window of opportunity before the declaration of cease-fire by embarking on an operation to simultaneously capture both the Israeli and Syrian posts on the Hermon. The plan went as follows: Sayeret Matkal, under the command of Major Yoni Netanyahu, would take position as a barrier between the two posts; a paratrooper brigade would seize the Syrian post and the Hermon peak. The Golani Brigade, commanded by Colonel Drori, would recapture the Israeli post.

The troops were weary after two weeks of fighting, yet the mission had to be carried out. The offensive was set for 6:00 P.M. Starting at two, Sikorsky helicopters transported 626 paratroopers from two reduced battalions, an engineering unit and a heavy mortar detail, to the departure point for the seizure of the Syrian post, located 7,812 feet above sea level. The Syrians noticed the paratroopers' airlift and dispatched 24 MiG-21s and five helicopters with commando troops against them, but IAF planes downed 10 MiGs and 2 helicopters.

The paratroopers' first objective was the capture of the Pitulim post, located at a critical junction between the roads to the mountain peak and the Syrian Hermon post. As they crossed the road to the junction, they took enemy fire and an officer was killed. Despite continuous shooting, the fighters charged the Syrian force, wiping it out. They continued their advance and three hours later reached the Syrian Hermon post. They clashed with the Syrian soldiers; twelve Syrians were killed and the rest retreated. The paratroopers crossed the fences surrounding the post, entered and discovered that it had been abandoned. The Syrian soldiers had opted to flee. Six trucks full of soldiers were immediately sent as reinforcements by the Syrian command and were hit by the paratroopers. At 3:25 A.M., the paratroopers' commander reported to his superiors that the Syrian post on the Hermon was in the IDF's hands.

But the main operation was recapturing the Hermon's Israeli post. It turned out to be much bloodier and more complicated. It would extract a heavy price in Golani blood, with fifty killed and eighty wounded.

Before they left for battle, one of the company commanders, First Lieutenant Yigal Passo, spoke to his soldiers: "Take care of yourselves; I need you whole. Work slowly, and use your heads. I don't want pointless charges and acts of heroism; we'll kill them one by one." Passo himself was killed hours later, during the punishing fight for Hill 16, part of the capture of the Israeli Hermon post.

Golani's soldiers ascended the mountain in three prongs. The main force was from the 51st Battalion, which started climbing on foot and was supposed to reach an elevation of 5,295 feet. The ascent was very difficult, lasting seven hours before they arrived, close to midnight, at a site nicknamed Tanks' Curve. The climb was quiet—so quiet that some believed the seizure would be smooth and easy, that the Syrians had already fled, that everything would soon be over. Just 2,600 feet separated them from the post, and nothing suggested that they were marching toward a firetrap. The IDF artillery blasted every hill on their way before they approached, but as the shells were falling too close to the advancing soldiers, the Golani commander instructed the artillery to skip a couple of hills. So it turned out that Hill 16 was spared by the Israeli cannon.

But on Hill 16, a large Syrian unit was hiding in fourteen trenches, as well as between the surrounding boulders. Golani's fighters knew nothing of what awaited them.

At 2:00 A.M., a fighter marching before the troops at Tanks' Curve heard noises. He crouched down and then, between the boulders, discerned the shape of a soldier who was wrapped in a blanket and wearing a stocking cap. The Syrian soldier, no less surprised, raised his head and asked, in Arabic, "Who are you?" The Israeli didn't hesitate, pulling his weapon out first and killing him. In response, gunfire came in on all sides, and on the radio, shouts of "Encounter!" broke out.

A brutal battle ensued. The Syrians, using MAG-58 machine guns plundered from Israel, shot with great accuracy at the Golani fighters on the mountainside, causing many casualties. Another Golani company also encountered Syrian troops, and during its charge, its fighters and their commanders were wounded.

David Tzarfati, a Golani fighter, later remembered: "From two-thirty, Hill Sixteen became another world. I heard screams of terror, shouting, crying, howling, like at a massacre. I told myself, 'This is it. No one can hear me now. This isn't a joke—it's death.' I disconnected from everyone and got my head down on the ground, hard."

The heroes of the Hermon—"the cannibals, the phalanges, the Indians . . ."
(Zeev Spektor GPO)

The deadly battle continued, with gunfire raining down on the hills from every direction. In the chaos and uncertainty over which positions were occupied by Israeli forces, artillery fire landed very close to IDF soldiers fighting on Hill 16. As shrapnel fell on the battalion commander and his aides, he radioed for a halt to the gunfire and ordered to use warning shots to ascertain where each unit was positioned, and only then to start shooting again. After a check, the batteries were ready to resume the gunfire, but an artillery-coordination officer, liaising between the units, was shot, along with his radio, and the artillery fire was held up.

Motti Levy, a Golani fighter, recalled, "The hill became a jungle: I can hear the screams of soldiers who've been wounded. I can hear my friend Hassan staggering on the mountain like a sleepwalker, yelling, 'Mother! I'm dead! Dead!' Eighty percent of the company is in critical condition; five meters above me I hear battle cries in Arabic. It's an awful situation."

At three, Brigade Commander Drori arrived at the site of battle with his staff and said to the soldiers, "Hold your positions. Reinforcements will be here soon." David Tzarfati shouted back, "We need to pull back! We need to pull back! There are many dead, many wounded!"

The brigade commander replied, "Quiet, soldier. Backup is coming. Maintain position."

At four, the brigade's reconnaissance company advanced toward the Hermon's upper cable-car station. Its members didn't know the size of the Syrian force opposing them. En route, Company Commander Vinick wanted to examine the roadway leading to Tanks' Curve, in preparation for joining the battle and assisting the 51st Battalion. While he was advancing along the road, Syrian soldiers concealed in a trench fired a continuous salvo at him. He managed to shoot several bullets before falling, drenched in blood. A signaler and a medic who tried to reach him were also shot and wounded.

As the battle claimed more and more casualties, the commanders of the Northern District instructed the paratroopers to prepare to complete the assignment given to Golani. After several minutes, the operation's commander instructed the paratroopers to descend from the Hermon Syrian post and assist Golani. The promise made to Golani that it would recapture the Israeli Hermon post was thus annulled. But Golani continued fighting.

At four-fifty, A Company found itself in battle on Hill 17. The fighters had prepared to charge but didn't realize they were about to attack a major Syrian formation comprising a considerable force, entrenched in thirty-five positions. The company began moving northward along a secondary incline, falling directly into a Syrian trap. Sixteen fighters were killed, and the company commander was fatally wounded, dying two weeks later in the hospital.

At five-fifteen, Brigade Commander Drori was wounded too; the 51st Battalion commander, Yehuda Peled, replaced him, but he also was wounded a few minutes later. Major Yoav Golan, the brigade operations officer, took over. Golan had been wounded at the Suez Canal, and by the time the Syrians captured the Hermon he had already been recognized as disabled by the IDF. Yet, he was fighting together with his comrades. He sent into battle a mechanized company and decided to activate heavy artillery on the Hermon post and on Hill 17, where Syrian commando forces had entrenched themselves. All that time the Golani fighters did not budge from the positions they had acquired for so much blood; two-thirds of the fighters had been killed or wounded. Benny Massas, one of the battle heroes, felt he and his comrades preferred to die on the mountain than to go back without conquering the post.

But the Syrians were first to break down. The artillery onslaught and the Golani desperately clinging to their positions determined the battle's outcome. At eight-fifteen, the Syrians began fleeing the battle zone. En route to the post, Golani fighters eliminated another ten Syrian commandos, and twenty were taken captive. Israeli soldiers entered the post with great caution, fearing that the site had been booby-trapped.

At ten-fifty, Yoav Golan radioed, "The post is in my hands! The Israeli Hermon post is in our hands! We're up there now, combing the site."

Minutes later, one of Golani's officers announced on the brigade's communication network, "All network stations throughout the world! The flag has been raised!"

Indeed, the flags of Golani and Israel were hoisted, following a bloody battle that had extracted a terrible price. Benny Massas and his comrades had recovered "the eyes of Israel."

A soldier named Alaluf summed up the fighting: "Who recaptured the Hermon? The brigade commander, Amir Drori? During the first wave, he got wounded and was down on the ground. The battalion commander? During the second round of gunfire, he fell, too. I'm not angry at them. They were my officers. But it was Yigal Passo and his ordinary soldiers who captured it. I, Motti Levy, Tzarfati, Eddie Nisim, Dahari, Azout, Blutstein: the so-called Cannibals, the Phalanges, the Indians."

GOLANI FIGHTER DAVID TZARFATI

"It was a hard, blood-soaked battle. I didn't think I'd survive. I had a sense that I belonged to the dead, that I would soon join them. . . . After the massive shelling, I lay down, unable to move or react. I was in a state of waking sleep, not wanting to live. . . . I was cut off from everything surrounding me, as if I were in a bubble.

"There's one moment that follows you your entire life—it's the truest, strongest moment, which gave me the strength to go on living, to continue functioning. . . . It was at eight A.M. as I was still lying down, useless, and my company commander, Yigal Passo, lay dying, after he was hit at four in the morning, and, in a weak voice, he tells me, 'David, you'll be the representative of those who died. You'll tell everyone about this battle.' And then he asked me to cover him, got up and, with his final bit of energy, started running toward the Syrian positions. Even in his final moments, he continued fighting. At the end of the battle, we evacuated those killed, and Yigal Passo's corpse was among them."

PART SIX

The Nuclear Danger

Opera, 1981

In 1977, Menachem Begin, leader of the right-wing
Likud party, wins the elections and dethrones Labor for
the first time. He regards the nuclear reactor Osiraq, which
Saddam Hussein is building in Iraq, as an existential danger
for Israel and decides to destroy it in spite of major objections.
This is Operation Opera.

Arizona, 2007

In 2001, Ariel Sharon is elected prime minister at the head
of the Likud; he then splits the Likud and creates a new party,
Kadima. After suffering a massive stroke, Sharon is replaced by
Ehud Olmert, who will launch Operation Arizona.

CHAPTER 19

"OPERA" IN BAGHDAD AND "ARIZONA" IN SYRIA, 1981 AND 2007

F riday, June 7, 1981, was the eve of the Festival of Shavuoth ("Pentecost"), the celebration of God giving the Torah to the Jewish people on Mount Sinai. Thousands of Israelis assembled in the synagogues, but thousands of others preferred to celebrate on the country's golden beaches. And so it was that at 4:00 P.M., the festive crowds sunning on Eilat's southern beach saw eight F-16s roaring in the blue sky, passing at low altitude over the Gulf of Eilat and continuing into Saudi Arabia. The F-16 had taken off from the Etzion airbase in Sinai. Eight F-15 fighter jets followed close behind. By coincidence, King Hussein of Jordan was, at that moment, sailing in his royal yacht in the Gulf and saw the jets passing overhead. He immediately transmitted a warning to his military, requesting that the armies of the surrounding countries be notified but, for whatever reason, the alert wasn't shared. This was a good thing, because Israel's air force planes were en route to Operation Opera, the destruction of the nuclear reactor being built next to Baghdad by Saddam Hussein.

The planning of the operation had begun years earlier. On August 26, 1976, Iraq had signed a deal with the French government for the construction of a nuclear reactor that the French called Osirak and the Iraqis referred to as Tammuz. The French also committed to supplying Iraq with eighty kilograms of 93-percent-enriched uranium, enough to produce an atomic bomb. When Israel found out, by its intelligence sources, it launched a diplomatic effort to prevent the reactor's delivery to Iraq. A nuclear weapon in the hands of Saddam Hussein could be a terrible danger for our very existence, the Israeli envoys explained to their counterparts in Paris. But all their efforts to convince the French that they were dealing with the devil failed miserably. According to foreign sources, the torch was then passed to the Mossad, which sabotaged several parts of the French reactor before they could be loaded onto ships for Iraq. But the damage was repaired and the construction of the reactor proceeded, to be completed within a short period. After his election as prime minister in 1977, Menachem Begin reached the conclusion that the only remaining option was military intervention. Defense Minister Ezer Weizman recommended a military operation, as did the IDF new chief of staff, Raful Eitan. Laying the groundwork for the mission was assigned to David Ivry, the commander of the air force. A brilliant colonel, Aviem Sella, would take on the meticulous planning of all aspects of the operation at IAF headquarters, along with several young officers. It soon became clear that the reactor would be fully operational by September 1981, and Begin decided to hit it in the spring. The program initially submitted by the air force was called Ammunition Hill.

An unexpected contribution to the planners' efforts came, of all places, from Iran. The Islamic Revolution had taken place in 1979, transforming Iran from a close American ally into a sworn enemy of the United States. Israel had concluded a deal with the U.S. government for the supply of F-16s, but the scheduled delivery was still far away, as other "clients" had a priority. After the Islamic Revolution in Teheran, however, the planned delivery of F-16s to Iran by the United States was canceled, and the White House agreed that the planes be given to Israel instead, ahead of schedule.

The F-16s turned out to be much better suited to the Iraq mission than Israel's other air force planes. According to the plan, eight F-16s would carry out the attack, with eight F-15 fighter jets escorting them while serving as a flying command station. The pilots and flight crews began training in secret, using a model of the reactor built in the Negev Desert. The IDF chief of staff himself participated in one of the simulated attacks, wanting to see from the navigator's seat whether the preparations could meet expectations. At the end of the simulation, General Eitan said nothing, taking off for home in his own light plane. Next to him sat Sella, who badly wanted to hear the senior commander's opinion. But Raful remained silent.

Raful Eitan had a place apart in the Israeli military elite. The tough, close-mouthed soldier was the descendant of a family of Subotniks, a sect of Russian peasants who had converted to Judaism and immigrated to Palestine at the end of the nineteenth century. The Subotniks settled in Galilee and became the best farmers in Israel. Raful, too, was born and raised on a farm at moshav Tel Adashim and remained an olive grower and a carpenter all his life, while emerging as a fearless fighter in the Palmach and the IDF. One of the first officers to join Arik Sharon's paratroopers, he had received the much coveted red ("battle") lining to his silver wings, after jumping with his battalion at Mitla and opening the Sinai campaign. He fought in all of Israel's wars, was severely wounded in the Six Day War, carried out several commando missions with his paratroopers and was among the staunchest defenders of the Golan Heights in the Yom Kippur War. In 1978, the tight-lipped, scarred warrior replaced Motta Gur as IDF chief of staff.

In the flight back north, he didn't speak for a long time, even though he knew what Aviem Sella wanted to hear from him. Finally, after half an hour in the air, he murmured, "The government will authorize this."

Aviem Sella let out a sigh of relief.

Yet, many major figures in the security establishment opposed the mission, including the head of military intelligence, Yehoshua Sagi; the head of the Mossad, Yitzhak Hofi; Ezer Weizman, who by then had left the defense ministry and changed his mind; and Deputy Prime Minister Yigael Yadin, who went so far as to threaten to resign. Patiently and methodically, Begin began convincing his cabinet of the operation's importance, persisting until he had won the ministers' support. Operation Ammunition Hill was set for May 8, 1981. That day, everything was in place. The pilots were sitting in their planes, already prepared for takeoff, when Begin received a letter from opposition leader Shimon Peres, a former minister of defense, pleading that he call off the attack, fearing that the international community would respond harshly and that Israel would be as isolated as, borrowing words from the Book of Jeremiah, "a juniper in the desert." Begin feared that if Peres, the opposition leader, knew about the top-secret mission, others might know as well and the secret would leak, jeopardizing Ammunition Hill. He therefore decided to delay the mission but was far from giving up. The operation was given the new code name Opera, and a new date—June 7.

Placed at the head of the octet of planes that would attack the reactor was Ze'ev Raz, a commander of one of the F-16 squadrons and a native of kibbutz Geva, in northern Israel. Leading the second group was the squadron commander Amir Nachumi. Among the pilots were Amos Yadlin, later the head of military intelligence, and Captain Ilan Ramon, the group's youngest member. Ramon was inexperienced but had served as the squadron's navigation officer, and had particularly impressed Raz when he calculated and then proved that it would be possible to carry out the attack without refueling in midair, despite the trip's 960-kilometer distance.

David Ivry decided that the planes would be gassed up when the engines were already running, an unusual and risky process. He also ordered the pilots to dump the detachable fuel tanks en route, despite the danger that they might hit the two bombs, each weighing a ton, that would be hanging under each plane's wings. The mission carried considerable danger: at that time, Iraq was deeply enmeshed in its brutal war with Iran, and it was reasonable to assume that the reactor would be defended by missile batteries and fighter planes. The pilots had no doubt that their F-15s would be forced to face off against numerous MiGs.

They knew they were taking enormous risks. If they were attacked by the enemy, their chances of survival were almost nil. Even if a pilot, whose plane had been hit, managed to parachute into Iraqi territory, hundreds of miles away from home, he would most probably be captured, cruelly tortured and put to death. Yet every pilot who heard about the mission volunteered to be among the chosen few.

On June 7, they set out, crossing the Gulf of Akaba, flying above the northern Saudi Arabian desert, bypassing Jordan from the south, penetrating Iraq and cutting across the Euphrates River as they neared their target. One of the prominent landmarks on the flight path was supposed to be an island at the center of a lake. Raz saw the lake and looked for the island, but it had disappeared. Doubts arose in his mind—perhaps they were flying over the wrong lake? Only later did the squadrons learn that the flat island had been submerged after heavy rains in the region caused the water level to rise.

The nuclear reactor eventually appeared to them, surrounded by high, thick defensive walls that were the pride of Saddam Hussein. Raz initiated contact with his comrades, urging them to increase altitude lest they run into electrical wires or tall power poles in the area. But one fact astonished everyone: no air defense was in place! Not a single MiG was visible in the sky nor was a single missile fired at them. A few negligible antiaircraft cannons fired some shells, but they missed.

The planes plunged toward the reactor, dropping their bombs at a thirty-five-degree angle. A portion of the explosives obliterated the dome covering the reactor; others carrying timed fuses penetrated deeper and blew up the center of the internal installations, the true core of the core. Most hit their target, and the reactor was completely destroyed. One pilot erred and dropped his bombs on an adjoining structure.

In total, the run over the reactor lasted eighty seconds, with the planes then immediately turning back toward Israel. As procedure required, the commanders called on each of the pilots to identify themselves, one after another, as "Charlie." All did so, except for Ramon. He didn't respond to the repeated calls of his commanders; only during his debriefing did it come out that he had feared a tardy MiG attack and had believed, being the last in the formation, that it was he who would be hit. He was so focused on the "imaginary battle" that he had ignored the calls on the radio. But he eventually opened his mouth, and the mission's lost boy was found. (Ramon was to become the first Israeli astronaut, but died tragically in 2003 in the crash of space shuttle *Columbia*.)

Nevertheless, the pilots felt certain that on their way home, they would encounter Iraqi MiGs scrambled to intercept them: planes that would take off from the H3 airbase, located in western Iraq and close to the Jordanian border, could easily attack them as they returned to Israel. But nothing happened. Not a single Iraqi plane raced to meet them, and all sixteen jets arrived home safely. A foreign attaché who had been staying in Baghdad at the time later said that the reactor's air-defense commander had been sitting in a Baghdad café, and his underlings hadn't managed to reach him. He was hanged in a public square in Baghdad the next day, under Saddam Hussein's orders.

The pilots, back from Baghdad. *(IDF Spokesman)*

In the course of the attack, ten Iraqi soldiers and a French engineer staying in the structure next to the reactor were killed.

Back home, news of the incredible operation was received with immense excitement. Those who had opposed the mission—everyone except Shimon Peres—acknowledged their error and heaped praise on the mission and the pilots. Not so with the foreign nations. Israel was harshly denounced at numerous international forums. U.S. President Ronald Reagan, a friend of Israel, joined the chorus of condemnation, even imposing sanctions on Israel: a temporary freeze on weapons deliveries.

The dark prophecies of the mission's opponents—that Saddam Hussein would build a nuclear weapon within two or three years—would prove completely false. Only in 1991, during the first Gulf War, did Israel's allies come to understand how important its mission had been. Dick Cheney, the Bush administration's defense secretary (and later, the U.S. vice president), thanked Israel during the war for its "daring, dramatic action."

The IDF chief of staff awarded a citation to Ze'ev Raz for the flawless mission. Raz insisted that all the participants deserved a medal, though one air force commander would claim, "What do they deserve medals for? They showed up at the game and the other team never set foot on the field." But the comment ignored the psychological effort, daring and determination of the pilots who had carried out the assignment.

After the mission was over, Israel published the Begin Doctrine, which stated that Israel would prevent any hostile Middle Eastern country from developing nuclear technology, because of the danger that an atomic weapon would be used against Israel.

ZE'EV RAZ, FIGHTER PILOT AND LEADER OF THE IRAQ ASSAULT

"Ironically, I'm proudest of something else. During the Yom Kippur War, I was sent from Ramat David to the Sinai to intercept enemy planes. I was flying a Phantom. Suddenly, a MiG appeared in front of us, and my navigator locked in on it; the missile's infrared radar also started buzzing, because it sensed the plane's heat. But I didn't fire the missile. My

navigator shouts, 'Ze'evik, why aren't you taking down the
plane? Bring it down already!'

"And I don't fire. Something seems unclear. Why is this MiG
flying alone? Why is it here? I came within a distance of four
hundred meters, cannon range, and suddenly he breaks off and
flies to the side. And then I saw: it's not a MiG. It's our Mirage!

"Several years go by, a short time after we established the
Hawk Squadron, and David Ivry, the commander of the IAF,
called me. It certainly couldn't have been easy for him because,
during my pilot training, I had struggled a bit, and he barely
gave me my wings. He asked me, 'Think about the reactor in
Baghdad. Long range, low altitude: can we do this?' I went to
my navigation officer, Ilan Ramon, and he told me it's possible.

"We did it without refueling in the air, and the Americans
truly couldn't believe it. Only afterward, when we returned,
did I find out that one of the pilots, Elik Shafir, had discovered
a glitch in his fueling system before takeoff. Instead of getting
off the runway and handing off his place to someone else, he
took off with less fuel and flew, carrying out the bombing and
landing on his last drops of fuel. I told him, 'Elik, that was
crazy, but in your place, I would have done the same thing.' "

Sixteen years later, Israel acted on the Begin Doctrine a second time.

In mid-2007, according to foreign reports, two Mossad agents sneaked
into a Kensington hotel room in London, where they hacked into the
laptop of a visiting senior Syrian official and viewed its contents. The laptop contained a trove of top-secret information. The most dramatic discovery of the Mossad was that Syria was secretly building a nuclear reactor.

The documents and photographs obtained by the Mossad confirmed
a strange, dubious report by another source, Iran's deputy defense minister, Ali Reza Asgari. Asgari had defected a few months before and been
debriefed by the Americans. He had revealed that a nuclear reactor was
being built in the Syrian Desert as a joint venture of Iran, North Korea

and Syria. Iran had financed the reactor, which was built and equipped by North Korea. Satellite images confirmed the information: in Dir al-Zur, in eastern Syria, a nuclear reactor identical to the one in Yongbyon, in North Korea, was being constructed. The Mossad also obtained photographs from the reactor showing North Koreans at the site. Israeli experts determined that the construction had reached an advanced stage, and that the reactor would be fully operational by September 2008.

The head of the Mossad, Meir Dagan, and Prime Minister Ehud Olmert urgently passed the information on to the United States. Syria was a sworn enemy of Israel, an ally of Iran and the Hezbollah terrorist organization. It could not be allowed to develop a weapon of mass destruction. Yet, when the intelligence was brought to the CIA and the White House, the Americans remained unconvinced and demanded additional evidence. President Bush asked that any operation be delayed until more reliable intelligence could be obtained.

In July 2007, the IAF carried out several high-altitude sorties and programmed its Ofek-7 spy satellite to photograph the reactor. The detailed photographs established clearly that Syria was building a nuclear facility identical to the North Korean reactor at Yongbyon. The Aman (the IDF intelligence department) listening service, Unit 8200, produced transcripts of intensive exchanges between Damascus and Pyongyang. The Mossad supplied photographs and even a video filmed inside the reactor. All these materials were dispatched to Washington but the White House still hesitated. The Americans wanted definite proof that radioactive materials had actually been placed in Dir al-Zur.

The IDF was ordered to obtain that definite proof. According to the international media, members of the Sayeret Matkal then flew in two helicopters to Dir al-Zur. The Sayeret commandos risked their lives, flying into one of the most secret and most heavily guarded areas in the most hostile Arab country. After landing, using special equipment brought over from Israel, the commandos collected radioactive soil samples from around the reactor. The samples were handed over to the Americans, proving that the danger was real. Stephen Hadley, George Bush's national security adviser, dubbed them the "smoking gun." But when Olmert spoke with Bush by phone and asked that the U.S. bomb the reactor, he received a disappointing answer: Bush responded that the U.S. couldn't attack a sovereign nation. Olmert, according to the same reports, replied that he was deeply troubled by such a response, and that he intended to act "in Israel's defense."

Indeed, Israel passed into action.

The Syrian reactor, before and after the visit from the Israeli Air Force.
(US Government)

According to Britain's *Sunday Times*, at 11:00 P.M. on September 4, 2007, fighters from the Air Force Shaldag ("Kingfisher") commando unit were sent on a crucial mission. They secretly penetrated into Syria and took positions around the reactor. Their mission was to "paint" the reactor's walls with laser beams in preparation for the anticipated attack, and in doing so, to signal its location for the air force. They spent the following night and day in hiding, On the evening of September 5 at eleven o'clock, ten F-15 planes took off from the Ramat David airbase, flying northwest to the Mediterranean Sea. On their way, three broke off from the pack and returned to the base. It's reasonable to assume that, at this stage, the IDF had activated electronic efforts to misdirect Syrian radar operators, who would have been left with the impression that all the Israeli planes had returned home. In fact, seven of them continued flying, moving eastward along the length of the Turkish–Syrian border and penetrating Syrian territory from the north. They reached their target and, from a distance, fired air-to-ground Maverick missiles and half-ton smart bombs toward the laser-painted walls of the reactor. The strike was precise, and the reactor was completely demolished. Planes and commandos safely returned to base.

According to reports published later, Israeli leaders following the mission from the Pit—the air force bunker and command post—feared a ferocious Syrian response; Syria was armed with thousands of missiles capable of causing major casualties in Israel. Olmert urgently spoke by phone with Prime Minister Erdoğan of Turkey—during a high point in relations between the two countries—and requested that he inform the Syrians that Israel wasn't interested in war.

The stunned Syrian government initially maintained complete silence about the attack; eventually, the Syrian state news agency released a statement that Israeli fighter planes had penetrated Syrian territory at night and "had dropped munitions above desert territory" without causing any damage; Syrian planes "had driven them away."

In contrast to the bombing of the Iraqi reactor, Israel kept silent this time. To this day, it hasn't admitted to wiping out the Syrian facility. But one of the clues left from the mission was the discovery of a discarded fuel tank from an Israeli plane, bearing a Hebrew inscription, in Turkish territory. Israel denied any violation of Turkish airspace, and Turkey accepted its claims at face value.

Officially, Israel did not admit its forces had carried out the strike at Dir al-Zur. But a confirmation came from then opposition leader Benyamin Netanyahu, who had been fully briefed about the mission by Prime Minister Olmert. Interviewed on a live newscast on the Israeli television, Netanyahu declared: "When the cabinet takes action for Israel's security, I give it my full backing . . . and here, too, I was a partner in this affair from the first moment and I gave it my full support."

The Syrian operation would have a strange epilogue the following year, on the evening of August 2, 2008. That night a festive party was held at a seaside mansion in Rimal al-Zahabiya, in northern Syria, close to the port of Tartus. It was the home of General Muhammad Suleiman, a close advisor to President Assad and a major figure behind the scenes of the Syrian security establishment. His office was in the presidential palace, adjacent to that of Assad, yet he was discreet and a man of the shadows; only a select few in the political and military establishment knew he existed.

Suleiman was among the initiators of the Syrian nuclear project. He had supervised the building of the reactor and managed (apparently not very successfully) its security. The Israelis had good reasons to believe that Suleiman would initiate the construction of a new reactor; he was also responsible for transferring missiles and other weaponry from Iran to Hezbollah, in Lebanon. As a result, Suleiman had placed himself in the IDF's crosshairs.

During the Rimal al-Zahabiya dinner, guests sat around a long table on the house's veranda. In front of them, the waves of the Mediterranean lazily rolled toward the beach. The image was peaceful and relaxing. The merry guests, however, didn't notice the sudden emergence, from the black Mediterranean waves, of two figures in divers' gear pulling out sniper rifles from waterproof cases and, after being given the signal, firing two bullets into Suleiman's head. The general collapsed forward on the food-laden table; only when some partygoers saw blood on his forehead did they realize that he had been shot. In the ensuing chaos, no one saw the shooters, who dived back underwater and returned to their mother ship, which took them— according to foreign media—to the base of Shayetet 13. British newspapers reported that the snipers had arrived at Suleiman's home on the deck of an Israeli-owned yacht, shot Suleiman, and disappeared.

The operation stunned the Syrian government. Was there nowhere in the country where Syria's leaders could feel safe? In their embarrassment, authorities announced that "Syria is conducting an investigation to locate those responsible." Meanwhile, in Israel, several months later, citations were awarded to Shayetet 13 without details, causing some to wonder if, perchance, one of the unnamed operations had happened to take place in the calm waters off Rimal al-Zahabiya.

PART SEVEN

The Lebanon War

In 1982, Begin and Defense Minister Ariel Sharon launch
the controversial operation Peace for Galilee against the
terrorist organizations in Lebanon. It is carried out by
the IDF under Chief of Staff Rafael Eitan. The war ends in
an Israeli victory, but it is marred by the massacre of hundreds
of Palestinian civilians by the Christian Lebanese Phalanges
organization at the refugee camps Sabra and Shatila,
in Beirut. An Israeli board of inquiry relieves Sharon of
his duties and harshly blames Eitan, even though they were
not personally involved.

CHAPTER 20

"DID THEY HAVE MACHINE GUNS?" 1982

"The morning after the night of fighting, when Beaufort was already in our hands and we knew the heavy price we'd paid, I looked from up close at the antenna—the antenna that, from every vantage point on Beaufort, I could see stick sticking out, threatening. I suddenly had a tremendous desire to knock it over, because, in my eyes, it symbolized all the evil possible. I asked Roni to hang a flag off the side. Roni took the flag from my armored personnel carrier and hung it on the tip of the antenna. This, for me, was a moment of enormous satisfaction, excitement, breathlessness . . . seeing the Israeli flag waving on the antenna that I had hated so much," recounted Lieutenant Colonel Zvika Barkai, who commanded the Golani Brigade's engineering company.

The battle for Beaufort took place during the first Lebanon War, which broke out on June 6, 1982. During the battle, Golani soldiers fought PLO terrorists at a fortress that had, over the years, become a symbol of the threat against Israel's northern towns and kibbutzim. Terrorists had fired every weapon at their disposal, including rockets, from the fortress toward the Galilee Panhandle, and especially at Metula, on the Lebanese border. On numerous occasions, Israel's air force had bombed the fortress but had never managed to dislodge the terrorists, who continued to embitter the lives of residents in northern Israel. It was with good reason that the fortress had earned the name "the Monster."

Built in the twelfth century on a mountain next to the Litani River, Beaufort had been a Crusaders fortress. Its strategic importance is tremendous: at just under four hundred feet in length and 2,350 feet above sea level, it overlooks southern Lebanon and the Galilee, as well as the routes leading to the Lebanese city of Sidon and the coastal plain.

Beaufort wasn't just a target to be captured; it was, for both sides, a symbol of power, control and strength. Everyone looked in fear at the fortress, which had taken on the image of a fire-breathing monster or volcano—except that, instead of lava and ash, it spewed smoke from missiles and cannons. As a consequence, the battles there were cruel and bloody, each side understanding that victory meant extending control over the entire region.

The task of capturing Beaufort and the fortified combat trench next to it had been assigned to Sayeret Golani, the brigade's commando unit. For a year and a half, it had trained and rehearsed for various conquest scenarios at different times of day, and using various methods: a raid with helicopters, armored personnel carriers or on foot. Another unit sent to the fortress was the brigade's engineering company, whose role was to seize the antenna post south of Beaufort.

At noon, IDF forces, including Golani troops, crossed the border fence and made their way into Lebanon to carry out the government's decision "to take all northern Israeli towns out of the range of terrorist fire from Lebanon." Menachem Begin and his ministers had made that decision after a prolonged period of restraint by Israel in the face of numerous terrorist attacks and unceasing shooting on northern towns by terrorist organizations, mainly Fatah, which numbered 23,000 terrorists under the leadership of Yasser Arafat. The terrorists were arrayed across the "Fatah Land," which included the western slopes of Mount Hermon, the area south of Mount Lebanon on the Nabatieh plateau, and in the region between Tyre and Beirut.

In 1978, Israel had launched Operation Litani. The IDF had pushed the terrorists to the northern shore of the Litani River; a UN force of peacekeepers had been created but had kept anything but the peace. The terrorists had recovered and reverted to their wicked ways. Their activity had reached its peak in July 1981, when they attacked Israel's northern towns with artillery and missile salvos. A cease-fire had been finally reached, but Israel knew well that this wouldn't last long, and the power of the terrorists in south Lebanon had to be eliminated; that's why the plans for Operation Oranim ("Cedars") were born in the operations centers of the IDF. Israeli agents and officers had secretly visited Lebanon and established close relations with the Christian community and its armed units, the Phalanges. Some Israeli leaders planned to join forces with the Christians, carry out the military operation together and later establish a "new order" in Lebanon.

What had brought about the end of Israeli restraint and the decision to go to war was an attempt on the life of Israel's ambassador to Great Britain, Shlomo Argov, by a gang of terrorists, which had left Argov critically wounded. Prime Minister Menachem Begin chose to ignore the fact that these terrorists belonged to a splinter group and not to Arafat's PLO. Begin and Defense Minister Ariel Sharon were determined to hit the PLO terrorists and to put an end to the terrorist attacks originating in Lebanon. Thus started Israel's military campaign, based on the Oranim blueprints, now dubbed Operation Peace for Galilee.

Long convoys of armored personnel carriers moved along the road to the Litani, creating long traffic jams and a delay in the timetable. Only at five in the afternoon did a Golani force cross the Litani en route to Beaufort. The fighters understood that the battle would take place in darkness. "During the trip, we started preparing the teams for nighttime combat. This fact didn't especially bother us, because our familiarity with the objective was total," Barkai said.

But a Sayeret junior officer, Nadav Palti, remembered it differently. "After a year of preparations and near-attacks on Beaufort, at the moment of truth, we weren't ready. The equipment hadn't come in; the soldiers weren't sufficiently awake following forty-eight hours without sleep. The tanks were causing problems, and Giora ["Goni"] Harnik, who had been the Sayeret commander for a year and a half and was considered 'the Beaufort expert,' had been discharged just a day before the war started."

In the early evening, while the Sayeret approached the Beaufort, its new commander, Moshe Kaplinski, was struck by a bullet in the chest in a sudden outburst of gunfire.

Goni Harnik immediately arrived in the area. Handsome and slim, with tousled hair, the son of a musician and a poetess, he was a charismatic leader, worshiped by his soldiers. He was a close friend of Gabi Eshkenazi, the deputy commander of the Golani Brigade; four years before, when Ashkenazi had been severely wounded during Operation Litani in Lebanon, young Harnik—a company commander in his battalion—had assumed command and successfully carried the mission to its end.

Tonight, hearing that Goni had returned to the battlefield, Ashkenazi urgently called him to take over the Golani Sayeret. As he sped toward his soldiers in an armored personnel carrier, in the dark and without lights, the vehicle hit the low stone fence of a mountain terrace and flipped over. Harnik, injured, ran the rest of the way.

When the soldiers and officers heard his voice on the communications network saying, "The Avenging Officer [Harnik's code name] reporting," they all breathed a sigh of relief. They believed in him and admired him, and felt calmer. He began by imposing order and coordinating the operation's next steps. Harnik and Barkai agreed that Barkai's soldiers would lead and Harnik would follow in their footsteps. Barkai's men set out on foot for their destination. "Going first on the ascent to Beaufort with an advance group of five people was an unpleasant feeling. It was obvious that, if they opened fire, I would be the first to get hit," he said. "I looked through my binoculars and could make out a terrorist lying in the central bunker, his weapon pointed at me. I gave the order to charge; at the same time, a heavy burst of fire came in our direction, the results of which I saw only later—it hit the Sayeret soldiers who were in the rear."

Barkai and his soldiers crossed a minefield and infiltrated the antenna station. In the trenches surrounding it, they fought face-to-face with the terrorists. The company's doctor and the patrol-team commander were wounded. Israel's fighters killed several terrorists at close range, and the engineering company eventually seized the antenna position.

Following the engineering company, Harnik's force advanced toward the fortress. As the soldiers started climbing, they crossed a white gravel path close to the road leading to the fortress. Their dark silhouettes stood out on the white background. "I received an order from Harnik: 'Forward!'" remembered Motti, a Sayeret detachment commander. "We started to run. We needed to pass along a firing zone on the western side of Beaufort. They opened hellfire on us. You see how the bullets are flying straight at you. I look back and see that there are seven or eight people left! When we started out, we were twenty-one. I tell Harnik that I'm missing soldiers, and he answers, 'Motti, go ahead. I'll send them after you.' In hindsight, I know that, during this sprint through the area, they were simply slaughtering us." Three Sayeret commandos were killed in the onslaught.

Nevertheless, the Sayeret continued toward the combat trenches leading to the fortress, moving under unceasing machine-gun fire. A team commander and a fighter were the first to jump into the trenches. The trenches were very narrow, and moving within them with full pack and a weapon was extremely difficult. The two continued without trouble until two bursts of fire mowed them down, and both fell to their deaths. But three other soldiers kept running toward the objective with a bag of grenades that they tossed into the ditches.

Meanwhile, Harnik had reached the entrance to the fortress with five soldiers. All around them, the shooting was fierce. Numerous terrorists were killed, others were seen fleeing the site. One stubborn terrorist, hiding at a small position covered in camouflage netting, fired a burst of bullets at Harnik, and the venerated commander was killed on the spot.

The remaining fighters continued clearing the site, aware that their principal problem was the bunker that spewed intense fire. Two soldiers crawled over to it, hurling a large explosive charge and retreating. The huge thundering explosion that followed left no doubt that the bunker had been destroyed.

By 10:00 P.M., the fighting was over. The soldiers counted the corpses of thirty terrorists. Golani had six dead and nine wounded. The news about Harnik's death left all of Golani and the supreme command in shock. Golan Heights' hero Avigdor Kahalani, now a commander of the Ga'ash Division, was unable to face the news. "I wanted to believe that there was a mistake, that I would receive another message cancelling the first, but it didn't come."

Goni's comrades were amazed to learn that his mother, Raya Harnik, had darkly foreseen her son's future. When he was just four years old, she had written a poem saying:

> I will not
> Sacrifice my first born
> Not me.

And when Goni was six years old, Raya had written these chilling verses:

> That day I'll stand, eyes wide open, facing the calamity
> My whole life freezes before this tomorrow
> A lodestone I am, iron doesn't cry
> I already feel the burning
> The dryness in my throat and the looks and the fury
> And night after night my life is crying the cry of that day. . . .

Ariel Sharon, with the Beaufort conquerors. *(IDF Archive)*

The day after Beaufort's capture, Begin's helicopter landed by the vanquished citadel. The prime minister was accompanied by Defense Minister Sharon. During a TV interview conducted at the fortress, Begin said that not one of Israel's soldiers had been killed during the battle, and that there hadn't even been any injuries. It later came out that no one had bothered to update the prime minister about the outcome of the fighting. This unfortunate comment—along with his question to the soldiers: "Did they have machine guns?"—provoked a harsh response from the public, and particularly among parents whose loved ones had been wounded or killed in the battle.

Meanwhile, during the first three days of the war, battles against the terrorists raged all over Lebanon. The Galilee Division moved on to the coastal plain, going as far as the Litani River. An armored force advanced toward Sidon; the Ga'ash Division progressed toward the town of Nabatieh; and the Sinai Division fought on the western slopes of Mount Hermon, but avoided conflict with the Syrians in the area, even when they opened artillery fire on IDF forces.

But on June 9, Israeli restraint toward the Syrians came to an end. Israel's request that they pull their forces back to their prewar positions went unanswered, and Israel decided to act with all its might. (See Chapter 11.)

GABI ASHKENAZI, DEPUTY COMMANDER OF GOLANI BRIGADE, LATER THE IDF CHIEF OF STAFF

"As a deputy commander of Golani Brigade, I went through several difficult moments during this battle. The first was when I was informed that Sayeret Commander Moshe Kaplinsky had been wounded. I sent Goni Harnik to replace him, and three or four minutes later, they're reporting that his armored personnel carrier has turned over in the village of Arnoun, near the Beaufort, and that he has started running on foot, his back badly hurting, to where his soldiers were located. I said to myself, the spine of the command has been hit, and now Goni has disappeared on me. . . . But within a few minutes, Goni shows up on the radio, we speak, the battle goes on and I have the feeling that the situation is under control.

"The second difficult moment was at the end of the battle, when they told me that Goni had been killed, together with five fighters. That really hurt. Goni and I had gone through a lot together, and I felt that I had lost not only an excellent commander but a good friend, as well as an exceptional fighter.

"Given that the battle had been planned for daytime and took place at night, in a situation in which the commanders had been hit, the Sayeret and the engineers company fought in a manner worthy of commendation, and all because of the quality of the fighters, the commanders and their familiarity with Beaufort.

"At the end of the battles, when I descended from Beaufort, I didn't believe that we would spend two decades there, and that in the year 2000, it would be me, as commander of the northern district, who would evacuate Beaufort and IDF forces from Lebanon."

The Syrian Army and Air Force treat Lebanon as if it
were part of Syria. They have established batteries of
ground-to-air missiles in the Lebanese Beqaa. During the
war with Lebanon, Israel will be confronted by
the Syrian missiles and fighter planes.

CHAPTER 21

"IT WAS A GREAT CONCERT WITH MANY INSTRUMENTS," 1982

n June 9, 1982, three days after the start of the first Lebanon War, IAF pilots waited with great tension and suspense for the signal to embark on one of the air force's most complicated missions: attacking Syrian missile batteries in Lebanon's Beqaa Valley. In Jerusalem, the government continued to discuss the operation, struggling over fears of an escalation with the Syrians, who were politically and militarily involved in Lebanon. The debate was tense and stretched on for many hours. The time set for the start of the operation was pushed back, and Air Force Commander David Ivry retired to his office to concentrate on the latest flashes from the battlefield. Colonel Aviem Sella, the head of IAF operations, circulated among the pilots, checking their readiness, providing encouragement and trying to ease the tension.

At 1:30 P.M., IDF Chief of Staff Rafael Eitan called the air force commander from the prime minister's office, telling him, "Time to act. Good luck!" At two, the offensive got under way.

When the green light was given, twenty-four F-4 Phantom jets from IAF Squadron 105 took off, armed with missiles. Soaring alongside them were Skyhawk fighter aircraft, Kfirs—Israeli-made combat jets—and F-15s and F-16s armed with heat-seeking air-to-air missiles. For Israel's electronic-disruption effort, the air force had enlisted Hawkeye early-warning aircraft, Boeing 707s and Zahavan drones. At the peak of the action, approximately one hundred Israeli planes were in the air.

The Syrians likewise threw roughly one hundred aircraft into battle—MiG-21s and -23s. Nineteen surface-to-air-missile batteries had been spread across the Beqaa Valley, where they were ready to launch SA-3, SA-6 and SA-8 surface-to-air missiles, among the most advanced, state-of-the-art engines developed by the Soviet Union.

Surface-to-air missiles were still a source of trauma for Israel's air force. The war of attrition with Egypt, followed by the Yom Kippur War, had left behind bad memories and a sense of powerlessness against Egyptian missiles. The former defense minister, General Ezer Weizman, had coined the famous phrase "the missile that bent the plane's wing," which had motivated IAF commanders to look for a solution to this difficult problem. For five years, the top minds in the air force had labored with members of the military industry to develop a technological response that would protect the planes from the enemy's missiles and bring the plane's wing back to its natural place.

Now the hour of judgment had arrived: Would the Jewish brain again come up with an answer? Would the pilots' nightmare come to an end? Would the IAF reestablish control over the region's skies?

The attack's opening move was the launch of drones over the Beqaa Valley, an act of misdirection. The aircrafts' radar profile had been designed to resemble that of fighter jets, and the Syrians fell into the trap. As Israel's military planners had thought, the Syrians immediately launched surface-to-air missiles at the drones, exposing the precise locations of their batteries, which in turn became targets for Israeli radiation-seeking missiles. Simultaneously, the IDF ground electronic sensors pinpointed the batteries' locations and its artillery began shelling them.

Twenty-four Phantoms then suddenly appeared, each carrying two

"Purple Fists," anti-radiation missiles that zero in on radar installations by detecting the heat from antiaircraft systems. The planes launched the missiles at the batteries from nearly twenty-two miles away; also fired were Ze'ev surface-to-surface missiles, a sophisticated short-to-medium-range weapon that had been developed in Israel. The entire time, drones circled above the area, transmitting the results back to the operation's commanders.

After the attack's first wave, the Syrian batteries went silent for several minutes, and then the second wave arrived. Forty Phantoms, Kfirs and Skyhawks fired various types of bombs, among them cluster bombs that destroyed the batteries and their crews. The third wave took on the few remaining batteries, and within forty-five minutes, the attack had ended as a complete success. Most of the batteries had been wiped out.

During the offensive, the Syrians had fired fifty-seven SA-6 missiles but had managed to hit just one Israeli plane. For several long minutes, the Syrian command had been in complete disarray, and when it realized its battery system had collapsed, scrambled its MiGs. During the aerial battles that ensued, Israel's F-15s and F-16s brought down twenty-seven MiGs using air-to-air missiles.

"From an operational standpoint, in contrast to what was planned, the attack on the missile batteries was one of the simplest missions I ever oversaw," said Colonel Sella, who had been charged with the operation's ground management. "Everything went like clockwork. As a result, even after the first planes successfully attacked the batteries, I ordered their continued bombing. The perception was that any change, any pause or shift, could only create turmoil that would disrupt the progression of matters."

Toward 4:00 P.M., Sella reached a decision that he later described as the most significant of his life: to halt the operation. "At this stage, we had already destroyed fourteen batteries. We were an hour before last light, and we hadn't lost a plane. I believed we couldn't achieve a better outcome. When I leaned back for a minute in my chair, I took in some air and said to myself, 'Let's stop—we've done our work for the day. They're going to bring more batteries tomorrow in any case.'"

Sella went to David Ivry, who was observing the mission with Chief of Staff Eitan. Sella leaned into Ivry's ear so that Eitan wouldn't hear and said, "I'm requesting authorization to stop the operation. We won't accomplish more today. We'll destroy the rest tomorrow."

Ivry thought for a moment and nodded in agreement. The handful of planes then en route to an additional attack returned on Sella's orders to their bases. Defense Minister Ariel Sharon didn't love the decision, to put it mildly, even criticizing it harshly during a meeting with Eitan. But Sella's theory that the Syrians would move additional batteries to the Beqaa Valley overnight proved correct.

Over the next two days, Israeli bombers, escorted by fighter jets, set out to strike the new SA-8 batteries relocated by the Syrians. Because of the paralysis of Syria's defensive batteries, its air force dispatched planes to intercept the Israeli aircraft. In the battles that followed, Israel's pilots again had the upper hand: eighty-two Syrian aircraft were downed over the course of the first Lebanon War. The Israeli Air Force lost two planes to ground fire. During the campaign, what became known as the "biggest battle of the jet age" took place, involving approximately two hundred planes from the two sides.

"This situation, in which our planes were dominant and the Syrians were in a state of panic, gave us a huge psychological advantage," Ivry said. "The aerial picture on the Syrian side was very unclear. We added in electronic means for disrupting their ability to aim and keep control, meaning that the Syrians entered the combat zone more as targets than as interceptors."

When Ivry, who had also been the air force commander during Israel's attack on Iraq's nuclear reactor, was asked what his most exciting moment had been, he answered without hesitation that it was the end of the missile attack during the first Lebanon War. "When it became clear that we had succeeded in destroying the Syrian missile apparatus and that not one of our planes was damaged, it was a moment of true spiritual transcendence. This was a struggle involving the entire air force—a big concert with lots of instruments of various types, and everyone needed to play in perfect harmony."

The missile batteries were wiped out. *(AF Journal)*

The operation's success gave Israel complete control over the skies of Lebanon and made it possible for air force planes to freely assist IDF ground forces. Nevertheless, the air force abstained from striking Syrian ground troops, in keeping with a decision made by the cabinet, which feared sliding into an all-out war with Syria. On June 11, 1982, following mediation by the American emissary Philip Habib, a cease-fire between Israel and Syria took hold.

The mission, Operation Mole Cricket 19, was considered one of the four most important in the history of the air force. (The other three were Operation Focus, the assault on the combined Arab Air Forces during the Six Day War; Operation Opera, the attack on the nuclear reactor in Iraq, in 1981; and Operation Yonatan, the rescue of hostages in Antebbe, in 1976.) Western air forces regarded the mission as an example of the successful use of Western technology against Soviet defense strategy. The results of the attack caused a great deal of astonishment among the military leaders of the Warsaw Pact, overturning their sense of confidence in the USSR, and particularly in the Soviet bloc's surface-to-air-missile apparatus.

AVIEM SELLA, SQUADRON COMMANDER

"For the sake of this operation, we developed, with the help of a great team of scientists from the Weizmann Institute, a computerized control and planning system that would make it possible to prepare and command a multivariable campaign: to manage hundreds of planes with hundreds of weapons facing dozens of missile batteries and dozens of radar installations. It was a dynamic system operating in real time with thousands of variables. The primary and most outstanding programmer was a Haredi [Orthodox Jew] who lived in Bnei Brak, Menachem Kraus, who had no formal education but immense and unique knowledge. He was involved in all of the operational programs and, at the moment of action, sat with us in the Pit, in his civilian clothes.

"At the end of the day, we would conduct a nighttime debriefing and discuss what we had learned. I arrived at one debriefing where all the squadron commanders were participating, as well as all the wing commanders and former air force commanders. And, all of a sudden, everyone is standing and starts to applaud me for the perfect operation. I was very moved, because this sort of thing is quite rare in the middle of a war. I also got a little statuette, which was inscribed, 'To Sella, the thinker behind the fight against missiles, your vision has been fulfilled and we're standing tall once again—the fighters of Air Force Base 8."

PART EIGHT

Fighting Terrorism

After the 1982 Lebanon War, the PLO terrorists and
their leaders have been exiled to Tunisia, where they live
with total impunity, protected by the Tunisian government.
But in 1988, Prime Minister Shamir approves a
mission to change that situation.

CHAPTER 22

"ABU JIHAD SENT US," 1988

March 7, 1988. The Mothers' Bus, so called because of the large number of women it carried, was on its daily morning trip from Be'er Sheva to the Dimona nuclear reactor. At a deserted stretch of the highway it was suddenly stopped by three men, standing in the middle of the road beside a military vehicle. Only after the men boarded the bus, waving automatic weapons, did the passengers realize that these were Arab terrorists. Panic broke out on board the bus, yet forty of the passengers, all of them workers at the Dimona reactor, managed to escape. The terrorists seized control of the bus and held hostage the remaining nine women and two men. Israeli Special Forces arrived almost immediately, and surrounded the vehicle. The terrorists began negotiating with them over the release of the hostages in exchange for Palestinian prisoners in the Israeli jails. They threatened to murder a hostage every half hour. First among those killed was Victor Ram.

The first intelligence reports that reached the Israeli unit indicated that the terrorists had crossed the border early that morning, coming from Egypt-controlled Sinai, and had hijacked a military jeep on their way. Order was given to the fighters of the Special Unit of Israel's border guard (Yamam) to raid the bus. Which they did, killing the hostage takers, but not before the terrorists murdered two of the female captives, Rina Pazarkar-Sheratzky and Miriam Ben Yair. During the negotiations, one of the terrorists shouted, "Abu Jihad sent us!"

Abu Jihad. The name was highly familiar to the IDF's intelligence services. Abu Jihad—or "Father of Jihad," whose given name was Khalil al-Wazir—was Yasser Arafat's deputy, and the head of the PLO's military wing. He was born in Ramleh, in then Mandatory Palestine, and grew up in refugee camps in Gaza. Before he was even twenty, he was organizing resistance groups composed of other Palestinian youths and was among the first to join Yasser Arafat's Fatah movement. Abu Jihad had participated in the first Fatah operation in Israeli territory, planting a bomb at a National Water Carrier facility on January 1, 1965. Following the Yom Kippur War, he planned a series of lethal terrorist assaults on Israel, including a 1974 attack in Nahariya that killed four Israelis and wounded six; a raid on the Savoy hotel in Tel Aviv on March 5, 1975, which killed eight hostages and three IDF soldiers, among them Colonel Uzi Yairi; a massive bombing in the crowded Zion Square in Jerusalem by a booby-trapped refrigerator that killed fifteen people on July 4, 1975; the Coastal Road massacre of March 11, 1978, in which thirty-five were murdered; and the killing of three Israeli sailors in Limassol, Cyprus, in September 1985.

By 1988, Abu Jihad was running the first Palestinian armed rebellion—the Intifada—from afar, and in the eyes of many Palestinians, had become a symbol of the struggle against Israel. He had married Intisar al-Wazir—also known as Umm Jihad, or "Mother of Jihad"—an impressive woman who was a leader in her own right. She gave him three sons and one daughter. Expelled from Lebanon with his PLO cronies after Israel's 1982 invasion, he was banished four years later from Jordan and settled in Tunis with the rest of the Fatah leadership.

Abu Jihad had already been marked for assassination a few years earlier; several operations had been planned but were abandoned at the last minute. However, with the Mothers' Bus attack of March 1988, the cup runneth over. Following the attack, the head of the military intelligence department, General Amnon Lipkin-Shahak, reached the conclusion that Abu Jihad should be eliminated. General Lipkin-Shahak knew what he was talking about: he was a decorated hero of Operation Spring of Youth in 1973. (See Chapter 14.)

The IDF new chief of staff, Dan Shomron, (the brain behind the Entebbe mission) approved an operation in principle and assigned its management and preparation to his deputy, Ehud Barak, the former commander of Sayeret Matkal. Outwardly, it appeared to be an incredibly complicated mission, more than 1,550 miles from home. The Mossad was asked to help. Ever since the Fatah leadership had settled in Tunis, the Mossad had been widening its effective intelligence network. Its agents in Tunis surreptitiously visited Abu Jihad's neighborhood, Sidi Bou Said, photographed his home and even succeeded in drawing up precise blueprints of the structure and its internal layout. A Mossad female agent had visited the house under false pretexts and submitted a report on its furnishings and interior: a corridor leading from the entrance to a couch and armchair-filled guest room; a door that led to Abu Jihad's study; another door, to the kitchen; and a staircase to the second floor, where the bedrooms of Abu Jihad, his wife, and daughter, Hanan, were located. The couple's baby, Nidal, a two-year-old, slept in his parents' room, while the family's two older boys studied in the United States.

The operation was planned as follows: the commandos of Sayeret Matkal would approach Tunisia's coast on Israeli naval ships. Members of Shayetet 13, the naval commando unit, would bring them to shore, and from there, they would reach Abu Jihad's home with the aid of the Mossad. The Shayetet and the navy had secretly mapped Tunis's coastline and located beaches for the Israeli landing. Air force jets were eventually dispatched for a surveillance flight, refreshing the IDF's intelligence before the operation.

Even so, the risks remained very high. Any encounter with PLO forces, Tunisian Army units or local police could lead to disaster, and it was clear that a retreat by Israeli forces or an evacuation of wounded participants would be much harder than in countries adjacent to Israel.

Abu Jihad's neighborhood was home to many PLO leaders on Israel's most-wanted list, and it was obvious that there would be a large presence of well-trained Fatah guards. Any misstep could end in battle or the entrapment of IDF soldiers. The operation could also lead to severe political consequences: Tunisia wasn't an active enemy of Israel, and it would be hard to explain an attack on Tunisians. One question kept Defense Minister Yitzhak Rabin particularly restless: how would it be possible to confirm that Abu Jihad was home on the night of the mission?

The Mossad had assured Rabin that it would have up-to-the-minute information about Abu Jihad's whereabouts within his home, which it hoped to secure via intelligence reports and careful surveillance. In the meantime, final preparations were under way. An exact replica of Abu Jihad's home was built in Israel, where Sayeret Matkal trained for the infiltration and assassination. Elite officers were selected for the operation, and each was assigned a precise role.

The team that would go up to the bedrooms and the officer who would shoot Abu Jihad were also chosen. Heading the operation would be Sayeret Matkal's commander, Moshe Ya'alon. Bogie, who had returned to active service as a sergeant after the 1973 Yom Kippur War, was now a colonel and considered one of the best Sayeret commanders. During the preparation for the mission Bogie decided to visit the area. He flew to Rome and from there, with a false passport, to Tunis. Once in Tunis, he was taken by Mossad agents on a tour near Abu Jihad's home. The next day, Ya'alon returned to Israel via Rome and joined his men.

The force set out in four missile boats, accompanied by a submarine, on Wednesday, April 13. Two of the boats transported the Sayeret Matkal and Shayetet 13 commandos, and were protected by the other two. One of the boats, containing a sophisticated electronics center, served as the operation's command post under Barak's command. A fully equipped and staffed medical operation unit had been set up in the other. The flotilla initially sailed northwest, toward the Greek islands, then turned west and later south, until it reached the coast of Tunisia.

That same day, three Mossad agents had appeared at a car-rental company in Tunis bearing false IDs. Calling themselves Ayish a-Saridi,

George Najib and Uataf Allem (the third was a woman), they rented three minibuses—two Volkswagen Transporters and a Peugeot.

The missile boats reached their destination on April 15. That day, Israel intercepted a transmission sent to the PLO by French agents, who warned that "the Israelis are cooking up something." This was a cause for concern, but Barak ordered that the operation move ahead.

That night, two Boeing 707s belonging to the Israeli Air Force arrived in the skies over Tunis, one a receptor for electronic transmissions and the other providing air cover and serving as a refueling plane for the fighter jets circling in the region.

The operation commenced. The submarine drew closer to the appointed beach—A-Rouad, next to Ras Carthage—and reported that it was completely empty. Two pairs of Shayetet fighters, aboard tiny "Hazir" ("Pig") submersibles, reached the shore, and met the trio from the Mossad, which had brought the rented vehicles. The Shayetet divers reported by radio that the beach was secure, and five rubber dinghies were immediately lowered into the sea, delivering twenty sayeret commandos to the shore. The landing point was a short distance from Sidi Bou Said. The commandos had been divided into four teams—A and B to carry out the operation, and C and D to provide protection. The fighters in A and B were armed with twenty-two-milimeter Berettas outfitted with silencers, as well as mini-Uzis. Several members of the C and D teams carried rifles and grenades. The Sayeret members wore coveralls concealing bulletproof vests and supple Palladium boots. Attached to their heads were communications devices with microphones and earphones, and their belts carried tiny pouches with ammunition and first-aid supplies. They were also equipped with surgical masks, to conceal their faces.

That evening, the Shin Bet had detained Fayez Abu Rahma, a relative of Abu Jihad who lived in Gaza. His interrogation had been cursory and unfocused, and he was released a few hours later. Actually, the arrest had a single, secret objective: to cause Abu Rahma to call Abu Jihad in Tunis, which would allow the Mossad and Military-intelligence's listening systems to confirm that the terrorist leader was in fact in the North African city.

But as H-Hour approached, a last-minute hitch occurred. While Sayeret Matkal was getting ready on the Tunisian beach, an urgent message was received from a Mossad agent. Abu Jihad wasn't home! He was in the city, at a meeting with another Palestinian leader, Farouk Kaddoumi. The unit was forced to wait. The risk was great: an elite unit of the IDF sitting tight on an isolated beach in an enemy country, thousands of miles away from home. A nerve-wracking hour and a half passed before Yaalon received word that Abu Jihad had returned home, escorted by two bodyguards—one who remained in the car, outside, and a second who went into the house. The sayeret fighters piled up in their vehicles and immediately departed for Sidi Bou Said, passing the darkened ruins of the ancient port of Carthage, where Hannibal had set sail to Spain, launching his legendary campaign against the Roman Empire.

The soldiers reached their destination shortly before 2:00 A.M. Abu Jihad's car was parked in front of his house, and his bodyguard was dozing off in the driver's seat. Two fighters approached the vehicle, one disguised as a woman. The "lady" was carrying a large box of chocolates that concealed his hand, holding a silenced pistol. When they reached the car, one of them shot the bodyguard through the head. The others moved into the garden surrounding the house, while members of the A team broke through a reinforced wooden door with the help of specialized, noise-reducing equipment. The A and B teams snuck into the house; in the basement, the commandos killed the second bodyguard, as well as an unlucky Tunisian gardener who had chosen to sleep there. Members of the A team ran upstairs, toward Abu Jihad and his wife's bedroom.

Abu Jihad wasn't sleeping. An hour earlier, he had kissed his sixteen-year-old daughter, Hanan, good night, and after leaving her room had sat at his desk to begin writing a letter to leaders of the Intifada back in Israel. A faint noise outside startled him, and he picked up a firearm—his special silver-handled pistol—and turned toward the door. Umm Jihad realized what was going on and called, "Verdun, Verdun," in reference to Verdun Street, in Beirut, the location of the building where terrorist leaders had been killed during Operation Spring of Youth.

Abu Jihad opened the door. Standing before him were masked men, their weapons drawn. He managed to push his wife into an alcove in the wall and raise his revolver, but the officer facing him shot an entire magazine into him, as did the rest of the group afterward. Abu Jihad collapsed in front of his wife. While the attackers still fired at the terrorist leader, Umm Jihad jumped toward her husband and bent over his body, embracing the corpse and eventually shouting at the attackers, "Enough!"

The shooters didn't harm her nor her daughter, Hanan, who had been awakened by the sound of the shooting and burst into the room. One blurted out in Arabic, "Go to your mother!" but she saw the attackers firing at her father on the ground and, for a moment, stood opposite one of the commandos entering the room without a mask. She looked at his face—a face, she said, that she would never forget. He, too, shot her father in the head. Umm Jihad and her daughter saw a woman who had accompanied the Israeli unit; she was videotaping the entire operation. The two-year-old baby, Nidal, woke up and burst into tears. Above him stood a Sayeret commando spraying gunfire into the ceiling, but he didn't harm the child. The PLO later claimed that the attackers had fired seventy bullets, and that fifty-two had struck Abu Jihad.

Retaking the hijacked "Mothers' bus." (GPO)

The commandos left the room quickly, descending the stairs, grabbing official documents and other papers they found, and ripping a small safe out of the study wall to take with them. Above them, Umm Jihad heard a woman's voice shouting at them in French to hurry: *"Allez! Allez!"*

The operation had taken less than five minutes. The commandos exited and stood in front of the house, where their commanders counted them, to ensure that everyone was there. From her window, Umm Jihad looked at them and counted twenty-four people. Their vehicles sped toward the beach; inside, the commandos found crates of soft drinks prepared by the Mossad. The boats awaited them at the beach, and they ventured out into the open sea, together with the Mossad agents who had taken part in the operation. Other agents had stayed in Tunis and called the police to report that the attackers' vehicles had been seen traveling toward the city—the opposite direction from the get-away route. Police in Tunis placed roadblocks on the roads leading out of Sidi Bou Said toward the capital, and the country's president scrambled ground forces and helicopters, also ordering the closure of the airport and seaport. But, with the exception of the three rented vehicles abandoned on the beach, not a trace of the Israelis was found.

By the following day, the episode made front-page headlines around the world; there could be no doubt that the operation had been the work of the Israelis. Abu Jihad had been killed, but his name wasn't forgotten. Years later, his talented wife, Umm Jihad, was appointed to serve as a minister in Yasser Arafat's government, after the establishment of the Palestinian Authority. She and her daughter would describe the assassination to Israeli writers and journalists.

THE FAMILY OF MIRIAM BEN YAIR, KILLED IN THE MOTHERS' BUS ATTACK

Miriam Ben Yair's daughter, Rachel, in tears: "When the terrorist turned toward my mother, she begged him, 'My daughter is getting married next month; please have mercy on me.' He shot her to death. She was on her way to the Nuclear Research Center, where she worked as an executive secretary. Invitations to my wedding that she had been planning to distribute to her friends were found in her bag."

Ben Yair's husband, Eliyahu: "Friends met me in the street and asked, 'What, you haven't heard? The Mothers' Bus was attacked!' I raced to Soroka hospital. My wife's sister, Frieda, a nurse there, told me, 'It's over.' "

Her son, Ilan: "My mom was a pretty woman, full of joy. She knew French very well and worked at the Nuclear Research Center from the time the French built the reactor. Her family was her entire world, and she dreamed of leaving one day, to raise her grandchildren. She didn't get to. She was forty-six at her death."

Eliyahu: "It was Major General Yitzhak Mordechai who comforted us. He would visit us often, talk to us. He was like a member of the family."

Rachel: "We knew that Abu Jihad was responsible for the murder. His death gave us a certain relief, but the pain remains deep and sharp, just as it was before."

Iran has become the major supplier of weapons,
mainly missiles, to the terrorist organizations in Gaza.
The weapons usually leave Iran aboard innocent-looking
cargo vessels; then they are either unloaded in Sudan and sent
to Gaza in truck convoys via Egypt and Sinai, or left aboard
the ships that traverse the Suez Canal and dumped in Gaza
waters, where local Arab divers recover them. One of the most
recent cases is the capture in March 2014 by Israeli commandos
of the boat *Klos C*, carrying a concealed load of missiles.
The most famous mission of this kind, however, is the
capture of the weapons on the ship *Karine A*.

CHAPTER 23

"WHERE IS THE SHIP?" 2002

A t 3:58 in the morning on January 3, 2002, two rubber Morena-type boats pulled next to the hull of the *Karine A*, a freighter making its way in the Suez Gulf. An electronic signal was flashed to the Shayetet 13 commandos on the Morenas, and they swiftly began climbing from the boats onto the deck of the ship. Suddenly, helicopters swooped down from overhead, and more fighters dropped out of them, sliding down on assault ropes. Quickly and without using weapons, the soldiers spread throughout the ship. They immediately started searching for a shipment of weapons purportedly sent from Iran to the Palestinian Authority.

Hovering simultaneously overhead were Israeli Air Force fighter jets; Sikorsky helicopters carrying members of Unit 669, the IDF's airborne rescue and evacuation team; a plane equipped for intelligence gathering, surveillance photography, and refueling; and a Boeing 707 serving as the command post for IDF Chief of staff Shaul Mofaz, Navy Commander Yedidia Ya'ari, Air Force Commander Dan Halutz, and additional senior officers, who would stay in the air for approximately two hours until the start of the operation, tracking what was taking place below. "It was a long flight," a senior officer recalled, "three hundred miles from the Israeli coast. The plane was crowded and very cold, and you could cut the tension with a knife. "

Until the last minute, the mission commanders feared that the raid would be called off because of the stormy weather. The waves were rising nearly ten feet, the winds reaching speeds of almost forty miles an hour. It was hard to sail in such conditions, and even harder to rappel down ropes from a helicopter onto the deck of a ship. But the *Karine A*, according to highly reliable intelligence, was in the Red Sea, en route to the Suez Canal, and the IDF needed to do everything in its power to take hold of the ship before it reached its destination.

The operation planner and field commander, Vice Admiral Eli ("Chiney") Marom, was assisted by a superb meteorologist. Marom understood that if they waited for the ship to reach the originally planned interception point, approximately twenty-five miles south of Sharm el-Sheikh, the storm would be at full force. After additional assessments and calculations, he decided that his forces would sail to a point twice as far from Israel as the preselected location, 150 miles south of the Suez Canal. The shayetet officers who heard his suggestion didn't believe it possible, as it carried a much greater risk that something would go wrong; they were also uncertain that the fuel supplies for the helicopters and boats would suffice. But Chiney persisted, suggesting that the fighters take with them barrels of fuel for refilling at sea, and that the helicopters, which couldn't circle for long in the air, would act in full coordination with the naval forces to best use the window of time at their disposal. The chips had fallen, and the mission got under way.

Chiney was forty-seven, a moshav boy, whose father had escaped his native Germany when the Nazis came to power, and landed in China. There he had wed Chai Lee, the daughter of a Russian-born Jewish woman and a Chinese man. The couple had immigrated to Israel and Chai Lee had changed her name to Leah. Young Eli had inherited her slanted eyes and his comrades at the naval officers' academy had nicknamed him Chiney. His Asiatic features made an American paper call

him the "Israeli Chinese Admiral." He was known as an excellent officer. "The fact that Chiney looked different," one former comrade said in
a press interview, "forced him to constantly show that he was better. He
became one of the best very quickly."

The night of the operation had been preceded by a long period of complex surveillance that combined multipronged intelligence gathering and
preparations. It had all begun when some top-secret reports were delivered to the IDF intelligence headquarters. The documents dealt with a
project to smuggle weapons by ship from Iran to the Gaza Strip. This
wasn't the first time the Palestinians had tried to smuggle weapons to
Gaza by sea. In May 2001, the Israeli Navy had captured a small boat, the
Santorini, as it sailed to Gaza from a Hezbollah base in Lebanon. On its
deck, the Israelis had found a small but significant cache of weapons: Russian Strella missiles with which the Palestinians intended to bring down
IAF planes. It was undeniable proof that Yasser Arafat was speaking out
of both sides of his mouth, talking about his people's desire for peace to
leaders in the West and, at home, in Arabic, about jihad.

A seemingly unimportant finding alerted the sensors of the Israeli
intelligence community: the Palestinians had paid too much for an old
ship. The navy head of intelligence recalled, "We realized that the ship
in question had been acquired for a task that wasn't innocent at all; they
had done everything to conceal their activities. They were treating this
like a secret mission, using special technology."

Intelligence operatives immediately began tracking the activities of
the people involved in the purchase and the handling of the ship, and
searching for any tiny piece of information that might lead them to crack
the mystery of the *Karine A*. In early December, they had assembled a
partial picture of the Palestinian operation: the ship had been purchased
in the summer of 2001 by Palestinians using multiple straw companies.
Fearing detection by the Mossad or other intelligence organizations, the
Palestinians changed the ship's name, *Rim K*, to *Karine A*. As eagle-eyed Israeli Mossad agents watched, the ship sailed from Lebanon to Port Sudan,
where it was loaded with large quantities of rice, clothing, toys and house-
hold appliances, with plenty of space left over for the weapons awaiting

the ship at its next destination—Kish Island, off the coast of Iran. Under the darkness of night, an Iranian ferry loaded the *Karine A* with eighty-containers, each holding nearly eighteen hundred pounds of weaponry.

The ferry's Farsi-speaking crew provided the *Karine A* captain with a list of the containers' contents, as well as clear instructions for the rest of the trip. The weapons had been loaded into eighty sophisticated, buoyant, hermetically sealed containers built by Iran's military industry. When the *Karine A* approached Gaza, its crew would dump the containers in the water. Each container was equipped with a compartment that could contain water or air. When the compartment filled with water, the container would submerge; a diver would later approach and turn a switch, compressed air would displace the water, and the container would float to the surface. At this stage, small boats would collect the containers and bring them to the beaches of Gaza, where they'd be collected by Palestinian police personnel and brought to the terrorists.

After the ship was loaded, it set sail for the crucial leg of its journey. However, it was forced to dock for eleven days at the port of Hodeidah, in Yemen, because of technical problems. The stop in Yemen gave the IDF the vital time window it needed to plan and prepare for the seizure of the ship.

The ship and its lethal cargo in the port of Eilat.
(Jo Kot, Yedioth Ahronoth Archive)

In Chief of Staff Shaul Mofaz's office feverish discussions started, with the participation of the Shayetet commanders and air force and intelligence personnel. Maps were spread and operational plans submitted; everyone understood that the pivotal moment was growing close.

"What are you calling the operation?" Mofaz asked at one of the meetings.

"Noah's Ark," replied the head of the navy's operations division.

"A nice name," Mofaz smiled.

In the lead-up to the final decision, Chiney explained to the chief of staff, "Everything is based on the discovery of the ship. The moment we found out about it, the rest was simply a matter of scheduling."

Mofaz remained uneasy. "Will you be on one of the patrol boats?" he asked Chiney.

"Yes."

"You'll know how to process all the intelligence about the ship?"

"Yes."

"You'll also be able to positively identify it, what's on it, its dimensions?

"Definitely."

"Were you ever in the Straits of Tiran?"

"Many times."

"Now, then, how would you sail the ship through the Straits of Tiran?"

"It's not too complicated. All we need to know is how to start the ship's engine."

Mofaz summed up his position. "I cannot risk that this mission would fail. If you see that conditions in the sea are such that it can't be done, you must stop and think it over again; or you put this on hold temporarily, and we wait, let's say, for a day; or we let the ship go away."

A few days before the operation, the team went to the home of Prime Minister Ariel Sharon, presenting him with the details of the mission. Sharon listened, asked questions, requested a look at the maps and praised the operation's daring. He then authorized it, aware that its success depended on the precise coordination between the Shayetet commandos and the pilots of the helicopters from which they'd be rappelling down. "This is like jumping onto a truck on a winding road," a member of the Shayetet later said.

There remained some unresolved questions: Was the ship's crew armed? Was the hidden weaponry booby-trapped or loaded with explosive charges programmed to be operated remotely? Were there Palestinian fighters on board? The mission could become a bloodbath, if Palestinian armed terrorists were protecting the ship. To address all the contingencies it was decided that a Shayetet doctor and a medic would be part of the takeover team, and that one of the helicopters would be fully equipped for emergency surgery, if needed.

One night, shortly before the mission, the chief of staff and the operation's commanders watched a simulation during which Shayetet commandos rappelled onto a commercial ship from two helicopters. Mofaz was highly satisfied with the exercise. The commandos then departed to Eilat, where they would wait for the green light. But Mofaz and the intelligence experts were still preoccupied with the ultimate question: Where was the ship? Why couldn't they locate it? They knew without a doubt that it was making its way toward the Suez Canal, but a definitive ID was missing. Only a few days later, on January 1, 2002, the chief of staff received word that the *Karine A* had been conclusively identified, forty miles north of Jedda, Saudi Arabia, at a distance of four hundred miles from the area where the takeover was planned. The last reports noted that the ship's name, *Karine A*, was written clearly and prominently on the ship's hull.

On the morning of D Day, the various units began moving toward their destination. Chiney boarded a "Dvora" patrol boat, while Shayetet commander Ram Rotenberg boarded a helicopter alongside his fighters. About two hours before H-Hour, Mofaz and officers from the navy and Air force climbed onto the special Boeing that would fly them above the Red Sea area where the takeover would unfold.

Even before the operation began, the Boeing's passengers were glued to their monitor screens; they watched Chiney and his command team at sea, trying to identify the *Karine A*, which finally appeared on the radar in the middle of a group of ships twenty miles from the takeover point. Using various indicators they attempted to determine which ship was the *Karine A* but without success. An IAF patrol plane was also unable to identify the target, due to a dense fog covering the waters. The navy's small flotilla drew closer to the group of ships. So as not to be identified, Chiney grouped the vessels in a unique formation, with a patrol boat in front and a patrol boat in the back and the rubber boats in between; from a distance, they looked like a single big ship.

The tension on the boats and in the Boeing kept growing. The window of opportunity was getting shorter—they needed to complete the mission by 4:15 A.M.; the choppers couldn't stay in the area a minute longer.

Chiney continued to calculate the timing and geographical issues, and decided the operation had to begin at 3:45.

"But where is the ship?" wondered a Shayetet officer. "Where the hell did it disappear? Could it have managed to get away?"

Suddenly, about 4.5 miles away, a Shayetet intelligence officer spotted a ship with a prominent smokestack, three loading cranes and a mast at its center, the distinctive characteristics of the *Karine A*. The report quickly climbed up the chain of command, and the excitement grew. The ship had been found.

It was three-forty. Now they began moving closer to the ship, which was growing increasingly visible. The Israeli force raised its speed and came within very close range, almost next to it. Shaul Mofaz asked again for clear confirmation. "That's the ship! That's the ship!" came the answer from below.

The moment of decision was approaching. All the senior officers on the Boeing remained glued to their monitors, where they could follow the takeover from start to finish; the process looked like a Hollywood thriller.

At four the electronic signal flashed through the flotilla receivers. That was the go-ahead for Noah's Ark, which began at once. From above, the officers in the Boeing could see the Shayetet fighters bursting from the sea and air onto the *Karine A* deck, surprising the thirteen-member crew, the majority of whom were asleep. They could make out that no gun battle was taking place on the ship, and could identify the Shayetet commanders conducting a preliminary search for the weapons. Most important of all, and unbelievably, the entire operation lasted just seven minutes.

A sigh of relief could be heard aboard the Boeing, and Chief of Staff Mofaz hurried to call the officers below. He congratulated them without concealing his happiness: "You did wonderful work! From above, it looked amazing. What now? What's the next stage?"

"We've completed the takeover, and our forces are doing a sweep," Shayetet Colonel Ram Rotenberg responded.

"Are you seeing anything yet?" Mofaz persisted, seeking a smoking gun, weaponry that would prove to the world—and to the United States in particular—that Yasser Arafat was engaged in smuggling Iranian arms into the Palestinian territories.

"Not yet—right now we're going down into the holds. We'll report back the moment we find something," the commander replied.

Chiney, who in the meantime had boarded the ship, rushed to the cargo hold with the Shayetet commander. With flashlights, they illuminated the area but couldn't find a thing. A few minutes went by, but the search bore no fruit. They saw nothing but bags of rice, bundles of clothes and children's toys. "We can't see anything, not a weapon and not a mortar," one of the searchers blurted out in despair. For a moment, an appalling doubt stole into their hearts: Had they captured the right ship? Was Noah's Ark a failure? Had they risked their lives for nothing?

And then came the turning point. A quick, rough interrogation of the ship's captain, Omar Akawi, an employee of the Palestinian transportation ministry, yielded results. A commando fighter considered the Shayetet tough guy began shaking him with no excessive gentleness, and the confession wasn't long in coming. "It's in the forward hold," Akawi ultimately blurted.

The commandos hurried to the bow. "We initially thought that we hadn't found anything," Lieutenant Colonel G recalled. "But we discovered the first crate, then the second, and a sense of great pride overwhelmed us. It was the first time we encountered such quantities of weapons. Every Katyusha launcher that was uncovered was accompanied by a round of applause, and the guys greatly rejoiced."

The soldiers took over the vessel commands and the ship was turned toward the Gulf of Eilat. One of the commandos ran to his officer. "We need to raise the Israeli flag," he said.

"But we don't have one," the officer countered.

"We do. I brought it from home," the commando said.

A few hours later, an Israeli flag flowing from its mast, *Karine A* docked in Eilat. The methodical search revealed that the ship had been loaded with sixty-four tons of weaponry, including Katyusha rockets, Sagger anti-tank missiles, Israeli-made mortars (that had been supplied to Iran before Khomeini's takeover), rocket-propelled grenade launchers, Ra'ad missiles, various kinds of rifles and land mines. "All this was an internal Iranian affair," a senior officer joked, "their Iranians were beaten by our Iranians, Mofaz and Halutz [both officers of Iranian origin]."

The day after the operation, Prime Minister Sharon hosted American General Anthony Zinni at his farm. At the end of the meeting, he told him, "You can tell Yasser Arafat, when you see him today, that he needn't worry about his weapons ship, the *Karine A*. We got it, and it's in our hands."

After the story went public, the United States cut its ties with the Palestinian Authority for an extended period. President Bush was furious that Arafat had lied to him, and that was one of the reasons the Americans would soon give their approval to Operation Defensive Shield.

SHAUL MOFAZ, THEN IDF'S CHIEF OF STAFF, LATER MINISTER OF DEFENSE

"The story of the *Karine A*, beyond the smuggling of fifty tons of weapons and terror supplies from Iran to the Palestinians, is about the agreement between them, according to which the Palestinians, in exchange for the weapons they received, would give the Iranians a foothold within the Palestinian Authority. Its significance was the entry of Iran's Revolutionary Guards into the cities of the West Bank.

"When we received the intelligence about this, it was clear

that we needed to take control of the ship in order to capture the weaponry and—no less important—to expose Arafat's true face as a terror leader to the world.

"After the Shayetet and the air force's amazing operation, Prime Minister Arik Sharon decided to send me to the White House to present Condoleezza Rice, the national security adviser, with all the intelligence that we'd acquired and to reveal the deal reached between Arafat and the Iranians. She looked over the material, astonished, and ran with it to President Bush. She asked if I could stay in Washington; I said that I could not because the Intifada was at its worst. This material led to President Bush's famous declaration that the Palestinian Authority is a terror organization.

"The central dilemma during the operation had been conclusively identifying the ship. The fear was that if we couldn't identify it with one hundred percent certainty, we might mistakenly capture another country's ship, something that could cause great trouble. Consequently, when I boarded the Boeing command post, the first thing I asked for was to see the ship's identification on the radar."

In 1993, Israel and the PLO have signed the Oslo Accords,
hoping to reach a peace solution soon. Unfortunately,
the accords fail and a new wave of terrorism sweeps Israel.
After a stunning increase in suicide bombings by Palestinians,
Prime Minister Sharon and Defense Minister Benyamin Ben
Eliezer launch a large-scale operation in the West Bank,
targeting the terrorist organizations. The operation is directed
by Chief of Staff Shaul Mofaz.

CHAPTER 24

HOLOCAUST REMEMBRANCE DAY IN THE NABLUS QASBAH, 2002

On the rainy, stormy night of March 29, 2002, an IDF force entered Ramallah, the capital of Yasser Arafat's Palestinian Authority. The troops' raid on his headquarters, the Mukataa, was carried out on foot, and wasn't met by particularly intense Palestinian resistance. Avi Peled, the commander of the Egoz Commando Unit, later remarked, "We knew that, for the Palestinians, the Mukataa was the end of the line, the holy of holies. We were sure that they would fight us till the last bullet. But apparently our entrance into the Mukataa and the Palestinian Preventive Security headquarters in Beitunia had broken them psychologically, and their resistance collapsed everywhere."

That was the start of Operation Defensive Shield, one of the IDF's largest-ever operations in the West Bank, territories also referred to by Israelis as Judea and Samaria. The goal was to strike at the area's terrorist organizations and to stop a wave of terror attacks that had reached unprecedented numbers. During the preceding month, referred to as

Black March, 135 Israelis had been killed by terror attacks, eleven of them suicide bombings within Israel's pre-1967 borders. The low point was a terrorist attack on a Passover seder in the Park Hotel, in Netanya: a suicide bomber entered the hotel undetected and killed thirty guests and wounded 140 others celebrating around the Passover table.

The horrifying images broadcast in Israel and around the world that night melted American objections to an Israeli military response. The next day, the government authorized Operation Defensive Shield and mobilized thirty thousand reservists. Called up for the operation were the Golani, Nahal, Yiftach and paratrooper brigades, as well as both regular soldiers and reservists in the infantry, armored and engineering corps. At the Knesset, Prime Minister Ariel Sharon explained the goals of the operation: "The IDF's soldiers and their commanders will go into cities and villages that have become shelters for terrorists, to capture and detain terrorists and, above all, those who dispatch them, to seize and confiscate weapons and fighting supplies intended to hit Israel, and to uncover and wipe out terror installations, terror laboratories, weapons-creation factories and hideouts."

In Ramallah. the IDF demolished the buildings of the Mukataa compound, except for the structure that housed Arafat himself. Fighters from the Egoz commando took positions in rooms along the corridor leading to Arafat's office, while outside, Israeli tanks encircled the site. Sheltered within the Mukataa's detention center were several fugitive criminals involved in terror activities against Israel. The head of Palestinian intelligence had ordered them clandestinely brought into Arafat's compound, under the assumption that they would be safe there from the IDF. After a lengthy standoff, the Americans had intervened, and the fugitives were transferred to a prison in Jericho under British oversight.

In Ramallah, the IDF had uncovered weapons labs and captured scores of fugitive men and materiel. Toward the end of the fighting, it had seized Marwan Barghouti, the commander of the Fatah armed faction, the Tanzim; Barghouti would be later sentenced to life in prison for his numerous terror attacks.

The siege in Ramallah. *(Yoav Guterman, GPO)*

From Ramallah, on to Nablus. Nablus was considered a stronghold of Palestinian resistance, and its Qasbah, a maze of narrow, tortuous streets and convoluted passages had become a source of dread for the IDF's General Staff, which was deeply concerned with the risks of fighting there. Densely populated, the Qasbah contained booby-trapped homes, sniper positions and a great number of terrorists. Hundreds of them hid in the crooked alleys, IEDs were planted everywhere and gas containers were buried in the ground, ready to explode. The IDF elite soldiers braced themselves before approaching the Qasbah, expecting bloody surprises at every street corner.

The assault on Nablus began on April 5, with the operation under the command of Brigadier General Yitzhak ("Jerry") Gershon, chief of the Judea and Samaria Division. He orchestrated the movements of the paratrooper brigade, which came from the west; Golani, which approached from the south, and the armored Yiftach Brigade, which occupied the eastern part of the city, including its hostile refugee camps. The Palestinians had planted dozens of mines within delivery trucks and water tanks lining the roadways, and IDF engineers systematically defused them, one by one.

The paratroopers attacked the Qasbah from all sides simultaneously. Their secret weapon was a revolutionary battle method: passing through walls. The paratroopers had developed various instruments allowing them to break walls with heavy sledgehammers or blow large holes in them and thus move from one house to another without even stepping into the murderous streets. That method had been used for the first time a month and a half earlier, during the seizure of the nearby Balata refugee camp. Aviv Kochavi, the commander of the paratrooper brigade, explained that, "in the crowded Qasbah, where the narrow streets contained numerous mines and obstacles, and where snipers could shoot from every corner, we developed an alternative system of fighting: we moved exclusively through the walls and buildings to surprise the enemy, who alone was left to circulate in the alleyways, becoming an exposed target. The strategy kept the enemy disoriented and vulnerable to our fire, which caught it off guard largely from the sides, from behind or from above."

In the Qasbah, the gangs of terrorists concentrated under a single command. Most of the fugitive Palestinian fighters, the majority of them Tanzim and the minority Hamas, had also holed up there. With great determination, the Palestinians fought with Kalashnikovs and M-16s, prepared to die as "martyrs."

But the soldiers of the IDF were also highly determined. The battle in the Qasbah moved from house to house. The goal was to limit, at all costs, the number of IDF fighters wounded in battle, and as a result, it was decided that a small operational force would be sent every few minutes to the houses where the terrorists were positioned. The terrorists would begin shooting, thereby exposing themselves to the fire of Israeli snipers waiting on the opposite side. The alleyways were left to the fugitive fighters, and the IDF made use of sniper positions in the homes. Israeli gunmen charged out of unexpected places and hit Palestinians who had prepared to fire on troops that were farther away.

By the third day of the war, the IDF was already in control of two-thirds of the Qasbah. Lieutenant Colonel Ofek Buhris, the commander of the 51st Battalion, had been deployed to Nablus with his soldiers after fighting in the Mukataa and Jenin, and was in charge of locating explosives' labs and capturing fugitives. He was assigned to entrap Ali Hadiri, one of Hamas's senior engineers, who had prepared the explosive that blew up at the Park Hotel in Netanya. During the raid on the house where the terrorist was staying, a hail of gunfire burst from within, killing a company commander in the Golani Brigade and badly wounding Buhris. Golani soldiers broke into the house and killed Hadiri and another terrorist.

On April 8 at about 7:00 A.M., all of a sudden, dozens of Palestinians emerged from one of the Qasbah houses, their arms in the air. The surrender of the terrorists had begun. Reports arrived hourly of additional groups turning themselves in; by the afternoon, further surrender deals were being proposed through the Shin Bet and the Civil Administration, Israel's governing body in the West Bank. By six-thirty that evening, the last of the armed men had left the houses of the Nablus Qasbah, their arms raised and waving improvised white flags as a sign of surrender. After seventy-two hours of fighting, seventy terrorists had been killed and hundreds arrested.

But the battle that would become most identified with Operation Defensive Shield would take place in Jenin, remembered because of the number of Israeli casualties—twenty-three dead and seventy-five wounded—and because of Palestinian claims of a massacre carried out by the IDF in the city's refugee camp.

The armed Palestinians, massed at the center of the camp, had laid a trap of thousands of explosive devices and had set up numerous ambushes in the camp's narrow alleyways. Israel's soldiers entered the camp with the assistance of tanks, assault helicopters and D9 bulldozers, which cleared explosives and opened booby-trapped doors. Progress was slow, with Palestinian snipers firing on the troops and making their advance difficult.

On the seventh day of action, a group of reservists from the Nahshon Brigade were caught in an ambush that killed thirteen soldiers. Their comrades charged the terrorists in an effort to rescue the wounded, but that resulted in more injuries. In the raid's aftermath, the IDF decided to change procedure and destroy every house in which terrorists could hide. The policy included a warning to armed Palestinian fighters to surrender before the bulldozers began their work, which convinced many, among them the most senior terrorists, to turn themselves in. A high-ranking member of Islamic Jihad, Mahmoud Tawalbeh, was killed after refusing to surrender, when a D9 bulldozer caused a wall to collapse on him in the house where he was hiding.

During the fighting, rumors were spread of a massacre carried out by the IDF in Jenin's refugee camp; the Palestinians even cited three thousand as the number killed. The international media accepted the Palestinian claims unquestioningly, until a UN investigative committee arrived on the scene and determined that the real figure was just fifty-six. The IDF claimed that the vast majority of the dead Palestinians were armed terrorists. It may be that the camp's complete closure to the media caused the proliferation of the rumors throughout the world.

The city of Bethlehem was seized by the Jerusalem reservist brigade. Immediately after their entry into Bethlehem, the troops detained dozens of fugitives and quickly gained control of the ancient town. But about forty armed terrorists barricaded themselves in the Church of the Nativity. The IDF, aware of the location's great importance for the rest of the world, had sent the Shaldag commando unit to block off the terrorists' entrance into the church. But the air force ran into delays while flying in the soldiers, and dozens of terrorists managed to hole up in the church, certain that the Israeli forces wouldn't enter or arrest them.

Leading the armed men was Colonel Abdallah Daoud, the head of Palestinian intelligence in Nablus, who took as hostages the forty-six priests staying in the church and roughly two hundred other civilians, among them children. The IDF imposed a blockade on the church for thirty-four days, disrupting the supply of food and water in order to break the will of the wanted men. The Vatican cautioned Israel not to damage the church.

On May 10, 2002, the standoff concluded after Israel agreed to the expulsion of 13 of the fugitives to 6 European countries, as well as the transfer of 26 others to Gaza. During the blockade, six Palestinians were killed, and Israel captured documents revealing that the residents of Bethlehem, principally Christians, had suffered from harassment by armed men belonging to the Tanzim and Al Aqsa Martyrs Brigades.

Over the course of Operation Defensive Shield, five of the six Palestinian cities in the West Bank were occupied. Within a short period, and at a cost of thirty-four dead soldiers, Israel succeeded in putting a stop to the vicious wave of terror, severely degrading the military capability of the Palestinian Authority, isolating Arafat, capturing a great number of fugitives and uncovering vast quantities of explosives and other weapons.

AVIV KOCHAVI, COMMANDER OF THE PARATROOPERS BRIGADE AND LATER THE DIRECTOR OF MILITARY INTELLIGENCE

"The battle of the Qasbah ended precisely on Holocaust Remembrance Day. The entire brigade was dispersed throughout the Qasbah and the rest of Nablus, after a series of intense battles and a decisive victory over the armed fighters. I decided that we wouldn't give up on marking this special day. We set up a public address system and high-powered speakers, and turned on the radio at the moment of the memorial siren, which echoed through the entire area. Just hours after the end of the battle, all the soldiers of the paratroopers brigade stood at attention in memory of the victims.

"It was a very emotional moment and has remained engraved in my memory for two reasons: first, because we proved—against the backdrop, fittingly, of Holocaust Remembrance Day—that there's no place we won't go in order to defeat terror and defend the citizens of Israel. And second, by implementing innovative, sophisticated tactics, we proved that it's possible to do battle in a manner that is simultaneously resolute, professional and ethical, despite fighting in a built-up, crowded area against numerous terrorists. More than seventy terrorists were killed by the brigade, and hundreds were wounded or captured.

"The battle ended with the surrender of the terrorists: after they were squeezed and surrounded on all sides, their leader called the representative of District Coordination, who was with me at the command post, and asked to organize his surrender with three hundred of his men. We arranged the terms, and the terrorists marched to a specified location, where they turned over their weapons and were arrested."

YITZHAK ("JERRY") GERSHON, COMMANDER OF THE WEST BANK DIVISION AND LATER OF THE HOME FRONT COMMAND

"An all-out war on terror was being waged in Judea and Samaria when I assumed my functions as commander of the West Bank Division. The IDF had been fighting terrorists for ten months but, for various reasons, hadn't looked its best. I felt that the weighty task of providing security had been placed on my shoulders, and I understood that it was me and the forces under my authority who would make the difference. We changed the operational paradigm and led hundreds of special operations, some in refugee camps.

"The change was felt on the ground and yielded meaningful operational successes. More and more commanders and decision makers at the level of the military staff reached the sensible conclusion that it was our obligation to decide the fate of this war that had been forced upon us.

"When Defensive Shield was authorized, two operations of the most sensitive nature were assigned to us: Ramallah and Nablus. Ramallah was the site and seat of Arafat's power and the center of the Palestinian Authority; Nablus was the terror capital. The character of the operations resembled that of the intensive activity that preceded Defensive Shield, requiring initiative and aggressiveness, determination and creative thinking. The operation highlighted the intelligent integration of all the components of military force, along with tight coordination with Shin Bet, the Internal Security Service.

"Defensive Shield achieved a physical and psychological turning point in the Palestinian terror in Judea and Samaria."

In 2005, Prime Minister Ariel Sharon unilaterally retreats from the Gaza Strip. The Jewish settlements are evacuated and the settlers forced to leave their homes and seek new homes in Israel. The IDF pulls out all its forces from the Strip. Israel's leaders hoped that Gaza, now fully independent, will devote all its efforts to building a thriving economy and a prosperous free society.

The opposite happens. The Hamas terrorist organization seizes power in Gaza and turns it into a base of bloody, incessant attacks on Israel's civilian population.

CHAPTER 25

THE NEVER-ENDING STORY IN GAZA: 2008, 2012, 2014

"Cast Lead," 2008

On December 27, 2008, at 11:30 A.M., several F-15 jets of the IAF dived over scores of targets all over the Gaza Strip. The lead plane launched its missiles on Arafat City, a large government complex in the center of Gaza. The attack targeted a graduation ceremony for police cadets, most of them members of the "Izz al-Din al-Qassam," Hamas's death squads. The other jets, and a few helicopters, launched massive aerial bombings on roughly one hundred Hamas targets across the Gaza Strip. In a few minutes they pulverized command posts, armories, underground rocket and missile launchers, and the organization's training sites. Operation Cast Lead had begun.

This first round of bombing caught Hamas completely off guard and unprepared. One hundred fifty-five terrorists were killed, eighty-nine of them at the police graduation ceremony.

As the campaign continued, the air force assaulted forty tunnels in the Philadelphi Corridor (a narrow strip along the border of Gaza and

Egypt) with bunker-busting bombs, in order to disrupt the smuggling of arms from Egypt. Strategic targets were also blown up, the objective being to undermine Hamas rule: government offices, television studios, the central prison, the general intelligence building, the city hall in Beit Hanoun, the Islamic University and more.

"We're talking about a great number of aircraft in a very small area with the goal of attacking buildings in very crowded places, where any misfire could hit a school or nursery," former IAF brigadier-general Ran Pecker-Ronen told the journalist Amir Bohbot. "Their accuracy was amazing, the execution perfect. I don't believe there's another air force in the world capable of carrying out these sorts of attacks at such a high level of precision."

The Israeli government, headed by Ehud Olmert, decided to launch Cast Lead after a large-scale, prolonged barrage of thousands of Qassam rockets on the towns and cities near Gaza. For many months, residents of the area had lived in fear, forced to sleep in safety rooms and bomb shelters. It was an absurd situation; no other nation in the world would have accepted being subjected to the daily firing of rockets on its civilian population. The cease-fire that had been reached via Egyptian mediation in June 2008 had collapsed completely, and Israel's southern region was subject to a real war, in which Palestinians fired rockets, Israel responded with bombings by the air force, and the pattern continued. The residents of the south were paying the price.

The objective of Cast Lead would be to end the Palestinian missile fire, destroy Hamas operational abilities and prevent its rearmament.

The IDF received authorization to carry out targeted killings, and eliminated senior members of Hamas and Islamic Jihad one after another, among them Said Siam, the Hamas government's interior minister; his brother Iyad Siam, another Hamas senior official; and Nizar Rayan, number three in Hamas's political wing. Rayan was killed when his home was bombed from the air; he died along with eighteen friends and relatives who had stayed in the house in spite of the IAF warnings. The building in which he lived had served as a command post, communications center, storage facility for weaponry and ammunitions, and a tunnel entrance.

The Southern District commander, General Yoav Galant, told the journalist Shmuel Haddad, "In the past, each Hamas commander built himself a three-story house, in which the basement level served as a storage area for materiel, the middle level as a command post, and the family lived on the third floor. For years, they assumed that the IDF wouldn't strike the building because of the family. We've changed the paradigm, warning the family by a telephone call and by firing a small, harmless 'knock on the roof' warning missile. Later, the building is bombed, and from then on the Hamas terrorist is left to worry about the fact that he has neither a command station nor a home for his family."

On January 3, the IDF launched the operation's second stage with the shelling of Gaza and the entrance of ground forces into the Strip's northern end. The offensive was intended to seize missile-launching areas, to cut off Gaza City from the rest of the Strip and increase the damage that the IDF was inflicting on Hamas, principally at points where the air force had no advantage—like armories, tunnels, bunkers and underground command posts. Ten thousand reservists fought alongside twenty thousand regular soldiers.

The forces fought primarily on built-up territory, facing ambushes, suicide bombers, and booby-trapped houses. It was a house-to-house— and, at times, face-to-face fight—battle. Homes used for terrorist activity or found to be booby-trapped were razed; during the fighting, roughly six hundred houses were destroyed.

Israel's offensive in Gaza began with the Golani, Givati and the paratrooper brigades breaking into the Strip from different and unanticipated directions. Merkava tanks of the armored 188th "Lightning" Brigade, which had defended the Golan Heights in the Yom Kippur War, blocked the passage from Rafiah and Khan Younis to Gaza City, thus disrupting the supply of arms to Hamas. The 401st Brigade, nicknamed "Iron Trails," established a buffer zone in the center of the strip, by the former settlement of Netzarim. IDF engineers, often employing mini-robots, defused explosives and booby-trapped houses. Saving the soldiers' lives was the mission's top priority; consequently, massive efforts were spent preventing unnecessary risks, even at the cost of civilians being hit.

Cast Lead—the fighters at the gates of Gaza.
(Neil Cohen, IDF Spokesman)

"The entry into Gaza was relatively quick," said a senior officer after the battle. "We felt that Hamas was in shock, which in turn significantly undermined the resistance they had prepared. The houses were packed very close together, with a portion of them booby-trapped. There were also motorcycles at the ready for abductions. Almost every other hour, there was an attempt by a male or female suicide bomber to run at us and detonate an explosive belt. In the booby-trapped houses, we found shafts leading to tunnels designated for kidnapping soldiers."

On January 6, the Palestinians claimed that an IDF mortar had killed thirty people sheltered at the al-Fahoura school, a facility run by UNRWA, the United Nations Relief and Works Agency. The shell had targeted the school yard, where a rocket had been launched at Israel; in response, the IDF had fired three mortars. Two hit the school yard, killing two of the terrorists in action, while the third errantly struck the neighboring school, thirty yards away. But an investigation by Canada's *Globe and Mail* revealed that, contrary to Palestinian reports, not thirty people but just three had been killed by shrapnel, when they had gone outside the building.

Hamas's ability to resist the IDF operation was weaker than the Israelis had anticipated. The Palestinians intensified the rocket fire into Israeli territory; over the course of Cast Lead, 730 rockets were launched into Israel, among them long-range Grad weapons that reached Ashdod, Ashkelon, Yavne and Be'er Sheva.

Hamas systematically fired from houses of civilians, whose lives it did not hesitate to put at risk. An IDF officer found a document that contained Hamas's battle plan, including the deployment of terror teams next to a mosque, the placement of large improvised explosive devices (IEDs) in a heavily populated area and even the booby-trapping of schools and the zoo. Yuval Diskin, then the head of the Shin Bet, Israel's domestic intelligence service, told journalists, "A considerable portion of the activists are hiding in hospitals, some at Shifa, some in maternity hospitals. A few are going around in doctors' and nurses' uniforms." The Shifa hospital director categorically denied his statements.

One incident seared into the public consciousness was the death of three daughters of Izzeldin Abuelaish, a Palestinian doctor who had for years worked in hospitals in Israel. Two IDF tank shells had struck his home in Jabalia, killing the three girls and injuring another. At the moment of the attack, Dr. Abuelaish was speaking with TV Channel 10 reporter Shlomi Eldar. Crying out hysterically, he pleaded with the journalist, a friend, to ask the IDF to stop shooting at his home. The IDF subsequently claimed that it had targeted the home because of shooting originating from there.

After twenty-two days of fighting, Prime Minister Olmert stopped the operation, rejecting the third stage proposed by General Galant—to cut off the Gaza Strip from Sinai. Olmert declared a unilateral cease-fire: "Hamas's military capabilities and control infrastructure have been hit hard. The present campaign has once again proven Israel's strength and deterrence capability."

On the Israeli side, thirteen had been killed, among them ten soldiers. According to IDF estimates, 1,166 Palestinians were killed, 709 of them members of Hamas. The Palestinians counted 1,417 dead. Four thousand homes were entirely destroyed, along with 48 public and government buildings.

Operation Cast Lead produced severe damage to Israel's international image. On September 15, 2009, Richard Goldstone, a South African former judge appointed by the UN Human Rights Council, submitted a scathing report to the UN portraying Israel as having committed war crimes and "crimes against humanity."

In April 2011, however, Goldstone made his mea culpa in a *Washington Post* article, admitting that his report hadn't been accurate and contained unjust accusations againt Israel. "If I had known then what I know now," he wrote, "the Goldstone Report would have been a different document."

YOAV GALANT, HEAD OF ISRAEL'S SOUTHERN COMMAND

"We embarked on the operation in order to hit Hamas and create deterrence, and to force it to halt its missile fire for an extended period. No less important, in my eyes, was the need to sear into its consciousness that it would pay a heavy price for targeting Israel's citizens and sovereignty. Hamas was surprised by the timing of the action, the force of the attack and the wide-scale entry of ground forces into its territory, as well as by the timing of the withdrawal and the speed with which it was carried out.

"This was the first time that the IDF struck at Hamas so comprehensively. The attack was carried out in a focused, continuous, intensive way, with thousands of bombs dropped on hundreds of targets, among them command posts, weapons caches, tunnels, bunkers and government offices. The ground maneuvers were performed by strengthened battalion forces, and at any given moment, there were seven thousand fighters within the Strip. The IDF achieved tight coordination between our intelligence and air, sea and land forces.

"Two weeks after the start of the operation, I recommended
to the chief of staff that we carry out the third stage of the
original plan: to cut the Gaza Strip off from Sinai by encircling
and occupying Rafiah. This process would have brought about a
disruption of the pipeline used for weapons smuggling, suicide
bombers and more. But the plan wasn't authorized because it
might have led to great losses."

Four years later...

PILLAR OF DEFENSE, 2012

The electronic signal flashed across the navigation system of the drone,
which, according to the London *Sunday Times*, was circling above the
mosques and refugee camps of Gaza. The drone dived toward Gaza City
center. Its cameras scanned the streets, focusing on a silver Kia carrying
a tracking device, which crossed an intersection and turned into Omar
Mukhtar Street.

The passenger of the Kia was Ahmed Jabari, Hamas's chief of staff.
He had become the commander of Hamas's military wing in 2003, after
his predecessor, Mohammed Deif, was severely wounded during an Israeli Air Force attack. Jabari, a member of a Hebron-based clan, had
been imprisoned in Israel for thirteen years because of terrorist activities. When he was freed, in 1995, he became a key Hamas figure, managing overseas relations, fund-raising and the planning of terror attacks.
As Hamas's military chief of staff, he oversaw weapons production, the
use of mortars and rockets, the smuggling of arms, and other military
and intelligence activity. Jabari had directed dozens of terror operations
against Israeli citizens, as well as the firing of Qassam rockets into Israeli territory; he was responsible for the kidnapping of Gilad Shalit and
had signed the agreement for his return.

To the IDF, Jabari, fifty-two, was mortal. He knew it and took meticulous security precautions. Foreign sources claim that he told no one
where he spent his nights or which vehicles he would use; he occasion-

ally even disguised himself by wearing women's clothes. In the past twenty-four hours, he had been closely watched with the help of Shabak agents; their reports revealed that Jabari had spent the night in a certain house in Gaza, parking his vehicle outside. Lurking in the skies above was a surveillance aircraft belonging to the air force's Squadron 100. And so, on November 14, at 3:45 in the afternoon, a Shabak operations director in Tel Aviv received a fateful telephone call from Gaza: within three minutes, one of the several cars serving Jabari would depart from a certain address in Gaza. The Shabak agent added that he would provide an additional warning thirty seconds later.

Without wasting a moment, the operative in Tel Aviv informed the head of the Shabak, Yoram Cohen, who in his turn called the IDF chief of staff, Benny Gantz, and Prime Minister Benyamin Netanyahu. When confirmation arrived thirty seconds later from al-Mukhtar Street, Amikam Norkin, head of Air Force Operations, was sitting, ready and waiting, in the command room at military headquarters in Tel Aviv. The air force drone was approaching Jabari's car. At 3:55, Norkin gave the order: "Go!"

The drone's systems zeroed in on the silver Kia. An electronic signal activated the drone's firing system. Two missiles detached from the fuselage, plunging toward the car. An enormous explosion echoed along the two-way street, and the car was obliterated in a cloud of fire. When the smoke dissipated, passersby pulled the corpses of Ahmed Jabari and another passenger, Raed al-Atar, a commander of Hamas's southern division. Thousands of Gaza residents streamed to the site, sounding calls for revenge.

That was how, at 4:00 P.M. on November 14, 2012, Operation Pillar of Defense began. The final unraveling at the Gaza border had begun a week earlier, when a few border skirmishes culminated with a massive barrage of rockets and mortars unleashed by Hamas, its rockets hitting Israeli communities near Gaza, as well as the larger cities of Ashkelon and Ashdod. Israel could no longer tolerate such assaults, which had increased in frequency during the previous months. Hamas had willingly violated the terms of the cease-fire with Israel, reached after Cast Lead.

Once again, the IDF had to deal a stunning blow to Hamas, to restore deterrence and quiet.

Pillar of Defense—back to Gaza.
(Gil Nehushtan, Yedioth Ahronoth Archive)

Jabari's assassination would be the crushing blow that would launch the operation, which had been decided upon just the day before by the Israeli cabinet—the inner circle of political leaders, headed by Netanyahu. Among them were Defense Minister Ehud Barak, Foreign Minister Avigdor Lieberman and Minister of Homefront Defense Avi Dichter. The decision had been obscured by a smokescreen of conciliatory declarations about Gaza by the prime minister and the defense minister during a visit to Israel's northern border. This deception was perhaps the reason that Jabari, typically so fastidious about his own security, felt such inexplicable confidence that day—a mistake that would cost him his life.

The task was assigned almost entirely to the air force. Israel had learned the lessons of Cast Lead, which had set off a surge of criticism around the world because of harm caused to Palestinian civilians. This time, Israel envisioned a surgical operation that would hit terrorists and their installations but would, as much as possible, spare the lives of civilians. Minutes after Jabari's assassination, the first wave of air force planes pounced on Gaza, attacking Hamas training camps in the north, as well as storage facilities and launch sites that housed long-range Fajar

5 missiles, which could travel seventy-five kilometers and hit Tel Aviv and Jerusalem. This was an impressive military and intelligence accomplishment, drastically diminishing Hamas's ability to fire into major population centers and wiping out years of intense, secretive efforts by the organization to smuggle and produce missiles. By the end of the first day, Hamas's long-range strategic capabilities had been almost entirely eliminated. But, after recovering from the initial shock, Hamas responded forcefully, firing more than sixty rockets at Israel's southern towns. In response, Israel immediately activated Iron Dome, its new missile-interception system, bringing down twenty-four rockets.

By evening, it had become clear to Israel's civilian population that the operation wasn't a one-off strike, but that it might last for several days. On the campaign's second day, Hamas and Islamic Jihad renewed the shooting toward towns near Gaza, with missiles also fired at several Negev towns and, for the first time, Tel-Aviv and Jerusalem. In Tel-Aviv, the sound of real sirens was heard for the first time since the first Gulf War, in 1991. But the hardest, most painful strike was on Kiryat Malachi.

At 9:52 A.M., a Grad missile hit a residential building, killing three people and wounding six, among them two children. "At the time of the siren," a neighbor said, "we went to the stairwell. After a few minutes, we heard a huge explosion in the building—we heard screams from the top floor and then saw our neighbor coming down with two wounded girls. . . . The neighbor who was killed had been standing on his balcony and had been trying to photograph the barrage of missiles. He took a direct hit."

Only a handful of the hundreds of missiles launched at Israel would hit their targets, but they caused heavy damage and trauma. Yet the Israeli public responded stoically, without panic, supporting the operation without regard to political outlook or social views.

By November 15, the air force had blown up 450 targets, among them seventy subterranean rocket-launch sites. But in the same period, more than three hundred rockets and mortars were fired at Israel. The leaders of Hamas, Egypt and Turkey boiled and raged against Israel, but the enlightened world took its side. Leaders of the European Union and others expressed unequivocal support for Israel's right to defend itself; the most effusive of all came from the president of the United States, Barack Obama, who took Israel's side while denouncing the terrorists of Hamas and Islamic Jihad. Under Obama's heavy pressure, President Morsi of Egypt changed course, ending his attacks on Israel and beginning feverish work to reach a cease-fire. But in the interim, the fighting continued. Day after day, air force planes and naval ships pounded Hamas nerve centers in Gaza, and day after day, Hamas and Islamic Jihad fired hundreds of rockets on Israel's towns.

Yet, the IDF had imposed strict limitations on its response. "Each day, I needed to struggle with dilemmas that arose during the operation," said General Tal Russo, commander of the Southern District. "For example: we received intelligence that a certain Hamas commander was in his home, and we had to decide whether we would hit him there. I decided not to attack, so as not to hit people who weren't involved. The IDF's sensitivity and caution about not hurting such people saved the lives of many Hamas and Islamic Jihad commanders."

Egypt's Prime minister, Hisham Kandil, arrived in the Strip, and Israel ceased fire during his visit. Upon his departure, terrorists shot two rockets at Tel Aviv and one at Jerusalem, with all three intercepted or falling in open territory. The Israeli air force attacked smuggling tunnels and government buildings, television stations and bridges, the Islamic Bank and pipelines funneling gas and oil to the Strip. IAF aircraft hit the office of Hamas prime minister Ismail Haniyeh. Haniyeh was not in his office, of course; he was hiding underground with his colleagues, while their people were paying with their lives the bloody cost of Israel's incursion.

A fifth Iron Dome battery was placed in Tel Aviv and, within an hour, shot down a missile. The emir of Qatar, Turkey's prime minister, and senior Hamas and Islamic Jihad officials rushed to Cairo for discussions with Egypt about restoring the calm. Secretly, Israel sent over the head of the Mossad, Tamir Pardo.

Nevertheless, Gaza continued shooting. November 20, perhaps the worst day of fighting, saw heavy salvos of rockets fired from the Strip. Despite Iron Dome's successes, rockets and mortars struck a house in Be'er Sheva and killed three soldiers at the Eshkol area. In Rishon Lezion, a rocket destroyed the top three floors of a residential building but only slightly injured three people.

The following morning, after intensive mediation by Egypt, a cease-fire was reached, with the Palestinians pledging to halt all hostile activities and Israel ending its air force attacks.

In total, the Palestinians suffered 120 deaths, most of them armed fighters. Roughly 1,500 rockets had been fired at Israel, with 413 intercepted by Iron Dome.

Operation Pillar of Defense was over, but without a decisive result. Israel had landed a tough blow to Hamas and Islamic Jihad, destroying rockets and launchers and eliminating senior Hamas officials, chief among them the leader of its military wing. But Hamas and Islamic Jihad hadn't been broken and had continued firing barrages of rockets until the cease-fire. In several southern Israeli cities, spontaneous demonstrations demanded that the government continue the operation. The protesters and their supporters insisted that the cease-fire would be fragile and temporary, and that it wouldn't be long before Israel was forced to open a more extensive campaign against the Gaza terrorists.

T he protesters were right. Barely twenty months later, Israel was on the warpath again.

Protective Edge, 2014

The police officer who received the call during the night of June 12, 2014, dismissed it as a prank. Only later, when a worried father called, it was established that three teenagers, Eyal Yifrach (nineteen), Gilad Shaar (sixteen) and Naftali Frenkel (sixteen), students in yeshivas in the Etzion Bloc of settlements, had disappeared while trying to hitch-hike home. One of them had used his cell phone but his call had been interrupted. Soon the police found a burned-out car by the Dura Arab village, west of Hebron. It was clear that the boys had been abducted and the kidnapping car had been set on fire, while the terrorists and their captives had moved to another vehicle.

An unprecedented search was launched throughout the West Bank. Soon, reliable field agents reported that the boys had been abducted by Hamas terrorists; the IDF started arresting notorious Hamas militants throughout the West Bank. Thousands of Israeli soldiers were dispatched to towns, villages, fields, orchards and other areas where the captives might have been hidden or buried.

The entire nation followed with bated breath the search for the missing. The IDF mission was named Shuvu Achim—"Come back, brothers." The three distraught mothers pleaded on radio and TV with the kidnappers to release their sons. They even traveled to a meeting of the UN Human Rights Council in Geneva, a notorious anti-Israeli body, whose members listened in frosty silence to the mothers' passionate pleas. The nerve-wracking search continued for eighteen days. IDF intelligence experts discovered the identities of the kidnappers, two Hamas militants. Caves were penetrated, wells and septic tanks drained, houses inspected, hundreds of Hamas militants arrested and interrogated.

The boys were finally found in a shallow grave in a rocky, sun-parched field just north of Hebron. Israel was devastated by the cruel, senseless murder of the three innocent boys. Three Israeli right-wingers, motivated by insane lust for revenge, kidnapped and savagely murdered a sixteen-year-old Palestinian boy, Mohammed Abu Khdeir. Even though the police found out and arrested the murderers, the rage in the Palestinian community was immense. Many Palestinians had danced in the streets when they had learned that three Israeli boys had been assassinated, but now they sought revenge for the death of one of their own. The worst—and most unexpected—reaction came from the Gaza Strip. Hamas and the Islamic Jihad started shelling the civilian Israeli settlements and towns with scores of deadly rockets. Prime Minister Netanyahu didn't want to confront Hamas again in a new round of senseless fighting. He publicly declared that "quiet will be answered by quiet." But the nice words didn't work. The attacks from the Gaza Strip only increased. The IDF first reacted by precise bombings of strategic targets in Gaza, while repeating its calls for a cease-fire. But Hamas would not stop. Israel, left with no choice, concentrated large masses of soldiers and armor by the border. Yet the army didn't cross the border fence into Gaza. Netanyahu, Defense Minister Yaalon and Chief of Staff Gantz willingly accepted a cease-fire proposed by Egypt, but Hamas rejected it outright.

Then, on July 17, the ninth day of the conflict, IDF spotters suddenly noticed a group of Hamas fighters, armed to the teeth, virtually sprouting from the ground in Israeli territory, close to kibbutz Sufa. IDF commandos charged at them, probably shooting some, but the intruders collected their dead and wounded and vanished as they had come—in a masterfully camouflaged hole in the ground. The hole, it turned out, was the exit of an underground tunnel, running for more than a mile from a Hamas entry point inside the Gaza Strip, deep under the border fence and almost to the very gates of the kibbutz.

Two other attack tunnels had been discovered and destroyed since October 2013, but the new tunnel posed a deadly threat to both civilians and military in Otef Aza—the area "enveloping" the Gaza Strip. After long and strenuous deliberations the cabinet ordered the IDF to launch a ground offensive in the Gaza Strip, with one main objective— finding and destroying the tunnels.

Thousands of IDF soldiers and scores of tanks crossed the border and entered the outskirts of Gaza City, supported by artillery and the IAF. They warned the civilian population to evacuate certain neighborhoods where they intended to operate; a massive exodus started, but simultaneously Hamas fighters occupied the areas, tended ambushes and planted mines, side charges and other explosive devices, booby-trapping the houses where concealed tunnel shafts were located. This caused heavy street fighting. During the following weeks the IDF discovered 32 attack tunnels that ran for hundreds of yards, sometimes a few kilometers, from Gaza, at 70 to 75 feet under the border fence and ended chillingly close to Israeli kibbutzim and villages. They were reinforced by concrete walls, equipped with electricity and abounded with weapons, ammunition and explosive caches and niches where Israeli Army uniforms and headgear had been stocked. What would have happened to the south of Israel if these tunnels had not been discovered? Hundreds of terrorists, maybe more, might have penetrated into the country and conquered peaceful towns and villages, slaughtering their populations or holding them hostage. The chance discovery of one tunnel had led to an astounding achievement for Israel's security, but it also triggered a wave of anger at the IDF since they hadn't acted earlier against the tunnels.

The price was high—the IDF lost sixty-seven of its best fighters, many of them officers charging ahead of their troops. The Gazan civilian population was painfully hit—over sixteen hundred dead, many of them terrorists, but also a large number of children. The IDF was criticized for destroying numerous blocks of houses, for its artillery shooting into densely populated areas and even firing at several UNRWA schools that had become refugee shelters. The IDF claimed that in several cases fire was opened on its soldiers or missiles fired on Israel from schools and mosques; yet the criticism, from within and without, did not abate.

It became clear that a regular army, trained to fight regular armies on the battlefield, was not prepared for fighting a terrorist organization entrenched in cities and towns. All the Israeli operations against the terrorist organizations—like Operation Litani, the first and the second Lebanon Wars, Operation Grapes of Wrath against Hezballah in South Lebanon (1996) and the three major missions in Gaza—had ended without a conclusive outcome. In the future the IDF had to develop new, creative methods of fighting terror organizations like Hamas, Hezbollah and ISIS, sparing as much as possible the civilian population.

The Protective Edge mission ended with a cease-fire, like other similar missions in the past. Yet all the demands of Hamas had been rejected and its leaders emerged from their underground bunkers to an image of terrible devastation and loss. Israel's victory was clear but not decisive. Hamas still had 20 to 30 percent of its rockets, most of its military units had survived and its leadership was intact. Israel's leaders had to cope with an angry nation, embittered by the feeling that once again, Hamas had been spared a decisive blow.

The real hero of the Protective Edge mission was the Iron Dome system, which during fifty days of fighting had succeeded in shooting down

735 Qassam, Grad and M-75 missiles fired at Israel's populated areas, disregarding the rockets falling in empty fields. Iron Dome had made its debut during the Pillar of Defense operation, but this time the results were even more staggering. During Protective Edge only 224 missiles fell in Israel's cities and villages, killing five people. The relatively light losses enabled the IDF to carry out its mission without any pressure from a battered and bleeding civilian population. By protecting Israel's civilians, Iron Dome had tipped the scales of the conflict.

Iron Dome—the star of operation "Protective Edge."
(Yariv Katz, Yedioth Ahronot Archive)

The Iron Dome was composed of a very sensitive radar that detected the firing of one or more missiles; a sophisticated computer calculated the exact trajectory of the enemy projectile, and a battery of Tamir anti-missile missiles, activated by IDF soldiers, would intercept the enemy rocket before it reached its target and blow it to smithereens in the clear blue sky.

The Iron Dome's father was a curly-haired, mustachioed and warm Moroccan Jew, Amir Peretz. A former paratrooper who had spent a year in a hospital after being severely wounded, he had later served as mayor of Sderot, a town located barely 3.7 kilometers from the Gaza border fence.

Shortly after being appointed defense minister in 2006, Peretz ordered the army—despite fierce opposition of the generals, the defense ministry, the media, learned engineers and scientists and a large part of the body politic—to launch a project for defending Israel from the Qassam and other rockets. The man charged with the project was a brilliant scientist, Dr. Danny Gold.

The objections were based on the then-limited threat of the rockets; the huge funds needed to develop another anti-missile system besides the Israeli-American joint Project Arrow for intercepting long-range missiles; the preference of many experts for the laser-based Nautilus system and the cynical disbelief that something would come out of the minister's project.

A popular newspaper, expressing the feelings of many, published a screaming front-page headline:

Iron dome—a failure known in advance.

Perhaps they were right. The minister of defense had been involved in the partly failed Second Lebanon War; he had been ridiculed by photographs published in the media showing him trying to watch IDF maneuvers through binoculars whose lens covers had not been removed. . . . And after all, he was a trade union leader, a politician, not a general; what did he understand about military matters?

That was 2007. But in 2014, during and after Protective Edge, the Israeli media and political leaders competed in showering kudos, compliments and flowery messages of gratitude on Peretz, who alone had made Iron Dome a reality and turned the small interceptor system into a game changer. The thousands of rockets still in the hands of Hamas had suddenly become obsolete.

During the Protective Edge mission, the Israeli military industries delivered the ninth Iron Dome battery to the army. "With thirteen batteries we'll be able to fully protect all of our cities and inhabited areas; when we put in place twenty-four batteries, all of Israel's territory will be safe," Peretz told the authors of this book. General Gabi Ashkenazi, a former chief of staff,who had been utterly opposed to the project (but had dutifully carried it out), quipped: "Binoculars or no binoculars, Amir Peretz saw farther than all of us."

O n September 23, about three weeks after the cease-fire, Israeli commandos located the two Hamas terrorists that had murdered the three teenagers on June 17, starting the vicious circle of violence. Amar Abu Aisha and Marwan Qawasmeh were killed in a firefight in Hebron.

AMIR PERETZ, FORMER DEFENSE MINISTER

"A month after I assumed my position, I summoned the General Staff and asked them, Why don't we have any means to counter the terrorists' most primitive weapon—the Qassams? They said there were two kinds of threats: tactical and strategic. The Qassams were not even a tactical threat: in seven years we had seven people killed. One a year—that doesn't justify spending millions.

"I said: Let me tell you a story I heard from an old man in a Sderot street. 'Long ago,' he said, 'in my native village in Morocco, a rumor reached the village elders. The Angel of Death was coming to the village to take a life sometime during the next two weeks! What to do? The elders decided to inform the population that, one, the Angel of Death was coming; two, he'll arrive during the next two weeks; three, nobody knows whose life he will take.'

" 'And what was the result of that?' the Old Man said. 'All the inhabitants of the village ran away, to the last of them!'

"I told the generals that the same thing happens with the Qassam rockets. We don't know when and where they would hit and who is going to get killed, but that disrupts the normal life of thousands of Israelis. Our duty is to guarantee them a peaceful life. So perhaps it is not a strategic or a tactical threat on our lives—but it is a moral threat.

"They didn't buy that; they were all against me. The army and the industries, civilians and military, media commentators and editorial writers, they all attacked me. I felt completely alone.

"When the matter was brought before Prime Minister Olmert, he washed his hands of it. 'You're minister of defense,' he said to me, 'it's your decision and your budget.' At least he didn't veto the project.

"When I finally made the decision to go ahead with the plan, I was attacked again for choosing the Iron Dome project instead of the Nautilus that was based on the destruction of enemy missiles by laser beams. I rejected that project for two reasons: first—at the time Nautilus was static, and the equipment couldn't be moved from one position to another. And the second reason—laser beams couldn't work properly when the sky was covered with clouds. That meant that for at least three months a year our towns and cities would be exposed and defenseless. Iron Dome, on the contrary, could easily be moved, and guaranteed protection in all weather and all through the year.

"I chose Iron Dome and once again found myself isolated and vilified. The following ten months were a nightmare.

"But today? The entire nation is praising the Iron Dome. It has also become a unique case in the U.S.-Israeli relations. The American president and lawmakers voted extraordinary budgets for the Iron Dome, beyond the annual help of three billion dollars to Israel. That was the first time that the U.S. financially participated in a project in which no American industries were involved, just 'blue and white,' a pure Israeli achievement."

The Lost Tribe Returns

CHAPTER 26

FROM THE HEART OF AFRICA TO JERUSALEM: OPERATION MOSES (1984) AND OPERATION SOLOMON (1991)

O n an October night in 1981, two Israeli naval vessels, the missile ships *Reshef* and *Keshet*, arrived secretly to the coast of Sudan. Fighters from Flotilla 13 descended from the ships on rubber rafts, embedding radar echo reflectors into the coral reefs as a way of indicating safe routes to the shore. The task was difficult; the reefs were spread over a wide area, and the fighters acted clandestinely because Sudan was an enemy country. Mapping the approach paths to the beach, they located four inlets that would facilitate their assignment: bringing the Jews of Ethiopia to Israel through Sudan.

The operation had in fact begun in 1977, when Prime Minister Menachem Begin summoned the head of the Mossad, Yitzhak Hofi, and told him, "Bring me the Jews of Ethiopia!" Begin knew about the unstable regime of Ethiopia's dictator, Mengistu Haile Mariam, the deep distress of the country's Jews and the longing of this ancient, legendary community to immigrate to Israel after living and preserving the commandments of Judaism in Africa. The Mossad was recruited for the task; initially, small numbers of Jews were brought to Israel from Addis Ababa, Ethiopia's capital, but Mengistu quickly locked the gates leading out of his country. Thousands of Ethiopian Jews had heard about the stirring idea—literally to "ascend," in the Hebrew, to Jerusalem—and had set out on foot toward neighboring Sudan. The trek would eventually lead to the deaths of thousands, who, for the length of the journey, found themselves at the mercy of thieves, wild animals, disease and hunger. The trip would become a saga of agony and heroism. Upon their arrival in Sudan, the majority would be absorbed into refugee camps, where they were forced to hide their Judaism, fearing the authorities and other refugees. The Mossad dispatched numerous agents to Ethiopia under various covers, and they did their best to get many of the Jews out of Sudan. At Begin's request, the Egyptian ruler, Anwar Sadat, reached out to the Sudanese dictator, Gaafar Nimeiry, to ask that he look the other way as Ethiopian Jews made their escape. Nimeiry agreed—in exchange for large bribes—but only a handful of Jews were able to leave his country with real or fake documents, while the vast majority remained in camps under terrible conditions.

Then an idea arose: to bring them out of Sudan by sea, with assistance from the IDF. Along with several former Flotilla 13 commandos, agents of the Mossad—among them Yonatan Shefa, Emmanuel Alon and others—acquired a resort named Arous on the Sudanese coast, running it as a diving and leisure center for tourists from Europe. The site served as a vacation village with an array of activities; but the visitors weren't aware that, on certain nights, the staff would drive hundreds of miles in antiquated, dilapidated trucks, picking up numerous Jews at secret meeting points and bringing them to the Sudanese shore. The operation—along with every other operation run by the Mossad in

Sudan at that time—was conducted by a young, courageous agent, a yarmulke-wearing blond by the name of Danny Limor.

On November 8, 1981, a civilian ship called the *Bat Galim* ("Daughter of the Waves") departed from the port of Eilat carrying a military commander, Major Ilan Buhris; also on board were medical equipment, field kitchens and roughly four hundred beds. Members of Flotilla 13 embarked with two commando boats known as Swallows, as well as nine Zodiacs, and the *Bat Galim* raised anchor. The Mossad dubbed the mission Operation Brothers—a fitting name, as its organizers indeed viewed the Ethiopian Jews as brothers.

On November 11, the *Bat Galim* reached its destination. That night, numerous Jews arrived on the beach in tarp-covered trucks, which had traveled many hours, risking interception by the Sudanese Army at any moment; they were even forced to break through Sudanese military checkpoints while making the trip. The passengers, exhausted by the long journey, and some of them quite afraid, were lifted onto the rubber boats and then brought to the ship. Many of them had never seen the sea in their lives; a few tried to drink the water. They were received on deck with bread, jam and hot tea. The Israelis subsequently organized a group sing-along as a way to calm them and even screened a movie; many of the passengers had never seen one. Two and a half days later, the ship docked at the Sharm el-Sheikh base in Sinai, where 164 immigrants descended onto the shore.

Preparations immediately got under way for a second voyage, which set sail in January 1982 and brought another 351 immigrants to Israel. The third, in March 1982, almost ended in disaster: one of the boats, transporting four Mossad agents, got stuck among the coral reefs at the same moment that Sudanese soldiers armed with Kalashnikovs suddenly appeared and threatened to shoot them. Fortunately, the mission commander responded with remarkable chutzpah, unleashing a verbal barrage at his Sudanese counterpart: "Are you crazy? You want to shoot at tourists? You can't see that we're here to organize a diving expedition? We're tourism-ministry employees, bringing visitors to the country, and you want to shoot them? Who's the idiot who made you an officer?" The

English-speaking commander was embarrassed, apologized, and took off with his soldiers. In fact, he had been looking for smugglers. *Bat Galim* set sail without further difficulties and delivered 172 additional immigrants to Israel, although the incident made clear that this method was too risky and wouldn't work anymore; it would be necessary to find another way of extracting Ethiopia's Jews.

One morning, tourists at the resort discovered that the entire staff, minus the locals, had disappeared. The "guides"—members of the Mossad—had left letters apologizing for the facility's closure, citing budgetary reasons. The tourists were flown back to their respective countries and received a full refund.

Meanwhile, back in Israel, it had been decided to transport the immigrants by other means, flying them on the air force's Hercules planes, known as Rhinos. Mossad agents found an abandoned British airfield south of Port Sudan, and a special air force team prepped it for landings. Ethiopian Jews would be picked up at a secret meeting place and brought to the airfield, where the landing strip was illuminated with special torches. But when the air force's Hercules landed, the Ethiopians were scared nearly to death. The flying metal colossus, which they were seeing for the first time in their lives, landed with a roar of the engines, moving straight at them. Many fled, returning only after the Israeli organizers won them over with heartfelt explanations. In the end, the plane took off with 213 Israel-bound Jews.

The incident at the airfield taught members of the IAF and Mossad several lessons: on the next trip, the plane would land and lower the ramp from its tail beforehand, and the truckloads of immigrants would go directly into the Hercules' open belly, without seeing the monster thundering toward them across the runway.

But Sudanese authorities discovered the operation, as well as the airfield. The Israelis found another landing area, roughly forty-six kilometers from Port Sudan, deciding then to arrange an airlift that would include seven Rhino flights, with two hundred Jews departing on each. Overseeing the mission would be the head of the Mossad and Brigadier General Amos Yaron, the paratroopers' chief officer. The operation was carried out between 1982 and 1984, during which fifteen hundred immigrants were brought to Israel.

On the eve of each operation, a truck would arrive at the landing area and light up the runway. The plane coming from Israel would touch down, run along the landing strip and turn around, opening its large tail door. Members of the air force's Shaldag commando unit would form two lines leading to the gaping door in the shape of a funnel, and when the trucks arrived, the immigrants would walk through the funnel, directly into the belly of the plane, where they would seat themselves on the floor. Many didn't even realize they were inside a plane.

On one of the flights, an elderly, distinguished Kess—a religious and social leader—got up and asked who the senior officer was. The flight crew accompanied him to Brigadier General Avihu Ben-Nun, of the air force. The Kess stood before him and slowly, ceremonially, pulled out an ancient sword from his belt and extended it toward him. "Until now, I've been responsible for their fate," he said, gesturing with his hand in the direction of his brothers. "From now on, you are," he continued, handing the sword to a visibly moved Ben-Nun.

At the end of 1984, the situation in Sudan destabilized even further; the country needed emergency humanitarian assistance and food. Israel took advantage of the situation, directing a request to the United States to aid Sudan—in exchange for Jewish immigrants. U.S. Vice President George Bush immediately responded, instructing the American embassy staff in Khartoum to initiate negotiations with Nimeiry. The talks proved a success, and Sudan agreed to the Ethiopian Jews' orderly departure by air, on the condition that they not fly directly to Israel but through a third country. The Mossad identified a small, Jewish-owned Belgian airline and launched Operation Moses: over the course of forty-seven days, the Belgian Boeings would complete thirty-six flights, transporting 7,800 Jews to Israel.

Following leaks by Israeli leaders to the world media, Nimeiry halted the operation. But Bush didn't give up, dispatching seven U.S. Air Force Hercules planes to Gadarif, in Sudan, in an operation called Queen of Sheba. The American planes flew five hundred remaining Jews from

Sudan directly to Israel's Ramon airbase. This mission crowned the close cooperation between the Israeli and American air forces in their common purpose—rescuing the Jews of Ethiopia.

Although Operations Moses and Queen of Sheba concluded successfully, thousands of Jews remained in Ethiopia. During the various stages of this exodus, many families were separated or torn apart, with children arriving in Israel without their parents and vice versa. The ruptures caused tremendous difficulties, and even tragedies, during the Ethiopians' absorption into Israel. At the same time, a lethal civil war had broken out in Ethiopia, and immediate danger loomed over the lives of the country's Jews. Emissaries of the Mossad and the Jewish Agency gathered thousands of Jews in makeshift camps in Addis Ababa, where they awaited a miracle that would bring them to Israel.

And the miracle happened.

In May 1991, seven years after Operation Moses, Operation Solomon was launched. It was carried out at the height of the civil war, as rebel forces opposing President Mengistu advanced from every direction on Addis Ababa. Israel was aided once again by George Bush, by then the American president, whose mediation produced an agreement between the Israeli government and the head of the collapsing regime several days before Mengistu's final defeat. Secret, dogged work by Uri Lubrani, of Israel's foreign ministry, acting under orders from Prime Minister Yitzhak Shamir, made it a reality.

As part of the agreement, Israel paid $35 million to Mengistu in exchange for bringing the Jews to Israel, while the Americans promised Mengistu and several senior members of his regime that they would receive diplomatic asylum in the United States. In exchange for an unknown sum, the rebel leaders agreed not to disrupt the operation and to observe a temporary cease-fire. The cease-fire, agreed upon by both government and rebel forces, was short: thirty-four hours. Israel had to fly all the Jews out of the country before the fighting resumed.

The mission was overseen by the IDF's deputy chief of staff, Amnon Lipkin-Shahak, who bore responsibility for flying approximately fifteen thousand Jews to Israel within thirty-four hours. The organization of the mission was exemplary, with Israel sending "anything that could fly" to Addis Ababa. El Al dispatched thirty passenger planes and the air force sent numerous cargo jets; leading them, of course, were the Rhinos. Hundreds of soldiers from various units, including infantry, Shaldag and the paratroopers, were sent to Addis Ababa to organize the immigrants and bring them aboard the planes. Especially prominent were soldiers of Ethiopian background who had arrived in Israel during Operation Moses and were now serving in the IDF. The sight of Ethiopian soldiers in IDF uniforms, many of them proudly wearing the red berets, red boots and silver paratroopers' wings, inspired great excitement among the new immigrants, and even the toughest Ethiopian-Israeli paratroopers couldn't stop their tears. The soldiers spread out to secure the airfield, leading the Jews onto the planes. They were divided into groups and each given a number; numbered labels were initially attached to their clothing, but a different process was subsequently discovered—sticking the labels on their foreheads. Within a few hours, 14,400 Jews were brought aboard the planes. Lipkin-Shahak oversaw the operation with his characteristic calm and composure.

As part of the operation, a Boeing 747 was going to break the world record, with 1,087 passengers on board. During the flight, a baby was born, and 1,088 immigrants deplaned in Israel.

The lost tribe returns on eagle's wings. (*Zvika Israeli, GPO*)

Many Jews remained in Ethiopia, still aspiring to immigrate to Israel. Ethiopian Jewry's fight to "ascend" had left many behind. In Israel, too, Ethiopian Jews were forced to struggle hard to be absorbed into Israeli society, to be recognized as Jews, to achieve true equality and to adapt to a modern society, where the worldview and traditions by which they had lived for thousands of years came apart.

BENNY GANTZ, LATER THE IDF CHIEF OF STAFF

"I took part in numerous assignments during my military career, among them secret operations. My life has been in danger more than once: I've been shot at, crossed paths with terrorists, lost fighters and saw friends die next to me. But the mission of bringing the Jews of Ethiopia to Israel, in which I participated as a Shaldag commander, was the most important, from a national standpoint, of all the operations I've taken part in. This mission, in substance, encompasses the entire concept of a national home for the Jewish people. The idea that you can carry it out—that's Zionism. It wasn't a heroic mission of individuals. It was the heroic mission of a country.

"I'm a son of Holocaust survivors, and during the evacuation, I couldn't not think for a moment about what would have happened if we'd had a country back then; perhaps everything might have been different. How might European Jewry have looked? There, in Ethiopia, I realized that the state of Israel was doing something great and powerful.

"There's a memory that I carry with me to this day: we're landing in the dark, leaving the plane, which looks like a terrible monster, reaching people sitting, folded on the ground, wrapped in blankets, carrying them in our arms into the belly of the plane, the door closing, taking off, the pilots turning on the lights, and then our eyes meeting, so many eyes looking toward you in fright, and it's impossible to communicate with them.

"The thing that most bothered me about the operation was the moment when the first caravan of immigrants came toward us on the airfield, and suddenly I could make out the stickers with numbers on their foreheads. That made me crazy, and I asked that the numbers be removed immediately.

"Since then, there've been moving moments of coming full circle. I met a singer in a military troupe who told me, moments before singing the national anthem, that she had been a baby during Operation Solomon."

AFTERMATH

Yitzhak Navon (1921 to): Ben Gurion's secretary since 1951, Navon became the fifth president of Israel (1978 to 1983) and later was elected minister of education and culture.

Yitzhak Rabin (1922 to 1995): Chief of staff (1964 to 1967). Ambassador to the U.S. Prime minister of Israel (1974 to 1977, 1992 to 1995). Was assassinated in November 1995.

David ("Dado") Elazar (1925 to 1976): Commander of the Northern District in the Six Day War. Chief of staff (1972 to1974), was forced to resign after the Yom Kippur War by decision of the Agranat Board of Inquiry. Died of a heart attack (1976).

Uzi Eilam (1934 to): Brigadier general in the IDF. Director general of the Israeli Atomic Energy Commission (1976 to 1985) and chief scientist and director (research and development) in the Ministry of Defense (1986 to 1997).

Moshe Dayan (1915 to 1981): Lieutenant general. Chief of staff (1953 to 1958). Minister of Agriculture (1959 to 1964). Minister of defense

(1967 to 1974). As minister of foreign affairs (1977 to 1979) he played a major role in negotiating the peace treaty with Egypt.

Ariel ("Arik") Sharon (1928 to 2014): Major general. Commander of the Paratroopers Corps (1954 to 1957). Discharged from the IDF in 1973, minister of defense (1981 to 1983), removed from his position by the Kahan Board of Inquiry after the War in Lebanon (1982). Served in several ministerial positions, elected prime minister in 2001, and as such carried out Israel's unilateral disengagement from the Gaza Strip. After suffering a stroke in 2006, he remained in a coma until his death in 2014.

Meir Har-Zion (1934 to 2014): Captain. A founder of Unit 101, member of the first paratrooper battalion, was awarded the Medal of Courage, lived on a farm in the Gilboa mountains named after his sister Shoshana; died in 2014.

Aharon Davidi (1920 to 2012): Brigadier general. Commander of the Paratroopers Brigade. Director and founder of Sar-El volunteer program of the IDF.

Shimon ("Katcha") Kahaner (1934 to): Colonel, member of Unit 101. Raises cattle on a farm in northern Israel, across the gully from his late friend Meir Har-Zion.

Mordechai ("Motta") Gur (1930 to 1995): Lieutenant general. Commander of the 55th Paratroopers Reserve Brigade, which captured Jerusalem in the Six Day War (1967). Israel's military attaché in Washington (1972 to 1973). Chief of staff during Operation Entebbe (1976). Minister of health (1984 to 1986). Deputy defense minister (1992 to 1997). Diagnosed with terminal cancer, he committed suicide with his handgun.

Yoash ("Chatto") Zidon (1926 to 2015): Combat pilot and commander in the Israeli Air Force. The head of weapon system and planning in the IAF. Member of Knesset (1988 to 1992).

Ezer Weizman (1924 to 2005): Major general, commander of the IAF (1958 to 1966). Minister of defense (1977 to 1980). Seventh president of Israel (1993 to 2000). Died at home in Caesarea.

Rafael ("Raful") Eitan (1929 to 2005): Lieutenant general. Chief of staff (1978 to 1983). Established the right-wing political party Tzomet. Deputy prime minister (1998 to 1999) then retired. Swept by a wave into the sea from Ashdod's wharf during a severe storm.

Shimon Peres (1923 to): Defense ministry director general and deputy defense minister under Ben-Gurion. Defense minister (1974 to 1977, 1995 to 1996). Minister of foreign affairs (1986 to 1988 ,1992 to 1995, 2001 to 2002). Prime minister (1984 to 1986, 1995 to 1996). Ninth president of Israel (2007 to 2014).

Rehavam ("Gandhi") Ze'evi (1926 to 2001): Major general, commander of the Central Military District. Established the right-wing Moledet party (1988). Minister without portfolio (1999). Minister of tourism (2001). Assassinated in the Hyatt Hotel in Jerusalem in 2001 by four Palestinian gunmen from the Popular Front for the Liberation of Palestine.

Avihu Ben-Nun (1939 to): Major general, Israeli Air Force (1957 to 1992). Combat pilot. Commander of the Israeli Air Force (1987 to 1992).

Mordechai ("Motti") Hod (1926 to 2003): Major general. Combat pilot. Commander of the Israeli Air Force (1966 to 1973).

Amichai ("Ami") Ayalon (1945 to): Admiral, commander of Flotilla 13 (1979), commander of the Israeli Navy (1992 to 1996). Recipient of the Medal of Valor. Head of Israel's Internal Security Service (the Shin-Beth) (1995 to 2000). Minister without portfolio (2007 to 2008). Senior fellow at the Israel Democracy Institute.

Haim Bar-Lev (1924 to 1994): Lieutenant general. Chief of staff (1968 to 1971). Responsible for the Bar-Lev Line, fortifications built along the Suez Canal. Several ministry positions, and ambassador to Russia (1992 to 1994).

Hadar Kimchi (1929 to): Commander of the Cherbourg Operation (1968). Deputy commander of the Israeli Navy (1971 to 1973).

Mordechai ("Moka") Limon (1924 to 2009): Admiral, commander of the navy (1950 to 1954). Head of delegation of procurement of the Ministry of Defense in Paris (1962 to 1970).

Nehemiah Dagan (1940 to): Brigadier general. Combat pilot (helicopters). Commander of the IDF education department (1985 to 1988).

Eitan Ben Eliyahu (1944 to): Major general. Combat pilot. Commander of the IAF (1996 to 2000).

Amir Eshel (1959 to): Major general. Commander of the IAF since 2012.

Benyamin Netanyahu (1945 to): Captain, Sayeret Matkal. Israel's ambassador to the UN (1984 to 1988). Minister of finance (2003 to 2005). Prime minister (1996 to 1999) (2009 to).

Uzi Dayan (1948 to): Major general. Nephew of Moshe Dayan. Fifteen years in Sayeret Matkal. Deputy chief of staff. Head of the National Security Council (2003 to 2005).

Ehud Barak (1942 to): Lieutenant general. Commander of Sayeret Matkal. Chief of staff (1991 to 1995). Prime minister (1999 to 2001). Minister of defense and deputy prime minister (2009 to 2013).

Amnon Lipkin-Shahak (1944 to 2012): Lieutenant general. Commander of the Paratroopers Brigade. Head of Military Intelligence (1986 to 1991). Deputy chief of staff (1991). Chief of staff of the IDF (1995 to 1998). Member of Knesset and Cabinet Minister.

Moshe ("Muki") Betzer (1945 to): Colonel. Deputy commander of Sayeret Matkal. First commander of Shaldag (commando of the Israeli Air Force).

Moshe ("Bogi") Ya'alon (1950 to): Lieutenant general. Commander of Sayeret Matkal. Commander of the Paratroopers Brigade. Chief of Staff (2002 to 2005). Minister of defense (2013 to).

Danny Matt (1927 to 2013): Major general. Commander of the Paratroopers Regular Brigade. Commander of the Paratroopers Reservist Brigade 247 (55). Chair of the IDF appeal court.

Yitzhak Mordechai (1944 to): Major general. Commander of the Paratroopers and Infantry Corps. Commander of the Northern Command (1993 to 1995). Minister of defense (1996 to 1999). Deputy prime minister (1999 to 2000). Retired from political life in 2001.

Amnon Reshef (1938 to): Major general. Commander of the Armored Corps. Chairman, Association for Peace and Security.

Avigdor Kahalani (1944 to): Brigadier general. Commander of the 7th Brigade of the Armored Corps. Decorated with the Medal of Valor, the Medal of Distinguished Service and the President's Medal. Minister of internal security (1996 to 1999). Chairman, the Association for the Soldiers' Welfare.

Tamir Pardo (1953 to): Communications officer, Sayeret Matkal. Head of the Mossad (2011 to).

Shaul Mofaz (1948 to): Lieutenant general. Commander of the Paratroopers Brigade. Commander of the Judea and Samaria Division. Chief of staff (1998 to 2002). Minister of defense (2002 to 2006). Deputy prime minister and minister of transports (2006 to 2009). Later head of the opposition in the Knesset. Retired from political life in 2015.

Dan Shomron (1937 to 2008): Lieutenant general. Commander of the Paratroopers and Infantry Corps. Chief of staff (1987 to 1991). Chairman of the Israeli Military Industries.

Meir Dagan (1945 to): Major general, various military positions. Medal of Courage. Director of the Mossad (2002 to 2010).

Gavriel ("Gabi") Ashkenazi (1954 to): Lieutenant general. Deputy chief of staff (2002 to 2005). Director general of the defense ministry (2006). Chief of staff (2007 to 2011).

Aviem Sella (1946 to): Colonel. Combat pilot. (Advancement arrested because of his involvement in the Jonathan Pollard affair.)

Eliezer ("Chiney") Marom (1955 to): Admiral. Commander of the Israeli Navy (2007 to 2012).

Aviv Kochavi (1964 to): Major general. Commander of the Paratroopers Brigade. Commander of military intelligence. Commander of the Northern District.

Itzhak ("Jerry") Gershon (1958 to): Major general. Commander of the Paratroopers Brigade. Commander of the Judea and Samaria Division. CEO of Friends of the IDF in the U.S. (2008 to 2015).

Dan Halutz (1948 to): Lieutenant general. Combat pilot. Commander of the IAF (2002 to 2004). Chief of staff (2005 to 2007). Resigned after the second Lebanon War.

Yoav Galant (1958 to):Major general. Commander of the Southern District during Operation Cast Lead. Appointed chief of staff in 2010, but the appointment was cancelled. Minister of Housing (2015 to).

Dr. Izzeldin Abuelaish (1955 to): Palestinian doctor. Since 2009, lives with his family in Toronto. Founder of the trust Daughters for Life, for the education and health of girls and women in Gaza and the Middle East. Active in promoting the peace movement.

SOURCE NOTES

The sources marked with an (h) are in Hebrew

1: Entebbe, 1976

"Operation Yonathan (Thunderball)—The full report," IDF Archives, November 1977. (h)

"The secret notes of Peres," Itamar Eichner, Yedioth Ahronoth, 17.7.2011(h)

"A rescue operation which shocked the world," Haim Isrovitz, Maariv, 27.6.2006. (h)

Parts from Motta Gur notes (Internet site: The heritage of Gur). (h)

"Exposure: The Mossad photograph, Operation Entebbe on the way," Sharon Rofe-Ofir, Ynet 1.7.2006. (internet site)

Bar-Zohar Michael, "Shimon Peres, the biography," Random House, New York 2007, pp. 313–348.

"Operation Entebbe," Journal of the Defense Minister, 27 June 1976, IDF Archives.

Peres Shimon, "Entebbe Diary," Yedioth Ahronoth, Tel Aviv, 1991. (h)

Rabin Yitzhak, "The Rabin Memoirs," Maariv, Tel Aviv, 1979, p. 527. (h)

Gur Mordechai (Motta), "The Chief of Staff," Maarakhot, Tel Aviv, 1998, pp. 236–288. (h)

Interview of Shimon Peres.

Interview of Tamir Pardo.

2: To Save Jerusalem, 1948

Yitzhaki Arie, "Latrun—the battle for the road to Jerusalem"; "Latrun, road seven is 'Burma Road'—the siege was broken," Kama publishers, Jerusalem 1982, volume 1, pp. 269–282, volume 2, pp. 321–339. (h)

Shamir Shlomo (Gen. res.) "At all costs—to Jerusalem," "Road Seven to Jerusalem," Maarakhot, Ministry of Defense, Tel-Aviv, 1994, pp. 415–454. (h)

Talmi Menachem, "The new route," Cultural service of the IDF, 1949. (h)

Oren Ram, "Latrun, the new hope," Keshet publishers, Tel-Aviv, 2002, pp. 309–332. (h)

Rabin Yitzhak, "The Rabin Memoirs," op.cit. 1979, pp. 52–56. (h)

"The man who discovered the Burma Road," Eli Eshed, E-magoo.co.il, Internet magazine, 28.5.2005. (h)

Interview of Yitzhak Navon.

3: Black Arrow, 1955

Eilam Uzi, "Eilam's Arch," Gaza raid—Black-Arrow Mission, 28.2.1955, Yedioth Books (Miskal) 2009, pp. 32–39. (h)

"Black Arrow—fiftieth anniversary to the unification of the mythological para-trooper unit 101," Kobi Finkler, Channel 7, 23.1.07. (h)

Bar-Zohar Michael and Haber Eitan, "The book of the Paratroopers," Levin Epstein publishers, Tel-Aviv, 1969, pp. 32–39. (h)

"We were here. The IDF attacks in Gaza, 1955," Yanai Israeli, Walla, 7.3.2008. (h)

"Black Arrow, a pierced heart: the paratroopers hero and the Gaza mission," Roi Mendel, Ynet, Yedioth Ahronoth, 7.3.2012. (h)

Interview of Uzi Eilam.

4: "Bring Down this Plane!" 1956

Tzidon Yoash (Chatto), "By day by night, through haze and fog," Maariv publishers, 1995, p. 216. (h)

"Hour of the bat," Elazar Ben-Lulu, Internet site of the IDF. (h)

Interview of Yoash (Chatto) Tzidon.

5: Kadesh, 1956

"Myths and facts," a historical research; The Mitla Pass 26th anniversary," Monitin Magazine, October 1981. (h)

"The Independence War was not a war of few against many—The Mitla Myth," Moshe Ronen, Yedioth Ahronoth, 4.8.1999. (h)

"The longest day in Sinai," Uri Dan, Maariv, 28.10.1966. (h)

"Being there—testimony on Sharon, Gur, Eitan, Hofi, Davidi and others," Monitin, November 1966. (h)

Ben-Gurion David, "A letter to the Ninth brigade, 6.11.1956," Ministry of Defense, IDF archives. (h)

Dayan Moshe, "On the Sinai campaign, 6.11.1956," Ministry of Defense, IDF archives. (h)

"Operation Steamroller, operation orders 64/56, 28.10.1956 including annex 4—A paratroop drop," IDF archive. (h)

"On the parachuting at the Mitla," Dr. Arieh Gilai, the Paratroopers' internet site. (h)

"The brigade's reconnaissance unit, a personal story of the Mitla battle," Uri Getz, the Paratroopers' internet site. (h)

"Heavy mortars battalion 332, testimony about the Mitla battle," Yakov Tzur, the Paratroopers' internet site. (h)

"Company A, Battalion 890, the cave mopping at the Mitla battle," Avshalom (Avsha) Adam, the Paratroopers' internet site. (h)

"Nahal squad commanders course 906, fighting route at Kadesh, personal testimonies," Shai Marmur and Rafi Benisti, the Paratroopers' internet site. (h)

"Machine-gunner company E battalion 88: At the Mitla battle I stood exposed on a half-track," Moshe Hassin as told to Dr. Arieh Gilai, the Paratroopers' internet site. (h)

"Fighter and Sergeant-Major, company A, A personal story about the Mitla parachuting and the caves' battle," Moni Meroz, the Paratroopers' internet site. (h)

"The Mitla battle," Shraga Gafni, Maarakhot, Ministry of Defense, number 113, 1960. (h)

Bar-Zohar Michael and Haber Eitan, "The Mitla trap," the book of the Paratroopers, Op. cit. pp. 132–140. (h)

Bar-Zohar Michael, "Ben-Gurion," Volume 3 (out of 3) Am-Oved publishers, Tel-Aviv, 1977, pp. 1207–1286. (h)

Bar-Zohar Michael, "Shimon Peres, the biography," Random House, N.Y. 2007, pp. 144–154.

Dayan Moshe, "Diary of the Sinai Campaign," New York, Harper and Row, 1966.

Eitan Rafael (Raful) "A soldier's Story," Maariv publishers, Tel-Aviv, 1985, p. 65. (h)

6: "Life or Death," Operation Focus, 1967

Cohen (Cheetah) Elazar and Lavi Zvi, "The Six Day War, The Suez is not the limit," Maariv, Tel-Aviv, 1990, pp. 263–291. (h)

"The Focus plan—as a thunderball out of a blue sky," Pirsumei Teufa (Aviation magazine) Rishon Lezion, pp. 55–80. (h)

Yanai Ehud, ed.; General (res.) Yiftach Spector, "Moked, Aerial Supremacy," Keter publishers, Jerusalem, 1995, pp.162–170. (h)

Churchill Randolph and Churchill Winston, "The air strike—the Six Day War," Houghton Mifflin, Boston, 1967, p. 82.

Rabin Yitzhak, "The Rabin Memoirs," Maariv publishers, 1979, pp.186–191. (h)

Weizman Ezer, "On Eagles Wings," Maariv publishers, Tel-Aviv, 1975, pp. 259–273. (h)

"The Focus Plan—how it was planned and how it was carried out," Zeev Shiff, Haaretz, 10.4.1981. (h)

"Our Air Force was annihilated—the picture was black," Yaakov Lamdan, "Laisha" (woman's weekly magazine), 5.6.1989. (h)

"A forced gamble," Meir Amitai, Haaretz, 4.7.1997. (h)

"Like a thunderball from a blue sky," Noam Ophir, the IAF magazine, 1.6.2002. (h)

A 1983 interview with Abd-El-Hamid Helmy, Commander of the Egyptian Air-Force, "Al Ahram" Internet site.

Steven Pressfield, "Lion's Gate," Sentinel HC, New York, 2014.

Interview of Colonel (res.) Yossi Sarig. (h)

Interview of General (res.) Avihu Bin-Nun. (h)

7: "The Temple Mount Is in Our Hands!" 1967

Narkiss Uzi, general (res.) "Jerusalem is one," Am-Oved, Tel- Aviv, 1975, pp. 160–163, 173–175, 200–201, 241–253. (h)

Landau Eli, "Jerusalem Forever," chapters: "The day of Jerusalem"; "Ammunition Hill;" "The temple Mount and the Western Wall are in our hands"; pp. 25–32,111–147, 161–171, Otpaz, Tel-Aviv, 1967. (h)

Nathan Moshe, "The battle for Jerusalem," Chapters: "Ammunition Hill"; "The Lions` Gate"; "The Victory Gate"; pp. 131–191, 293–333, 334–349, Otpaz, Tel-Aviv, 1968. (h)

Dayan David, "From Hermon to Suez"—History of the Six Day War. Chapter: "Jerusalem of Iron"; "Here is the Western Wall"; pp. 144–154, 155–161. Massada, Ramat-Gan, 1967. (h)

Weizman Ezer, op. cit. pp. 283–297. (h)

Kfir Ilan, "The Fighting IDF- Military and Defense Encyclopaedia," Volume 4, chapter: "Jerusalem of Iron," pp. 89–99, Revivim Publishers, Maariv, Tel-Aviv, 1982–1986. (h)

"Motta made History," Moshe Bar-Yehuda, Military Magazine, 24.5.1968. (h)

"We've got the scoop," Ravit Naor, Maariv, 18.4.1997. (h)

"The hill was acquired by blood," Yoram Shoshani, Yedioth Ahronoth, 8.1.1968. (h)

Oren Michael, "Six Days of War," Presidio Press, 2003.

"Jerusalem of blood, songs and prayers," Yehuda Ezrachi, Maariv, 13.6.1967. (h)

"Jerusalem will be built," Yehuda Haezrachi, Maariv, 16.6.1967. (h)

"Against fortified bunkers and 120 mm. mortars," Amit Navon and Moshe Zonder, Maariv, 18.4.1997. (h)

"The battle for Jerusalem continued because of lack of communication with the IDF forces after the Jordanians broke the ceasefire," A. Gazit, Maariv, 8.6.1972. (h)

"The Battle over the Bridge," Hotam magazine, 18.1.1974. (h)

"The blowing of the Bunker at Ammunition hill," Shimshon Ofer, Davar, 25.8.1967. (h)

"Ammunition hill in retrospect," Haim Fikersh, Hatzophe, 17.5.85. (h)

"Dayan ordered me: Take my picture when I enter the old city," Ilan Bruner, Maariv, 18.4.1997. (h)

"This year in built Jerusalem!," Menachem Barash, Yedioth-Ahronoth, 8.6.1967. (h)

Gur Mordechai (Motta)—"The Temple Mount is in our hands—Victory Parade, 12.6.1967," Defense Office publications, p. 335. (h)

8: "I felt I Was Suffocating": The Raid on Green Island, 1969

"Tens of Egyptians killed on IDF invasion to Green Island," Eitan Haber, Yedioth Ahronoth, 20.7.1969. (h)

"The Canons of Green Island"—Haolam Haze, Magazine, 23.7.1969. (h)

"At Least 25 Egyptians killed on IDF attack on Green Island." Military correspondent, Davar, 21.7.1969. (h)

"On Green Island 25 years ago," Yehuda Ofan, Al-Hamishmar, 21.7.1969. (h)

"The hottest day in Suez," Eitan Haber, Yedioth Ahronoth, 21.7.1969.

"Heroes of Green Island," Zeev Shiff, Haaretz, 13.3.70. (h)

"Green Island: First attack," Uriel Ben-Ami, Bamahane, 27.7.1977.

"In fire and water," Judith Winkler, Haaretz, 27.6.1979. (h)

"Exodus of the naval commando fighters," Bruria-Avidan-Barir, Laisha, 17.4.1989. (h)

"50 critical moments," Meirav Arlozorov, Bamahane, 23.3.1994. (h)

Eldar Michael (Mike), "Flotilla 13—The story of the Naval commandos," Maariv publishers, Tel-Aviv, 1993, pp. 386–414. (h)

Mustafa Kabha, "The Egyptian attrition and the Israeli counter-attrition," Egyptian sources, Yad-Tabenkin, Institute of Research, pp. 79–100.

Interview of Ami Ayalon. (h)

9: The French Defense Minister: "Bomb the Israelis!" 1969

"Suddenly, one morning, 6 boats disappeared," Sigal Buhris, Between the Waves magazine, no. 89, 20 years to the operation.(h)

"The 48th soul," Uri Sharon, Davar, 9.8.1991. (h)

Limon Moka, Tzur Miron, "Jewish Pirates—Boats of Cherbourg," Maariv publishers, Tel-Aviv, 1988, pp. 138–184. (h)

"They had a general rehearsal," Idith Witman, Hadashot, 25.12.1988. (h)

"In memory of the boats on their way," Ilana Baum, Maariv, 26.12.1988. (h)

"The story of A.M. Lea," Joseph Michalsky, Davar, 23.12.1979. (h)

"Five boats are about to arrive today," Lamerhav Daily, 31.12.1969. (h)

"Egyptian spokesman: we are confident that France is not to blame for the smuggling of the five boats," Shmuel Segev, Maariv, 31.12.1969. (h)

Rabinovitz Abraham, edited by Effi Melzer, "The boats of Cherbourg," Effi Melzer Publishing House, Military research, Reut Publishers, 2001. (h)

Interview of Hadar Kimchy.

10: "Why Bomb if We Can Take?" 1969

"The night of the Radar," Eitan Haber, Yedioth Ahronoth, 8.1.1971.

Kfir Ilan, op. cit. Paratroopers, Volume 4, pp. 123–125

Fiksler Yoel, "Rooster 53—Operation for bringing the radar from Egypt, December 26–27, 1969," S.H.R. publishers, Rehovot, 2009. (h)

Cohen Eliezer (Cheeta), Lavi Zvi, "The sky is not the limit," "Imaginary, crazy rooster," Maariv publishers, Tel-Aviv, 1990, pp. 387–392. (h)

"An American request for information about the Egyptian radar is expected," Nissim Kiviti, Eitan Haber, Yedioth Ahronoth, 4.1.1970. (h)

"Remember, you are entering the Lion's lair!" Eitan Haber, Yedioth Ahronot, 28.12.1969. (h)

"Expiatory Rooster," Dani Spector, Yedioth Ahronoth, 30.12.2009. (h)

"Heritage paper 66—The snatching of the Egyptian radar," Oded Marom, IAF friends Magazine, 2012. (h)

"Operation 'Rooster'—Israel Captures Egyptian Radar in War of attrition," Jewish Virtual Library, December 26–27 ,1969.

Interview of Nehemiah Dagan.

11: "The Enemy Speaks Russian!" 1970

Yonai Ehud, "No Margin for Error," op. cit. pp. 231–134.

"The Russians did not believe it's happening," Amir Rappaport, Omri Assenheim, NRG, 13.8.2005. (h)

Cohen Eliezer (Cheeta), Lavi Zvi, op. cit. pp. 411–415. (h)

Amir Amos, "Fire in the sky," Defense ministry, Tel-Aviv, 2000. (h)

"Our pilots overcame the Russian pilots," Arie Avneri, Yedioth Ahronoth, 2.8.1970. (h)

"Commander of the Russian Air Force investigates the interception of the MiGs," Egyptian news agency, Yedioth Ahronoth, 2.8.1970. (h)

"The four MiGs that were shot down yesterday were flown by Russian pilots," Yedioth Ahronoth, 31.7.1970. (h)

"Will the USSR accept her fighters being hurt?" Eitan Haber, Yedioth Ahronoth, 3.8.1970. (h)

Interview of Amir Eshel.

12: White Angels on Jacob's Ladder, 1972

"Brilliant 90 seconds of The Matkal Commandos," Moshe Zonder, Maariv, 25.3.1994. (h)

"23 hours of anxiety ," Yedioth Ahronoth reporters, 12.5.1972. (h)

"We released Sabena," Moshe Zonder and Amit Navon, Maariv,16.5.1997.

"That is how I shot The prime Minister," Yossi Asulin, Southern local paper, 25.4.1997. (h)

"The breaking into Sabena," Yosi Argaman and Zvi Elchayani, Bamahane, 20.5.1992. (h)

"Kidnapping Diary: hour by hour," Zeev Shif, Haaretz, 12.5.1972. (h)

"The hot line between Lod and Jerusalem," Yosef Harif, Maariv, 12.5.1972. (h)

Kaspit Ben, Kfir Ilan, editor: Dani Dor, "Netanyahu—The road to power, the break through into Sabena airplane," Alfa Communication, Tel-Aviv, 1997, pp. 65–70. (h) Birch Lane Press, USA, 1998.

Interview of Benjamin Netanyahu.

13: "Stop! Halt! Hands Up!" 1972

Argaman Yossef, "Intelligence and Israel's security,"—"Kidnapping of the Syrian Generals—Top Secret," 1990, pp. 32–42. (h)

"Trapping the five Syrians—great victory of the Israeli Intelligence," Yedioth Ahronoth, 22.6.1972. (h)

"Syrian Intelligence officers have more influence than other officers," Ilan Kfir, Yedioth Ahronoth, 22.6.1972. (h)

"Frightened and distraught, the five high-rank Syrian officers were taken prisoners," Yehezkel Hameiri and Eitan Haber, Yedioth Ahronoth, 22.6.1972. (h)

Zonder Moshe, "Sayeret Matkal, the Uzi Dayan era," Keter, Jerusalem, 2000, pp.182–183. (h)

Kaspit Ben , Kfir Ilan, Dani Dor ed., "Netanyahu—The road to Power," Alfa communication, Tel-Aviv 1997, pp. 68–70. (h).

"The Kidnapping of the Syrian Generals," Yosef Argaman, Bamahane, 29.7.1987. (h)

"Heroes of operation Crate reveal: that is how we kidnapped the Syrian officers," Shaul Shai, Moria Ben-Yosef, "Israel Defense," Internet site, 25.3.2012. (h)

Interview of Uzi Dayan.

14: That Lady Means Trouble , 1973

Documents of the IDF Archives, file 401 (papers 4,6–16)

Bar-Zohar Michael, ed., "The Book of Valor," Yaakov Hisday on Avida Shor, Ministry of Defense publishers, Magal, Tel-Aviv, 1977, pp. 184–187. (h)

Bar-Zohar Michael, Mishal Nissim, "Mossad—The Greatest Missions of the Israeli Secret Service," The Quest for The Red Prince, Harper Collins, New York, 2012, pp.186–213.

"We heard a huge explosion, the building was cut in two," Tal Zagraba, "Shavuz," Internet site. (h)

"The autumn of 'Spring of Youth'," Onn Levi, Davar, 23.4.1993. (h)

"Bravery does not console," Oded Liphshitz, Al Hamishmar, 24.4.1993. (h)

"Mental strength is our weapon," Ehud Barak, Yedioth Ahronoth, 25.4.1993. (h)

"Barak dressed like a woman entered the terrorist buildings," Dani Sade, Yedioth Ahronoth, 25.4.1993. (h)

"General Barak, dressed like a woman, on a lovers' stroll to the terrorists' homes in Beirut," Gil Keisari, Haaretz 11.4.73. (h)

"The raiding force captured important papers regarding the terrorist organizations in Israel and in the occupied territories," Haaretz reporter on Arab subjects, Haaretz, 11.4.1973. (h)

"Six Israeli Mossad agents arrived in Beirut—a few days before the IDF raid," David Herst, The Guardian, quoted in Maariv, 11.4.1973. (h)

"I heard shootings in the corridor and I said: Certainly the Israelis are attacking," Zvi Lavi, Maariv, 13.4.1973. (h)

"If we would have learned a lesson from this," Uri Milstein, Hadashot, 29.3.1985. (h)

"Western papers on the IDF raid in Beirut, Reuters, AFP, UPI; Daily Express, London: "The Israeli intelligence is the most efficient in the world," as quoted in Hazofe, 12.4.1973. (h)

"I'll never forgive Ehud Barak for taking part in the killing of my husband," D'isi Adwan, in Amman, Zoher Andreous, Maariv, 16.5.2000. (h)

"IDF Raid—Shock treatment," Eitan Haber, Yedioth Ahronoth, 13.4.1973. (h)

"Prime minister of Lebanon demanded to fire senior officers after the raid; He retired after his demand was rejected," News agencies in Beirut, Yedioth Ahronoth, 12.4.1973. (h)

"Israeli Agents arrived in Beirut on Friday to prepare the operation," Arthur Chatsworth, Daily Express, as quoted in Yedioth Ahronoth, 12.4.1973. (h)

"Chief of Staff Elazar confirms important documents were captured in Beirut; 900 terrorists were hit in 1972," Reuven Ben-Zvi, Yedioth Ahronoth, 12.4.1973. (h)

"Mission impossible in the heart of Beirut," Dan Arkin, Maariv, 11.4.1973. (h)

"The Mercedes cars were rented in Beirut seven hours before the raid," News agencies' correspondents in Beirut, Maariv, 11.4.1973. (h)

Interview with Kamal Adwan, a week before he was killed, Robert Stephens, The Observer, as quoted in Maariv, 15.4.1973. (h)

"The Operation in Beirut (the full story as told by the participants)," Benjamin Landau, Bamahane, 6.9.1972. (h)

Interview of Amnon Lipkin-Shahak.

Interview of Ehud Barak.

15: The Bravehearts Land in Africa, 1973

"Bridge over troubled waters," Uri Dan, Haolam Haze, 16.9.1991. (h)

"The Crossing of the Suez Canal," Uri Milshtein, Maariv 7.10.1974. (h)

"Luckily, Erez managed to steal 30 command cars and Nahik found the boats," Ariela Ringel-Hoffman, Yedioth Ahronoth, 2.10.1988. (h)

"A bridge over Suez," Uri Milshtein, Haaretz, 27.10.1978. (h)

"The bridgehead was captured," Ilan Kfir, Yedioth Ahronoth, 16.11.1973. (h)

Oren Elhanan, Lieutenant Colonel (res.), "History of the Yom Kippur War"—The crossing; IDF History Department, December 2004, pp. 205–232. (h)

Kfir Ilan, "My glorious brothers of the Canal"; Chapter 14: "October 15–16: Acapulco"; Chapter 15: "October 16: Africa"; Chapter 21: "October 17: Heroes of the bridges," Yedioth Ahronoth Publishers, Tel-Aviv, 2003, pp. 205–213, 214–222, 270–283. (h)

Bergman Ronen, Melzer Gil, "The Yom Kippur War real time"; Chapter 3: "The Crossing." Yedioth Ahronoth Publishers, Tel-Aviv, 2003, pp. 221–288. (h)

Dan Uri, "Bridgehead," Chapter 23: "The paratroopers are crossing," A.L. Special Edition, Tel-Aviv, April 1975, pp. 157–169. (h)

Herzog, Chaim. "The War of Atonement," Greenhill Books, London, 1988.

Interview of Moshe (Bogi) Yaalon.

16: "Commander Killed ... Deputy Commander Killed ... Second Deputy Commander ..." 1973

Segal Maozia, "Testimonies from the sandy battlefield: the paratroopers' combat in the Chinese Farm," Modan publishers. Ben-Shemen, 2002, pp. 80–230. (h)

Ezov Amiram, "Crossing—60 hours in October 1973," Dvir Publishers, Or Yehuda. 2011, pp. 55–220. (h)

"Bloodshed in the Chinese farm," Ilan Kfir, Yedioth Ahronot,24.4.1974. (h)

"The hell was here," Yael Gvirtz, Yedioth Ahronot, 17.6.1994. (h)

"Slowly, slowly, they tell about the night when they were sent to the slaughter," Batia Gur, Haaretz, 17.9.1999. (h)

"Itzik, here is Ehud, I'm coming to help," Shiri Lev-Ari, Hair, 29.1.1999. (h)

"The Deputy company commander mumbled: It's over, the battalion is gone . . . 890 is gone . . . everybody was killed," Yael Gvirtz, Yedioth Ahronoth, 17.9.1991. (h)

"Regiment 890 at the Chinese farm," Eitan Haber, Yedioth Ahronoth, October 1985.

"The battle of the Chinese farm, a wound that won't heal," Nava Zuriel, Maariv, 4.2.2006. (h)

"The Armor fighters demand that their part in the Chinese farm battle be recognized," Dana Weiller, Maariv, 7.10.2008. (h)

"History, memory and rating," Zeev Drori, Maariv, 28.4.2004. (h)

"Overlooked but not forgotten," Abraham Rabinovitch, Jerusalem post, 3.10.2007.

Interview of Itzhak Mordechai.

17: "I See the Lake of Tiberias!" 1973

"Back to the Valley of Tears (Emek Habacha)," Yaron London, Yedioth Ahronoth, 6.10.1992. (h)

"The battle in the Valley of Tears," Renen Shor, Bamahane, 19.12.1973. (h)

"Why was Barak's brigade abandoned?" Emanuel Rozen, Maariv, 24.9.1993. (h)

"Syrian Documents captured: The Golan Heights have to be taken within 24 hours," Davar 19.4.1974. (h)

"The fighting of Division Mussa," Amir Oren, Bamahane, 30.1.1974. (h)

"The battle of the Golan," General (res.) Chaim Herzog, Yedioth Ahronoth, 30.9.1974. (h)

"Destroy Damascus," Igal Sarna, Yedioth Ahronoth, 17.9.1991. (h)

"Look at the Syrians, how brave they are," Avigdor Kahalani, Yedioth Ahronoth, 24.9.1993.

"Bravery or death," David Shalit, Haaretz, 7.8.1993. (h)

Milshtein Uri, "The Yom Kippur War"; the Paratrooper Corps; The blood-line; The breaking of the war," Yaron Golan Publishers, Tel-Aviv, June 1992, pp.162–222. (h)

Interview of Avigdor Kahalani

18: The Eyes of the Nation, 1973

"That's how the Hermon fort fell," Eitan Haber, Yedioth Ahronoth, 28.12.1973. (h)

"Here lie our corpses," Igal Sarna, Hadashot, 24.9.1985. (h)

"We captured. We the cannibals," NRG Internet site, 24.9.2004. (h)

"The monster on the mountain," Haolam Haze, 14.11.1973. (h)

"It was very important for them not to walk the way of the paratroopers," Gadi Blum, Hair, 13.9.1991. (h)

"File Operation Dessert is published—that's how the Hermon was taken," Ahikam Moshe David, Maariv, 12.5.2012.

Lieutenant Colonel (res.) Oren Elhanan, op. cit. pp. 276–279. (h)

Asher Dani, ed., "The northern command in the Yom Kippur war, Operation Dessert"; Re-capturing the Hermon, The Syrians on the fences, Maarakhot Publishers, 2008, pp. 261–289. (h)

Shemesh Elyashiv, "Slow and wise with quick success (Paratrooper brigade 317 in the battle for capturing the Syrian Hermon, October 21–22, 1973)"; The hell with you, move forward! (On speed in the battlefield), Modan publishers, Maarakhot, 2011, pp.48–67. (h)

Becker Avihai, "Indians on hill no.16, a company at the Hermon battle," Ministry of Defense publishers, Jerusalem 2003.

Interview of David Zarfati, Golami brigade fighter.

19: "Opera" in Baghdad and "Arizona" in Syria, 1981 and 2007

"Opera," -1981

"IAF Commander, at the time of the nuclear-reactor bombing, David Ivry," from an interview published in the IAF magazine, Aharon Lapidot, Journal 118, 1.12.1997. (h)

Nakdimon Shlomo, "Tamuz in Flames," Yedioth Ahronoth Edition, 1986. (h)

"We made a bet which one of us will stay in Baghdad's central square," Alex Fishman, Amit Meidan, Yedioth Ahronoth, 1.8.1997. (h)

"Comparison: Entebbe, Iraq, Tunis," Hadashot, 3.10.1985.

"The pilot who led the attack on the nuclear reactor, the pilot who planned the operation," Yedioth Ahronoth reporters, 16.6.1981. (h)

"A special interview with an unnamed Colonel—the planner," Yaakov Erez, Maariv 12.6.1981. (h)

"Operation Opera, Lieutenant General Aviem Sella, one of the planners," Ron Ben Ishai, Yedioth Ahronoth, 28.4.1995. (h)

"Opera," Shlomo Nakdimon, Bamahane, 1.6.2001. (h)

"Israeli aircraft attacked the Iraqi nuclear reactor from Iranian territory—claims a British writer," Amos Ben-Vered, Haaretz, 9.8.1991. (h)

"The Government communique," Maariv, 9.6.1981. (h)

Interview of Zeev Raz.

"Arizona," 2007

"Attacking the nuclear reactor in Syria—step by step," Gordon Thomas, Epoch times, 21.11.2008. (h)

"The Story of 'Operation Orchard'—How Israel destroyed Syria's Al Kibar nuclear reactor," Erich Follath and Holger Stark, Der Spiegel, February 11, 2009.

"Israel thwarted Syria's plan to attack," infolive.tv, September 17, 2007.

"Sayeret Matkal collected nuclear material in Syria," Ynet, 23.9.2007. (h)

"Israel forwarded intelligence to the USA prior to the attack," Ynet, 21.9.2009 (h)

"Due to secrecy Syria did not protect the site which was bombed," Arie Egozi, Orly Azulai, Yedioth Ahronoth, 4.11.2007. (h)

"Report: a Commando unit landed in Syria a month before the bombing of the nuclear reactor," Yossi Melman, Haaretz, 19.3.2009. (h)

"The Iranian connection," Alex Fishman, Yedioth Ahronoth, 16.9.2007. (h)

"Sayeret Matkal collected nuclear samples in Syria" Jerry Louis, as quoted by Yossi Yehoshua and Idan Avni, Yedioth Ahronoth, 23.9.2007. (h)

"The night of the bomb," Michael Bar-Zohar and Nissim Mishal, Yedioth Ahronoth, 13.8.2010. (h)

20: "Did They Have Machins Guns?" 1982

"I knew that we had to conquer the Beaufort," Mazal Mualem, Bamahane, 8.6.1988. (h)

"Conquest of the Beaufort," Brigadier General (res.) Avigdor Kahalani, Maarakhot 413, July 2007. (h)

"Revenge Commander calling," Igal Sarna, Yedioth Ahronoth, 6.1.1987.(h)

"Hadad raised his flag over the Beaufort and said: We are here with the help of God and the IDF," Joseph Walter and Shaya Segal, Maariv, 9.6.1982. (h)

"Battle over the Beaufort restarted," Moshe Zonder, Tel-Aviv magazine, 2.7.1993. (h)

"Cannon crews facing the fortress," Igal lev, Maariv, 11.6.1982. (h)

"Battle of the Beaufort—the officers were the first to attack," Shira Ben-Zion, Bamahane, 14.7.1982. (h)

"I started advancing and got scared. Darkness, night, moving shadows," Tal Zagraba, Bamahane, 11.1.2008. (h)

"The battle for the Beaufort, Lebanon war, Arab documents and sources," Collecting materials, editing and analysis: Reuven Avi-Ran, Maarakhot, Tel-Aviv, 1987, pp. 20–25. (h)

Tamir Moshe (Chico), "A war with no medals," Maarakhot, Ministry of Defense publishers, 2006, p. 28. (h)

Interview of Gabi Ashkenazi.

21: "It Was a Great Concert with Many Instruments," 1982

Rosenthal Rubik, "Lebanon: the other war," Sifriat Poalim, Hakibutz Haartzi, Hashomer Hatzair, 1983, pp. 67–75. (h)

Cohen Eliezer (Cheeta) and Lavi Zvi, op cit. pp. 604–620.

Ben David Ofer Colonel (res.), "The Lebanon campaign," Tel-Aviv, pp. 68–72. (h)

Reuven Avi-Ran, op. cit. pp. 91–93.

"Six Days in June," Lior Shlain and Noam Ofir, IAF Magazine, no.145, 1.6.2002. (h)

"David Ivry, the ninth Commander (October 1977–December 1982)," Aharon Lapidot, IAF Magazine, no. 118, 1.12.1997. (h)

"How we destroyed the disposition of land to air rockets in the first Lebanon war—1982,"Major General (res.) David Ivry, Fisher strategic research institute, air and space, 2007. (h)

Interview of Aviem Sella.

22: "Abu Jihad Sent Us," 1988

Zonder Moshe, "Sayeret Matkal, the assassination of Abu Jihad," Keter Publishers, Jerusalem, 2000, pp. 238–248. (h)

"Liquidation of Abu Jihad: a professional work in less than 5 minutes," Uzi Mahanaimi, Dani Sade, Edwin Eitan reporting from Paris; Yohanan Lahav reporting from London, Yedioth Ahronoth, 17.4.1988. (h)

"The Liquidation," Noemi Levitzki, Yedioth Ahronoth, 5.4.1993. (h)

"The Jihad against Abu Jihad," Ronen Bergman, Yedioth Ahronoth, 23.3.2012. (h)

"The Israelis shot my father and mother shouted: Stop!" Semadar Perri, Yedioth Ahronoth, 22.4.1994. (h)

"That is how Abu Jihad was killed," Al Hamishmar, 17.10.1990. (h)

"4000 Israelis took part in the elimination of the terrorist Abu Jihad," according to Robert Fisk, The Independent, as quoted in Maariv, 13.4.2001. (h)

"Um Jihad, his widow, talks . . ." Yassar Muassi, Emza Natania, 29.10.1993. (h)

Interview with family members of Miriam Ben- Yair.

23: "Where Is the ship?" 2002

"Disclosure: That's how the Shayetet captured the weapons-carrying boat Karine A," Hannan Greenberg, Maariv, 13.1.12. (h)

"The old man and the sea," Amir Oren, Haaretz, 11.1.2002.

"Suddenly, out of the dark, the commando fighters appeared," Yoav Limor, NRG Internet site, 6.1.2002. (h)

"Seized arms would have vastly extended Arafat's arsenal," James Bennet, New York Times, January 12 2002

"The weapons-carrying boat Victoria, accompanied by IDF forces, docked in Ashdod port," Amir Buhbut, Maariv, 16.3.2011. (h)

"The Navy captured the weapons-carrying boat that made its way from Turkey to Gaza," Amir Buhbut, Maariv, 15.3.2011. (h)

"The Idf forces captured a weapons-carrying boat from Syria to the Gaza strip," Ron Ben Ishai, Yoav Zeitun, Ynet, 15.3.2011. (h)

"What brought to the capture of the Karine A," Jacky Hugi, Maariv, 22.1.09. (h)

"Broke the waves," Nahum Barnea, Yedioth Ahronoth, 29.9.2004. (h)

"Israel recorded Arafat talking about buying the weapons-carrying boat," Ilan Nachshon, Yedioth Ahronoth, 17.1.2002. (h)

"I have been on many enemy boats," Igal Sarna, Yedioth Ahronoth, 11.1.2002. (h)

Lecture by Admiral Eli (Chiney) Marom at a conference in the Israel Intelligence Heritage and Commemoration Center, 29.2.2012. (h)

Interview of Shaul Mofaz.

24: Holocaust Remembrance Day in the Nablus Qasbah, 2002

Harel Amos, Issasharof Avi, "The seventh war," Yedioth Ahronoth publishers, Tel Aviv, 2005. (h)

The battle over the Qasbah in Nablus: 13 armed Palestinians were killed," Amira Hess, Amos Harel, Aliza Arbeli, Haaretz, 7.4.2002. (h)

"You are alive and fighting like in a movie," Felix Frish, 8.4.2002. (h)

"Two soldiers were killed in Jenin camp," Amos Harel. Amira Hess, Haaretz, 8.4.2002.(h)

"At 6.30 the last wanted terrorists surrendered in the Nablus Qasbah," Amos Harel, Haaretz, 9.4.2002. (h)

"A senior military Fatah commander was killed in the Qasbah," Globe's, 7.4.2002. (h)

"Between the walls" Alex Fishman, Yedioth Ahronoth, 30.3.2012. (h)

"Lieutenant Colonel Ofek Buhris is expected to be the first decorated soldier of operation Defensive Shield," Yoav Limor, NRG, 31.5.2012. (h)

"The terrorists did not notice us, they walked calmly like reserve soldiers on leave," Tal Zagraba, Bamahane, 20.3.2009. (h)

"Adventures of the naval commando in the alleys of Jenin," Yoav Limor, Israel Today, 30.3.2012. (h)

"Ten years to Defensive Shield," Ron Ben-Ishai, Ynet, 30.3.2012. (h)

"Did we defeat Palestinian terror?" Bamahane, 1.4.2012. (h)

Interview of Aviv Kochavi.

25: The Never-Ending Story in Gaza: 2008, 2012, 2014

Cast Lead 2008

"Head of UNRWA: There are members of Hamas in the organization. It's not a problem," Diana-Bachor-Nir, Ynet, 4.10.2004. (h)

"Gaza: 10 killed in IAF attck: Senior Hamas commander killed," Amir Buhbut, NRG, 29.12.2008. (h)

"IAF attacked targets at the strip northern part," Nir Yahav, Yehoshua Breiner, Walla!, 31.12.2008. (h)

"Galant after the liquidation: we pressured Hamas heavily," Shmulik Hadad, NRG, 15.1.2009. (h)

"Mashal offered Quiet for lifting the siege," Reuters, Ynet, 29.12.2009. (h)

The government confirmed recruiting thousands of reserve soldiers," Walla!, 28.12.2008. (h)

"IDF opened artillery fire: hundreds of shells were fired," Ynet, 3.1.2009. (h)

"The ground operation started: IDF hit tens of terrorists," Ynet, 3.1.2009. (h)

"The ground operation started: IDF forces entered the Gaza strip," Hanan Greenberg, Ynet, 3.1.2009.

"Palestinian report: The IDF split the Gaza strip into three parts," Or Heller, Allon Ben David, Nana 10 Internet Site, 4.1.2009. (h)

"The target—attacking Gaza. The result—perfect," Amir Buhbut, NRG, 27.12.2008. (h)

"General Security service: Hamas activists are hiding in hospitals in Gaza," Rony Sofer, Hanan Greenberg, Ynet, 31.12.2008. (h)

"Head of a Gaza hospital: Diskin Lies," Daniel Edelson, Ynet, 31.12.2008. (h)

"Han Yunes: two Hamas senior commanders were liquidated in the attack," Amir Buhbut, NRG, 4.1.2009. (h)

"IDF to the Supreme Court: Rockets were launched from the hospital, that is why it was bombed," Shmuel Mitelman, NRG, 15.1.2009. (h)

"The Chief of staff visited secretly the fighters in Gaza," Yehoshua Breiner, Walla!, 8.1.2009. (h)

"General Galant, Commander of the southern district, returns to the sea of Gaza," Amir Buhbut, NRG, 9.1.2009. (h)

"IDF: Fire was opened from the doctor's house and UNRWA compound," Hanan Greenberg, Ynet, 17.1.2009.

"Commotion in Sheba hospital: The doctor from Gaza is spreading propaganda," Dudi Cohen, Meital Yassur Beit-Or, Ynet, 17.1.2009. (h)

"Olmert declared ceasefire: mission accomplished," Rony Sofer, Ynet, 17.1.2009. (h)

"With bared teeth: Oketz dogs to catch stone throwers," Amir Buhbut, Maariv, February 4 2010.

"Israeli commander: 'We rewrote rules of war for Gaza conflict'," The Belfast Telegraph (Jerusalem), March 6, 2010.

"Rockets hit Israel, breaking Hamas truce," Isabel Kershner, International Herald Tribune, June 25, 2008.

"Israel Rejected Hamas Ceasefire Offer in December," IPS, January 9 2009.

"Gaza-Israel truce in jeopardy," Al Jazeera, December 15, 2009.

"In Gaza, Both Sides Reveal New Gear," Defense News, January 5, 2009.

"Israeli troops, tanks slice deep into Gaza," Ibrahim Barzak and Jason Keyser, Associated Press, January 4 2009, azcentral.com., February 18, 2009.

"Israeli arsenal deployed against Gaza during Operation Cast Lead," Journal of Palestine Studies (Institute for Palestine Studies), XXXVIII (3): 175–191. ISSN 1533–8614. Esposito, Michele K. (Spring 2000). March 6, 2010.

"Israel enters Gaza: Negotiating with extreme prejudice," Klein Aaron, Time, January 3, 2009.

"Palestinians: Mother, 4 children killed in IDF Gaza offensive," Amos Harel, Yanir Yagna and Yoav Stern, Ha'aretz, January 3, 2009.

"Reconsidering the Goldstone report on Israel and war crimes," Richard Goldstone, Washington Post, April 1, 2011.

Interview of Yoav Galant.

Pillar of Defence

The IAF Commander said "Kill the bastard." The missiles were fired at Jabari. The Sunday Times report, Uzi Mahanaimi, as quoted in Maariv, NRG, 18.11.12. (h)

"Hamas Military leader Ahmed Jabari killed on a missile strike by Israeli Defense force," Ted Thornkill, The Huffington Post UK, November 15, 2012.

"IDF refrains from killing civilians, but still has not learned the nature of Hamas," Amira Hess, Haaretz, 16.11.12. (h)

"The assassination and the state of alert," Nahum Barnea, Sima Kadmon, Alex Fishman, Eitan Haber, Yoaz Hendel, Yedioth Ahronoth, 15.11.12. (h)

"The Hamas commander was killed; a large scale operation in the Gaza strip," Amos Harel and Avi Issasharof, Aluf Ben, Amir Oren, Yossi Verter, Haaretz, 15.11.12. (h)

"A smokescreen," Alex Fishman, Yedioth Aharonoth, the Magazine, 16.11.2012. (h)

"Efforts to reach a ceasefire," Nahum Barnea, Shimon Shiffer, Alex Fishman, Yedioth Ahronoth, 18.11.2012. (h)

"A defense of iron," Eitan Haber, Yedioth Ahronoth, 18.11.12. (h)

"Netanyahu: I agree to a general ceasefire, but if the [rocket] firing does not stop, we'll invade Gaza," Barak Ravid, Haaretz, 18.11.12. (h)

"In our field," Alex Fishman, Yedioth Ahronoth, 21.11.12. (h)

"Rockets fall in two schools in Ashkelon; A senior Jihad commander killed," Gili Cohen, Yanir Yanga, Haim Levinson, Jacki Hugi, Haaretz, 20.11.12. (h)

"A night meeting of the "Nine"; Obama presses for a ceasefire," Yedioth Ahronoth, 20.11.12. (h)

" 'Red Paint' from Beer-Sheba to Tel-Aviv," Yedioth Ahronoth, 16.11.12. (h)

"Israel and Hamas agreed to a ceasefire under Egyptian patronage," Barak Ravid, Jacki Hugi, Haaretz, 22.11.12. (h)

"The Mediator of the agreement: The head of the Mossad," Itamar Eichner, Yedioth Ahronoth, 22.11.12. (h)

"The light behind the cloud," Alex Fishman, Yedioth Ahronoth, 23.11.12. (h)

"Release Order," Eitan Gluckman, Matty Saiber, Zeev Goldshmidt, Yedioth Ahronoth, 23.11.12. (h)

"The Star War," Amir Shuan, Amira Lam, Yedioth Ahronoth, the Magazine, 23.11.12. (h)

Protective Edge

"Eitan's heroism," Yossi Yehoshua, Yedioth Ahronoth, 4.8.2014. (h)

"From depth I thee called," Eitan Glikman, Yedioth Ahronoth, 6.8.2014. (h)

""The hero who chased the terrorists," Yossi Yehoshua, Yedioth Ahronoth, 4.8.2014.

"Hamas tunnel in Gaza," Yossi Yehoshua, Yedioth Ahronoth, 31.7.2014. (h)

"The bombers," Ariela Ringel-Hoffman, Yedioth Ahronoth, 1.8.2014. (h)

"Fighting above and under the houses," Gili Cohen, Haaretz, 31.7.2014. (h)

"Advancing in the pace of the bulldozer," Amos Harel, Haaretz, 31.7.2014. (h)

"Hamas members coming to sting and disappear," Odded Shalom, Yedioth Ahronoth, 25.7.2014. (h)

"The light at the end," Alex Fishman, Yedioth Ahronoth, 12.8.2014. (h)

"Death tunnels," Semadar Perri, Yedioth Ahronoth, 12.8.2014. (h)

"Exposure to the future: new technologies," Haaretz, 1.8.2014. (h)

"I would have jumped into the tunnel—Colonel Ofer Winter," Yossi Yehoshua, Yedioth Ahronoth, 13.8.2014. (h)

"A non-choice war," Sima Kadmon, Yedioth Ahronoth, 15.8.2014. (h)

"An operation getting confused," Alex Fishman, Yedioth Ahronoth, 15.8.2014. (h)

"Bank of targets and reality?" Asaf Hazani, Haaretz , 15.8.2014. (h)

"Sorry we have told you to return home," Yedioth Ahronoth, 14.8.2014. (h)

"IDF has lost its creativity," Michael Bar-Zohar, Ynet, opinions, 11.8.2014.

"ISIS (Dai`sh) in Gaza," Michael Bar-Zohar, Ynet, opinions, 24.8.2014. (h)

Interview of Amir Peretz.

26: From the Heart of Africa to Jerusalem: Operation Moses 1984 and Operation Solomon 1991

Adega Abraham, "The voyage to the dream," self-edition, Tel-Aviv, 2000. (h)

Shimron Gad, "Bring me the Jews of Ethiopia," Maariv publishers, Hed-Arzi, Or-Yehuda, 1988. (h)

Shimron Gad, "The Mossad and the Myth; the best smugglers in the world," Keter, Jerusalem, pp. 207–233. (h)

Toren Yaron (editor) "Operation Solomon: Beita Israel coming back home," The Jewish agency—Department of Immigration and Absorption, Jerusalem, 1994, pp. 28–35. (h)

"The price: 4000 dead," Ronen Bergman, Yedioth Ahronoth, 3.7.1998. (h)

"The one responsible for Operation Solomon: All the Falashmura should be brought to Israel," Bareket Feldman, Haaretz, 28.5.2006. (h)

"The Shayetet and the Mossad in a rare documentation, in Operation Moses," (Hadashot), channel 2, Israeli TV. (h)

"Military Operations behind enemy lines, Shaldag unit," Michal Danieli, PAZAM, Internet site, 1.7.2011. (h)

"Third place: Shaldag," Yoav Limor and Allon Ben David, Ynet, 14.2.2008. (h)

"Operation Solomon," IAF Internet site. (h)

"Flotilla 13 landed in Sudan," Arie Kiezel, Yedioth Ahronoth, 18.3.1994. (h)

"There was no one who was not moved, even me," Ravid Oren, Yedioth Ahronoth, 20.5.2011. (h)

"The IDF rescued the Ethiopian Jewry," Hadashot, 26.5.1991. (h)

"Shai said no," Orit Galili, Haaretz, 3.6.1991. (h)

"Exodus from Ethiopia," Tudor Perfitte, Yedioth Ahronoth, 1.11.1985. (h)

"Following him in the desert," Smadar Shir, Yedioth Ahronoth, 17.7.2009. (h)

Interview of Benyamin (Beni) Ganz.

ACKNOWLEDGMENTS

The story of the perilous missions described in our book is based on a multitude of sources: books and articles; archival documents, some of which had never been published before; Internet sites; interviews with a great number of past and present IDF officers, soldiers and statesmen. We thank the IDF Archives, the authors of the books and articles presented in our bibliography and the fighters themselves—some of them still in uniform, many of them retired or holding major civilian positions. The IDF spokesman, General Yoav ("Poli") Mordechai, together with his devoted staff, gave us very useful assistance from the moment this project was born.

We are also very grateful for the help of Ms. Nily Falic, chairperson of the FIDF—"Friends of the IDF"—association; General (res.) Gershon ("Jerry") Yitzhak, former director of the FIDF in New York, and his successor, General (res.) Meir Khalifi; the Hecht Foundation; and General (res.) Avigdor Kahalani, the ultimate Israeli hero, today chairman of the Association for the Israeli Soldiers' Welfare.

Our project was encouraged and supported by our excellent agent, Al Zuckerman, "Mr. Writers' House"; his foreign rights magician, Ms. Maja Nikolic; and our publishers, Dov Eichenwald of Yedioth Aharonoth Books for the Israeli version, and Dan Halpern at Ecco/Harper-Collins. The English manuscript, translated together with Nathan K. Burstein, took its final shape after additional research and rewriting; once again, the contribution of our home editor, Nilly Ovnat, was invaluable. In New York we got the devoted and efficient assistance of our editor, the excellent Gabriella Doob; and Katherine Beitner was incomparable in spreading the good word. Special thanks to Ecco's associate publisher, Craig Young, for his wise counsels and ideas.

And finally, thanks again to our superb ladies, Galila Bar-Zohar and Amy Korman, who stood by us while this second book—after Mossad—was researched, written and saw the light of day.

INDEX